What Women Want

Also by Maxine Mei-Fung Chung

The Eighth Girl

What Women Want

A Therapist, Her Patients, and Their True
Stories of Desire, Power, and Love

MAXINE
MEI-FUNG CHUNG

**GRAND
CENTRAL**

New York   Boston

Copyright © 2023 by Maxine Mei-Fung Chung

Cover design by Arsh Raziuddin. Cover image of flowers by Universal History Archive/Getty images. Cover images of lips, fire, and hand © CSA Images. Cover copyright © 2023 by Hachette Book Group, Inc.

Grand Central Publishing
Hachette Book Group
1290 Avenue of the Americas, New York, NY 10104
grandcentralpublishing.com
twitter.com/grandcentralpub

Originally published by Hutchinson Heinemann, a division of the Penguin Random House group of companies, in 2023

First Grand Central Publishing Trade Paperback Edition: September 2023

Grand Central Publishing is a division of Hachette Book Group, Inc. The Grand Central Publishing name and logo is a trademark of Hachette Book Group, Inc.

The publisher is not responsible for websites (or their content) that are not owned by the publisher.

The Hachette Speakers Bureau provides a wide range of authors for speaking events. To find out more, go to hachettespeakersbureau.com or email HachetteSpeakers@hbgusa.com.

Additional credits can be found on page 289.

Grand Central Publishing books may be purchased in bulk for business, educational, or promotional use. For information, please contact your local bookseller or the Hachette Book Group Special Markets Department at special.markets@hbgusa.com.

Library of Congress Cataloging-in-Publication Data has been applied for.

ISBNs: 978-1-5387-5828-1 (trade paperback): 978-1-5387-5829-8 (ebook)

Printed in the United States of America

LSC-C

Printing 1, 2023

For women and all marginalized communities
who want and desire *their* way.

We have been raised to fear the yes within ourselves, our deepest cravings. For the demands of our released expectations lead us inevitably into actions which will help bring our lives into accordance with our needs, our knowledge, our desires. And the fear of our deepest cravings keeps them suspect, keeps us docile and loyal and obedient, and leads us to settle for or accept many facets of our oppression as women.

Audre Lorde, *Uses of the Erotic: The Erotic as Power* (1978)

Introduction

In Pursuit of Wanting My Way

May 1980

I saw the fish before I heard the word. *Sensitive.*

It had been spoken many times when I was a child, the claim made by my father any time I cried, which was often, unpredictable, and, apparently, embarrassing. I was *too sensitive to live* he would say, the comment sometimes chased with a sharp slap. I was my father's second child and his first daughter, who, unlike my brother, took pleasure in the Asian delights offered in Chinatown's restaurants.

I want to look at the fish, I shined; I pointed.

My father took my hand and guided me to the enormous domestic fish tank planted in the center of the restaurant and beckoned a waiter to accompany us. As I stared at the kaleidoscopic fish, their tangerine tails swirling, I quickly forgot that my father and I had company. Seconds later I was pulled from my technicolor trance when the waiter, tall and stinking of smoke, tapped me on the shoulder. For drama, he licked his pen and flicked the page of his slim notepad with nicotine-stained fingers. Both men leaned in, snickering.

She'll have the one hiding at the back. Lots of garlic, my father said, smiling and pointing at one of the fish. Then he broke out into laughter that grew to a roar.

Was my wanting to gaze and be dazzled by the fish the reason for their cruelty? My small body began to shake.

I didn't challenge their joke; I was too scared. My father's message was loud and clear: my desire, unless possessed, "allowed," and guarded by him, would be ridiculed—killed.

Back then, the word *want* was a ghost lodged at the back of my throat that I dared not say out loud. Spoken now, it conveys liberation, love, and growth. I want to desire my way, it insists.

And even though I lost the word for a time in my late adolescence and early twenties, it eventually, and thankfully, resurfaced. Much later, I'd claim it and make it my companion. I'd own it and hold it in my body. I realize now that the restriction, possession, and shaming of my desire as a child led me to realize as an adult how much my wanting mattered.

This is the engine and inspiration behind the conversations in *What Women Want*. For the past fifteen years I have worked as a psychotherapist, choosing a method of practice in which my passion for civic life and social justice takes its rightful place beside work and love in the consulting room. During this time, I have had the important task of listening, learning, teaching, and writing about psychotherapy, and my fascination for what women want has been at the center of my inquiry.

Sigmund Freud once said: "The great question that has never been answered, and which I have not yet been able to answer, despite my thirty years of research into the feminine soul, is *'What does a woman want?'* "

As a psychotherapist-in-training, I was puzzled by Freud's declaration. Why the founding father of psychoanalysis couldn't answer this fundamental question was a mystery. Perhaps psychoanalysis was not as I'd imagined after all, and concerned itself instead, as Freud had, with the wranglings of detective work—patients' life stories shoehorned into neat theories.

Was Freud's question, though—primarily aimed at women of the Victorian era—still an enigma? Are we still perplexed by women's desire? It is evident to me that in modern relational psychotherapy we do know what women want—if we are prepared to listen and connect in a deep and meaningful way.

Since those early days of learning Freud, I have been committed to deepening my practice by thinking about how the social and clinical intertwine: the ways socioeconomics impact one's ability to access psychotherapy; and about the urgent problems of class, race, and gender, and their impact on patients and society as a whole. I have reached into new worlds, new theories, and new understandings of psychotherapy with each patient, who brings their own unique shape, essence, and energy to therapy. It is easy to imagine that Freud's classical and remote analytical approach through the view of his male, heteronormative, and white privilege didn't allow him to enter women's worlds. How could it? Was he even truly listening? That snipe perhaps made you smile, but when we listen through ears attuned to race, ethnicity, sexual orientation, class, and age, we can hear women and how they claim their desire.

Women are not a mystery and neither are our wants or needs. But there is complexity attached to our desire—there is more to it than simply figuring out what women want. What I want to understand more deeply is what keeps us from having what we desire, and what keeps us in denial, loveless, or in a constant state of longing.

As I have seen in my clinical work, women's forbidden desires foster feelings of shame and depression, which can lead to self-harm, low self-esteem, emotional starvation, and anorexic love. Each of these longings is equally heartbreaking and infuriating to bear witness to as a therapist.

Ultimately, to want is to connect with ourselves and with

others. Having desire ignites hope and opens up healing in the dark and dire times when we are warned *Do not want; it's not safe*. Ask yourself what will happen if you choose to live with your creative desire empowered. How will it feel? What will it change? What is possible? And then ask yourself if the fear of the longing inside yourself is worth challenging.

What Women Want: Conversations on Desire, Power, Love, and Growth is a collection of true, intersectional stories that examine women's lives and their relationships with desire. It is also a gently opened window into the intimate relationship between psychotherapist and patient. My hope is that the next time your desire feels like a foreign island, you'll find yourself pausing with a new consciousness and perhaps reaching out.

What Women Want is a love letter to seven patients I cannot name. These are true stories, but I have made changes to protect the owners' identities. The dialogue is not precisely word for word, but the essence is true to what we have shared together. Each patient has read a draft of their story and given me their consent for publication and their approval of the disguise. Some patients offered editorial suggestions. In some cases, my patients even believed the disguise too deep and extensive and encouraged me to bring a more exacting description to their story. One patient, whom I have named Ruth, offered the title for her chapter. Another shared that she felt she knew me better having read her story and has since been able to take greater risks in our work together. One patient was unsettled by the racist attacks I experienced as a child.

Each of the seven women featured in this book is someone I have worked with for many hours and was selected on the strength of her desire, the relatability of her story, and the way her reason for seeking therapy has remained embedded deep within her body. "Love in the Afternoon" looks at a patient's experience of finding love late in life, while "My Father, the Jerk" asks whether "daddy issues" still have a place in modern psychotherapy. In "White Noise," we address how the issue of structural racism demands a comprehensive response in the practice of psychotherapy.

For many years psychotherapy has been eclipsed by thoughtful and well-intentioned secrecy. And while I appreciate and understand the concern that psychotherapy not be misrepresented, distorted, or misinterpreted, I believe archaic taboos no longer serve the greater and much valued interest in society at large about the growth and change psychotherapy can bring about.

It is my hope that *What Women Want* will ignite and invite conversation about women and desire. And I believe we learn best with an open heart and through the respect and understanding of each other, but I am equally awake to the reality that we do not always arrive at therapy with such openness or trust. This takes time, as you will see reflected in the story "My Body, My Rules."

These are stories of modern women in modern times. It is my hope that you will relate and recognize in yourself some of their universal struggles. Exploring what women want is an ongoing inquiry for all of us. And one of the great gifts of beginning this conversation is it bypasses the question *What do women want?* to settle on the premise that *women want*. Period.

So with this in mind, give yourself time to experience desire *your* way, be aware of the risks involved with your wanting, make wanting your answer and not your question. When I think now of those words: *too sensitive to live*, I feel myself rise. I am no longer thwarted by such tyranny, such oppression. Now I am proud of and own my sensitivity. I claim and respect my desire. To do this I have had to unshackle myself from the male gaze, the misogynist outpouring. So remember, when you are free enough to be your full self, take another woman's hand, hold it, squeeze it, and invite her to join you in deliberate conversation, friendship, and life. It is through our talking, listening, claiming, and rising with each other that together we will be empowered and free of patriarchy's reach.

What does a woman want?

Ernest Jones, *The Life and Work of Sigmund Freud* (1953)
In a footnote Jones gives the original German:
"Was will das Weib?"

I'll tell you what I want, what I really, really want
So tell me what you want, what you really, really want
I wanna, (ha) I wanna, (ha) I wanna, (ha) I wanna, (ha)
I wanna really, really, really wanna zigazig ah

Spice Girls, "Wannabe" (1996)

Mothers, and Other Lovers

The aliveness of a spring fevered night slicing through. She arrives, low-slung jeans, a tight-fitting vest. Mouth outlined and filled in with plum lipstick. The strap of her black bra is showing—but Terri knows this already—encourages it to fall like sin; all casual, all ease, an indicator of her carefree and confident self.

She rides her feeling of desire and strides toward the under-lit bar. Patiently she waits for the bartender: *Jack D, straight up*, and downs the amber liquid with one swig.

Her legs, hidden and long, have been scraped and moisturized, but the hot place between them has been stripped with wax because she honors that tender spot. *It* deserves a more dedicated removal; not the quick whizz of a blade in a hurried shower.

Earlier she was undecided—*jeans or skirt?*—and settled on the former because tonight she feels tall, edgy, a cool slice of androgyny thrown in for the thrill. Another night she might have chosen a silk dress and suede ankle boots, perhaps a pale lip. But she used that look last week and tonight felt the urge, the desire for something a little harder, grittier, *more tomboy, less girlie girl.*

She'd also removed her engagement ring: a pear diamond, three carat. Placed it in the tiny crystal bowl that she keeps in the bathroom, next to the toothpaste and razors. She struggled to feel the necessary guilt when deleting the ring—that will come later—and instead smiled at her reflection. She watched herself smile back.

Leaning into the bar, Terri notices a woman with long shiny hair, an eel of waist-length black. Tanned, demure shoulders and pretty eyes. She is talking with two friends, both women, and all three of them are sipping beer—pale and bottled. Terri notes how the woman laughs openly, tucks her jet hair behind an ear full of rings, and gazes just long enough for the woman to notice her watching. Then come the smiles.

Last week Terri's desire carried her to a different woman with severely bobbed hair who glided over to say how much Terri reminded her of *a young Demi Moore in* A Few Good Men, *but with red hair*. Terri shined and spoke, *I think Demi Moore is beautiful,* and flicked her keen eyes to the floor. An hour later they were both dancing in a club, doing tequila shots. Kisses mingled with lime. When they eventually fell into bed together there was laughing, wrestling and goofing around. Terri enjoyed their tangling of limbs and the way her body hung loose the following morning. But this feeling was interrupted, stolen. Because Richard was due back after a weekend at a friend's stag party and she'd made plans to meet him for brunch to discuss wedding plans. Their wedding plans.

Richard sensed her distant gaze over their eggs, fried and poached, and put it down to nerves and mild hysteria. Terri thought him teetering pathetically toward complacent and entitled. A satisfaction felt when she reached under the table and cupped her palm between her legs. The night before was still there, pulsating and needed—like a shot in the arm. *So, what did you get up to last night?* he asked. *Nothing much,* Terri lied. *Just a quick drink after work, I was home by ten.* Then a smile. A sip of freshly pressed juice.

Terri is not always comfortable at the ease with which her lies are told. They happen mostly when Richard—eighteen years her senior, boyfriend of four years and fiancé for two—is out of town on business. Richard is kind and reliable. High-born and rich. Once incredibly hot with very few kinks that she's aware of. He is also a photographer: commercial, pedestrian, and unfulfilled.

Terri loves Richard.

At 7 a.m., Terri arrives for her session.

I'm bad, just plain wrong, she says, before even making contact with the chair. *Tell me what I need to do.*

I ask that she pause, breathe, take a seat. *What's happened?*

She stares at me from beneath her red, ruler-straight fringe, her pale skin and jaded eyes payback from the night before. Cheeks hollowed out with stress. It is early, and Terri wears last night like a fresh cut, inescapable and raw.

I did it again, she confesses, voice curling at the edge. *I can't help myself.*

As a psychotherapist for close to twenty years, I've witnessed lies told in personal relationships to be risky, dangerous even, but not uncommon. We may excuse a white lie for an easier life or to save face, but most people are uneasy about the purposeful liar. Lies dismiss feelings and hurt lives. They claw at the psyche and slash the safety net of trust knitted between two people. A therapist walks an artful line when observing lies told by patients, but it is the lies patients tell themselves, along with their denial, that walk an even tighter line. These are the types of lies that can cause the patient to slip from a far greater height. And I believed Terri's safety net was unraveling, the tightrope loosening. The fall, I sensed and feared, was just moments away.

Terri talks of her desire and how it infused her body last night as she removed her engagement ring, devoid of emotion or attachment to Richard, whom she is due to marry in less than six months' time. She wonders aloud why she has found herself recently skyfalling into sex with several perfect strangers—more than two and less than six—whom she's picked up in various bars across town, all women. *I'm terrified,* she says, *I feel so claustrophobic at the thought of marriage.*

I lean forward in my chair. *We touched on this last week,* I say, *your fear of what you believe is the doomed fate of romance over time. You mentioned how risky it feels fusing love and desire?*

Terri stares at her feet. *No change there,* she whispers.

This isn't the first time Terri's infidelity has gate-crashed the session. It is becoming uncomfortably familiar, almost domestic. I sense a wave of compassion buried in my chest for her marching, unfolding fear.

She tells me about Richard's last-minute flight, a shoot for an advertising campaign—*face creams.* How she'd spent the night in a bar with a woman and her two friends who left around eleven, leaving Terri and the woman alone. She shares how alive she'd felt, the night ending at her place in Chelsea. Clare was soft and beguiling. Her tender strokes and keen mouth alive and delicious. When Terri left this morning, Clare asked if she had *a girlfriend, a wife? No,* Terri replied. Happy, for once, to be speaking the truth.

Clare kissed Terri square on the mouth and handed her a phone number written on the back of a brown paper bag that Terri inhaled on her way to my office: the almond croissant shared earlier with coffee still expelling its sweet marzipan smells. In six months' time Terri will reckon with swallowing a jar of pills and thankfully survive her dark thought of suicide. And I will wonder if she remembers this moment of joy, her connection with Clare, the smell and taste of cloying almond paste. Clare's mouth on her mouth. *I guess,* Terri will shrug in response, *but if I'm honest that whole period is a blur. I wish I could hold on to the connection we had, but somehow it gets lost. It disappears.*

Now Terri wipes her enormous gray eyes with the back of her hand. They are sad and afraid, damp and weary; an immediate appeal to respond to her. I do.

Do you want to help yourself? I ask.

Yes. No. She looks away, wet leaking from her eyes. *I am so fucked,* she says.

The Rules. Never work harder than the patient. A therapist who rushes in, fails to listen. Still, I find myself yielding.

Fucked, perhaps, I offer. *But not powerless.*

She leans forward, her body full of unnatural energy and purpose. *I love Richard,* she allows. *But I don't want him. I don't desire him.*

Have you ever wanted, desired him? I ask.

I guess; in the beginning. When we were fresh. You'd think we'd be so hot for each other, what with him working away the whole time. But there's barely a sizzle. He suddenly feels very old to me.

Terri hangs her eyes on me in silent inquiry, while I contemplate the meager sizzle and do the maths: old, plus lack of sizzle, equals boundless sex with many women—and a likely runaway bride.

They met four years ago at an art gallery in the West End. An exhibition of challenging portraits of people having undergone cosmetic surgery. Terri stared at the gigantic monochrome prints, a fish-eye lens used to capture unloved faces: skin with black pen marks, bruises and tiny thin scars. She felt a longing to stroke the portraits with her fingertips, wishing the subjects were more accepting of the features they were born with. And when she arrived for her session the following morning, Terri wondered what messages, -isms, and possible cruelties had been forced upon each of them.

Introductions came by way of the gallery curator, Joel. *Hey, you guys must know each other, right? Terri here works in production at* Blaze. *Didn't you do some test shoots over there too, Richard?*

Richard had worked for *Blaze*, but way back, way before Terri was offered the role of producer on a popular series of fly-on-the-wall documentaries. Terri and Richard shook hands. Two hours later they were screwing in the bathroom. Richard had grinned, freed Terri's blouse and placed their bodies in a unique position, cupping her chin in his hand as protection against the cold ceramic cistern. It was over way too quickly, Terri thought, adjusting her body and rebuttoning her blouse. Afterward they walked to Chinatown and ate dumplings.

Terri entered the relationship with a burst of desire and enthusiasm but quickly found her interest waning. She called it *Couple-Cozy* and rainbow-rolled her eyes. Weekends away swiftly descended into watching television with takeaway food, bottles of mid-range wine and a foot massage. Flirtatious phone calls were cut to perfunctory, with only the occasional flash of risk. Nicknames were agreed: *Tezzi, Dimples*. Terri missed the excitement, the zeal, the unpredictability. She wanted it all back, she said. But she also wondered whether she wanted it with Richard, given her attraction to women. I suspected Terri was using sex as a balm, or an antidepressant, a means of momentarily replacing her emptiness and loss with the excitement of being desired by other women. If Terri's self-medicating was an attempt to disavow the reality of being gay, how long could she sustain her denial, and at what cost? I was beginning to feel a sense of urgency for her compromised and conflicted life.

Recently during sex with Richard, Terri had taken to

creating fantasies in her head. Images of half-naked women—combative, and tender—crawling aimlessly over each other. To reach orgasm she would close her eyes, call back the picture that often ended with a woman holding her tightly. This confession made her cry. She had also started to explore how much of what she wanted in a lover came from what she needed from her mother, a functioning alcoholic. These painful insights had unsteadied her, sent her zigzagging into bars in search of women, in search of answers and in search of love. The kind of love her mother was, and is, unable to give her.

Richard suddenly feels very old to me, Terri repeats, and I wonder if she senses that my attention has wandered—and she'd be right. Moments of mindful diversion and internal reflection by the therapist are often sage reminders that a patient never arrives to therapy alone. She enters the consulting room with a blueprint of her interpersonal relationships—a world of family, friends, acquaintances, enemies and loved ones, past and present.

Old? I say, thinking of Richard. *Say more?*

He feels—a pause—*really old, distant. We want different things. It's as if we're living on completely different islands.*

And where's your island?

Over there, she points, *and Queer,* she smiles. Terri stares at the bay window where she has pointed, her gaze adrift, at sea.

I wait, sensing Terri needs space to remember, forget, or possibly daydream. A moment to reflectively feel the words she has just spoken.

Where have you gone? I finally ask.

I was just thinking about Rebecca, Becks. She speaks softly. *You remember, right?*

I do, you've spoken of Rebecca often, I reply. *You imagined your island and Rebecca followed? Is that what just happened, Terri?*

Terri nods. *Why couldn't I just accept it then—when I met Rebecca. Why has it taken me this long to admit I prefer the company, and touch, of women?*

Silence.

I reflect on the times during our ten months of working together when Terri has shared her longing to feel loved, seen and wanted by her mother. The bribes, the conditions and the threats her mother made in an attempt to deny her the love and touch of other women. Of the times when her sneaky palms were used to slap Terri's face. What becomes of a woman when she is unbeloved by her mother; when her desires are killed, or made invisible; when she is told that her life is wrong?

Well . . . I say, pausing for effect. *There was the complicated issue with your mother.*

Together, Terri and I revisit a memory.

It had been a sweltering September night. A tent hammered into the ground. Terri's mother was entertaining—a flurry of *hot single women and mostly married men.* Her latest *man-friend* was a guy called Rick who wasn't married this time and worked in sales. Rick traveled a lot, up and down various motorways selling air-conditioning units, and ate microwaved fast food from polystyrene cups. Terri watched her mother reach out to touch Rick's arm with her fingertips while chugging down her third tumbler of *vino.* She noted her mother's sway in a dress that she might have worn.

He's a keeper, slurred Terri's mother, *so be nice. And make sure you play with Rebecca.*

I'm not a child, spat Terri. *And you're drunk—again.*

Rebecca was Rick's daughter. Blush hair, gold hoops, freckles. A slim waist. She lay on the grass beside the tent, tearing the heads off dozens of daisies and checking her nails as though they might fall off—acrylics, square and French-tipped.

Go talk to her, said Terri's mother, wrist flicking the air like she was shooing a dog.

She'd like that, sweetie, added Rick, wine moving in his glass.

Irked, Terri walked toward Rebecca and asked if she wanted a drink.

Got any vodka? said Rebecca.

How old are you? said Terri.

Sixteen, why?

Same. And your dad lets you drink?

As the night wore on, Terri and Rebecca—Becks—had some fun. They teased the curiously attentive men; the loose straps of their fitted dresses casually dropping from their shoulders; a quick flash of teeth and legs. The men looked on, trying to disguise their thrill, then moved in closer, inquired about school. *School's good,* they both chimed and giggled, then gawked at the men with clear distaste before charging their plastic cups. *You're both so pretty,* one man said. He had small animal teeth and wore a large Hawaiian shirt, a foam of silver hair fizzing out like a gray cloud. At some point Terri and Rebecca escaped the garden and climbed the soft stairs to Terri's bedroom. An hour or two spent on the Xbox, a change of lip gloss and drunk dancing to Justin Timberlake. Outside, an outdated sound system leaked Phil Collins and Chris Rea. Old people music. *The grays love that crap,* scoffed Rebecca.

Terri leaned out of her window and spotted Rick's hand disappear beneath her mother's dress and winced. She distracted Rebecca by asking her to pass the remaining vodka. No point in both of them suffering, she thought.

The rest is a pleasant, drink-fueled blur.

Terri felt Rebecca's hand reach for her bra strap, snapped it right open. Rebecca's fingers touched her back lightly, possessively, and a welcome quiet fell over Terri, like it would in class, or at church. They watched each other move with pleasure. Hands, teeth, tongues. Scissoring their soft parts until a tremble reached their throats. Then, finally, intoxicated wonders and sleep.

The morning was wrenched open with a scream and a yank. Terri stared at the twist of black lace underwear on the floor. Her arm pulled so violently that she'd howled. Becks—or rather, *Rebecca, get up. Now! What do you think you're doing with my daughter?!*—tried to cover herself with the cotton bedsheet. Both naked, the girls cowered and fawned under the gaze of a raging banshee. Terri watched her mother's hand opening and closing a fist before she finally relented and slapped her daughter's face.

You're disgusting, her mother screamed. *Get out!*

Shame. Terri and I visit shame frequently. Often she will ask me the same question, over and over: *What's the opposite of shame?* And each time I pause, offering again: *Beloved.*

I remind her that she has asked me this question many, many times. But today she has no recollection of such a question, no recall of even thinking it.

She reaches inside her bag, collects the familiar red notebook and fountain pen that she uses for our sessions. Her memory to date has been faltering, sporadic, and frequently amiss. I have reflected upon this in clinical supervision, her struggle to digest and remember our conversations. What else have you forgotten, Terri? What other happenings are too distressing to recall?

All too often, fixed points of memory are denied, ignored, disbelieved and dissociated from to protect the self, to conceal what was too painful to feel before. The role of the therapist is to create a secure base from which difficult memories can tentatively return. This requires special care and attunement. Because in this endeavor one discovers that no feeling is final, that further challenging feelings will most likely follow. Truths and realities return and are tended to with devotion and care.

Terri licks her finger and swipes the pages of her tiny red notebook, again writing the word: *Beloved.* I contemplate asking her to pause, to see whether she might find the word repeated—an agony of organized words—but quickly decide that further exposure, further potential shame, can perhaps wait for another day.

When Terri was a child she was called *disgusting, worthless, a big fat waste of space.* When the *vino* was really flowing, words tended to be even crueler, if that's possible, because they hammered, chipped away and drowned out who she was. Who she *is.* They attempted to rock her core self. And shame her for preferring the touch of, firstly, a girl named Rebecca, Becks. Later, more young women—too many to mention—who were made into formidable secrets because her mother would disown her, throw her out, and wreck any remaining scrap of self-worth Terri was desperately clinging on to. Terri has whispered the words *dyke, lezza, lesbo, fucking queero.* Her mother's words. And I have attempted to hold my nerve, my rage for the violence and injustice forced against her. It is still alive, and searing, *beloved* Terri.

I'm so sorry for the loss of what ought to have been a good enough childhood. It must have been incredibly painful for you as a teenager, trying to make sense of your desire.

She hesitates, and casts her damp eyes about the room, landing them finally on my eyes. *I'm sorry, too.*

After her session, Terri makes a call to Richard's mobile phone. *We need to talk,* she barely speaks.

Richard senses that something is wrong, the note in his voice rising when he reluctantly asks, *Have you just been to therapy?*

She says that she has, but that's not the reason she needs to talk, *It's something else, something really important.* They agree to have dinner at home after work, around eight. *Shall I pick anything up on my way home?*

No, Terri says, *I'll make dinner.* She figures it's the least she can do.

For the rest of the day Terri seems to go in and out of consciousness. Almost like she's living and existing outside of her body. She takes out her tiny red notebook and flicks to the page with the word *dissociation* and reminds herself what is happening: *Dissociation is one way that the mind copes with too much stress, such as during a traumatic event. It is a mental process of disconnecting from one's thoughts, feelings, memories, or sense of identity.*

Terri steadies herself. Makes a mug of sweet tea. Removes her boots and prepares her body to cry. The office is quiet today, so she cries, and drinks her sweet tea, and forces her thick-sock-covered soles down hard into the rough, carpeted floor. Later she calls her best friend Kirsty who knows everything: what's been keeping Terri awake at night, why her drinking wine has turned to spirits for the past six months. *I love you,* says Kirsty, *you're doing the right thing.* Terri ends the call on a slight smile and feels mildly better after that.

At eight-thirty Terri calls Richard. A simple meal of chicken and leeks prepared and resting in the oven. No wine. Just fizzy water, because she needs to keep her head and hold her nerve. *I'm five minutes away, Tezzi, sorry,* Richard puffs. *Tubes; they're a living hell.*

Terri feels her stomach clench. The smell of food-keeping-warm not helping in the slightest. She refrains from saying, *Okay, Dimples*, because that would be misleading and cruel. Instead, she offers, *Okay, see you shortly. We're having chicken and leeks*. She also misses out the *I love you* part, because that would also be cruel. Instead, she lassoes a memory of the time when, on their third date, she'd told Richard, *I love your dimples, they're gorgeous*. He'd grinned, the dimples even more delicious and pronounced. *I didn't know you could see my ass*, he'd beamed. They had both laughed. The memory has Terri temporarily off-balance. Perhaps wine would have helped.

The front door opens. The clanking of keys. *I'm home*, he sings. *Sorry I'm late, Tezzi. Something smells good*. Terri is standing when Richard enters the kitchen and the look on her face, ashen and frightened, must worry him because he sits before kissing her cheek, as he so often does when arriving home from work.

There's no easy way to say this, she musters.

What is it, Terri? What's wrong?

I can't marry you. I want out. Please forgive me.

7 a.m. again. Morning larks. Terri adjusts a stubborn leather glove. Contact lenses have been switched for her large, heavy-framed black glasses. I know she does this when she's been crying and the lids of her eyes are too sore to be touched or messed with. Today, I can see clearly there is something in her eyes, her gait—a live wildness—that disquiets me. *How are you?* I ask.

Her gaze wanders toward the bay window. Without make-up she appears humble and much younger than her thirty-two years, and the clothes she has chosen—gray marl sweatpants and a matching hoodie—give off the delicate scent of fresh soap.

Not good, Terri says.

The session is almost wordless. The occasional sentence offered to describe Richard's hurt and confusion; his angry need to move out; the burnt chicken and leeks; their wedding plans—killed. I cast my eyes low, but their focus lets Terri know that I'm here. That I am listening.

When I began practicing as a psychotherapist back in the early 2000s, prolonged silence would unsettle me. A rookie need to feel engaged with my patients, I guised my fledgling anxieties of not being a good-enough therapist with words. Effectiveness often resembled, in my mind at least, action; alongside audible engagement that turned into conversations, suggestions, and sometimes—I wince writing this—*interpretations*. Back then, the therapist who guided me while training and with whom I was in therapy for eleven years had asked what it was about silence that unsettled me. I'd responded that it brought to my mind both a disconnected life and feelings of aloneness. He had frowned, tipped his head. *Can you say more?* he'd encouraged. I recalled times of longing for connection through respectful conversation, rather than the frequently feared and challenging demands made on my voice as a child when it was suggested that I not *bring any dead air to the dinner table; entertain us; for God's sake say something interesting, or leave.* Fearful of annihilation and going hungry, I instead carried the fire and desirous feelings I held inside my body, which later resurfaced when I began training to become a psychotherapist.

Over the years I have grown more comfortable with silence, perhaps because I now welcome, wholeheartedly, solitude in my life. For therapy at least, these silences afford valuable reflection time for both therapist and patient and allow feelings to surface that otherwise might be disavowed when words, superfluous or futile, enter the room. I have come to regard moments of busy audio as a "wall of words" that prevent intimacy and connection. The busy therapist misses much.

Terri shifts in her chair. We have been silent for five minutes.

I miss him, says Terri finally, shifting again in her chair. *I feel like a child. It's just like the times when I needed Mum but she wasn't there for me—not in the way I wanted and needed her to be.*

She wipes her damp cheek. *Different islands,* she says.

For the bereaved, nothing but the return of the lost person—or the longed-for mother in Terri's story—can ever bring true comfort. Should I fall short of this request, I fear I will almost definitely insult her. Instead I choose to let her know the pain will pass, that no feeling is final, that loss is a process, that she will not have to go it alone.

We must enter the necessary, painful, and complicated process of grief together.

I think the terror of letting Richard go is tied up with my longing to do the right thing by my mother, she says. *My desire is something entirely different. I'm ready and petrified of what lies ahead.*

This moment of self-reflection and ownership is important in and of itself. *And the desire to do so is a gift you give to yourself,* I say.

So what happens now? she asks.

Now, we work.

Terri forgets to cancel the cake. *Of all the things to forget,* a giant ass cake arrives at her home the night before her killed wedding. Richard had wanted vanilla sponge with lemon curd but she'd convinced him to change his mind to red velvet, her favorite—Kirsty's too. When it arrives Terri senses a sudden shock in her chest; the sheer beauty of it stains her eyes and leaves a terrible taste in her mouth. She is alone, the feathery tick of a clock suddenly very loud and very frightening. Eager for connection and safety she calls Kirsty. *Come over,* she pleads, *the cake's arrived. You have to help me eat it.*

There is an important and recurring dream that Terri enters on her manic nights alone, without Richard. The images stay with her for days. They are brilliant and clear. Through a semi-consciousness, the dream connects with her mother and Terri's childhood pet rabbit, Barbara.

Barbara was a white lop-eared gift handed to Terri by her father on the day he decided to give up. A cedar hutch purchased and planted at the bottom of the garden among the pampas grass and climbing Chilean lanterns and opposite a baby apple tree.

In the dream, Terri remembers feeling dread at watching her father escape. A tan, plastic suitcase gripped in his fist that she suspected was carrying nothing but relief. Terri was ten years old when he left, and she would not see him again until the eve of her eighteenth birthday. A lot can happen to a daughter in the time it takes to grow a tree swelled with apples: a broken elbow, changed hair, explored sexuality, winning a hockey match, a stolen bike, a close brush with the police, a mother slapping her face with her palm—many, many times.

In the dream he told Terri he was leaving London to start a new life with his new friend. *Bunny here will keep you company,* he said.

I'm going to call her Barbara, she spoke, fighting back her tears. Terri squeezed Barbara tight, a carrot sawn in half and offered to her twitching nose and mouth.

Her father kissed the top of her head. *You'll be fine.*

Please don't leave me, she begged.

I have to, Terri, he spoke gently, *you'll understand one day.*

Take us with you. We won't be any bother, will we, Barbara—I promise.

Terri knew in the dream that when he'd turned away, he had cried. *How could he not?* But by the time he'd locked the boot of the car and keyed the ignition his tears had dried, and Terri realized then that she and Barbara were already forgotten. Much like a fading picture on a turned-off and abandoned television screen.

In the dream, Terri pulled and collected dandelion leaves from the grass verges that grew wild and plenty along the riverbank close to home. She liked to watch Barbara nuzzle the stems of thick green and was soothed when she stroked the full length of the rabbit's innocent, velvety ears. Barbara had gotten all plump and there was a certain joy Terri felt when she lifted her, placing her in the playpen she'd built using old vegetable crates and chicken wire. Sometimes she carried Barbara to her bedroom when no one was watching, wrapping her in an old sweater, a faded pillowcase. Terri was careful to clean up the hard pellets from her bedroom carpet, not wanting to give her mother further reason to hate.

Terri's mother didn't like Barbara. *She stinks and shits everywhere. Typical of your father to leave me with yet another thing to look after.*

Thing. There it was. Terri took the word in and made it her master. A lifetime of feeling hated and unwanted is hard to unlearn.

In the dream, her mother's drinking was on wheels. Skidding out of control. Terri was told that the house vodka must never touch her lips, and instead should be poured into her mother's morning juice before she headed out to school. Terri remembers feeling hungry and thirsty, stealing limp sandwiches and ginger cake from a supermarket even though she had money—the genius invention of a pillowcase sewn into her puffa jacket to hide the embezzled food. *Stealing was a way*

to have some control, to take back what was rightfully mine. My life.
It was my life.

Wishing for her own escape, the dream had Terri staying
out late one night with a school friend. When she eventually returned home, she noticed the hutch door ajar. Barbara
was gone. Terri searched everywhere: next door's gardens, in
the choke of hedgerows, across the street in the local park. A
smiling lunatic, she rapped on her neighbors' doors, enlist-
ing their help. A search party for Barbara. But the dream had
her defeated, and she eventually returned home exhausted and
alone.

In the dream her mother was standing at the porch, arms
laced around a stranger's waist, laughing. The bottle of house
vodka drained. She wiped her mouth with the back of her
hand. *Barbara said she'll see you around,* she sniggered. *Apparently*
she's gone to find your useless father.

Terri had wanted so badly to hurt her mother in the dream.
To scratch her eyes out. Yank on her weak peroxide hair.
Instead, she held all the pain inside her. A giant, jagged edge
of glass splintering and filling her small, shaken body.

A dream? I ask. *Are you sure this is all a dream?*

Terri sighs into her tiny red notebook, a look of dolor and
defeat. *No,* she admits, *it's not a dream, I know that now. It really*
happened. She let Barbara escape, but not me.

The first phase of grief: shock, and denial.

She moves through feelings of pain, guilt, then anger and
bargaining with relative ease. It is another symptom of grief
that I fear: depression. I fear her chance of breakdown. And
for a moment my confidence is lost.

I present the idea: *Depression is unresolved loss,* and she tells me
that she's decided to go cold turkey, take a break, and ignore
her weekly fix of sex with women in bars. I suggest a pause,

not a break. *A break is something you may want to forge rebellions against that could have you acting out, or leaning into old habits,* I say.

She leans forward and trails her fingers through her red fringe, growing out. Her body appears small and injured like a tiny sparrow. Her eyes are wide and startled, dark rings, hollowed out cheeks.

A pause, I continue, *will offer you time to figure out what you want without satiating your longings, and your aloneness.*

I don't understand, she says.

Perhaps avoiding distractions will afford you the space to grieve, I say.

Got it, she half smiles.

For days there is total blackout. Collapse. She cuts her hair mega short. *I want to wear my grief,* she says. Terri doesn't tell anyone, not even Kirsty, that she's stopped eating, working, or bathing. Instead, she spends her hours adrift, with Prince Valium. Dreams—real this time—take her to grief in wild chariots. Her well-being, she believes, is in the lap of the gods. Night sweats. Delirium. Hallucinations.

The dreams, so many . . .

Her mother refuses to die.

Vexed and beautiful, she takes charge of the reins, wine pouring from her eyes, and rides the chariot into feral fires, iced-over cities and towns. The horse's quick flesh is whipped by her strong hands. Here she rules and reigns, clasps Terri's wrist so tightly that it bleeds. Below, Richard and the women leaning against underlit bars. Love waits for Terri to escape years of hurtful journeying.

Rebecca, Becks, is lying on the wet grass counting the moving marshmallow clouds. Tangerine dahlias at the edge of the riverbank, a cool fragrant wind. Terri and Rebecca gaze at each other. A pretty stroke, a kiss. *Please, never leave me,* Terri pleads. Nothing dark will kill their shining hour.

Richard in his ordinary clothes. *Dimples,* she says, *something smells delicious.* He plates up chicken and leek pie, adds a slither of gravy. The gingham check tablecloth tucked in his collar for amusement. He offers Terri more wine and she agrees, but as he turns back around to face her, the bottle of wine morphs into a large carving knife and is driven straight through her heart. *Eat your fuckin' pie, bitch,* he yells.

The woman, Clare, with pretty eyes and long shiny hair, an eel of waist-length black, is driving a low, fast car, the roof down. She and Terri reach a junction. *Where now?* asks Terri. *To the moon,* says Clare, *wanna come?*

Her mother, again. This time no chariot. She is standing in Terri's childhood garden, next to the pampas grass, the crowded apple tree. Her face is a mixture of puzzle and mania. Terri reaches out her palms like the Virgin Mary, a need felt for her mother's misplaced love. Terri watches her mother's frantic look morph into defeat. Her mother smiles, places Barbara in her daughter's palms and walks away. *I just want you to love me,* Terri calls to her mother's turned back. All the while knowing her words, her choking aloneness and longing, has fallen not only on deaf ears, but on a deaf heart.

I notice the speed of her weight loss first. Then the dull of her hair—once red, now turned Titian. She contemplates additional pharmaceutical help, a work sabbatical, more sessions. Suicide.

Some of our sessions simply require my listening and understanding. My presence. Other times, intervention, like the time when she called my mobile after a flurry of emails went unanswered. It was 4 a.m. But she and Prince Valium knew nothing of time back then—days into nights into days. It was agreed that Kirsty would move in for a while, and it was Kirsty's physical holding and caring of her, our extra sessions and an acceptance of her love for women that eventually got Terri through—just. Now, depression takes hold.

Her limbs feel heavy, *like dragging a cow's carcass through treacle,* she says. Her mind, too, feels sludgy and uncooperative. We discuss what it might mean for her to pause, to suspend herself in time until she can figure out how to own and accept her feelings, to honor her body and reflect on her past life. *I want that, I need that,* she says. But she worries that the time it's taken for her to accept her parents' neglect, her longing for a romantic relationship with a woman, will evoke suspicion, that it's all too late. *People won't believe me, or trust me,* she says.

I believe you, I trust you, I say.

She cries for at least half the session, every session. But this is good. It is healing. There is a lifetime's worth of tears to be mourned and felt. Two years into our work, I monitor her ability to greenlight her desire for healing. A letter of apology written to Richard, explaining in detail that she's currently working through some painful memories, a hope that one day they can talk, maybe even be friends again. He doesn't reply, but that's okay. *What did I expect,* she says, *a friggin' pen pal? I broke the poor guy's heart.*

You did, I say, *and actions have consequences. But let's not be punitive. It's important to keep moving.*

Reluctantly, Terri considers my suggestion and turns to exercise: cardio, speed-walking, and team sports. But the chaos of too many people, too many voices and too many bodies has her retreating to yoga—a yellow mat purchased *because yellow is encouraging and jolly. Did you know the fewest car crashes happen to those driving yellow cars,* she informs me. *I did not know that,* I say. The bizarre distraction an indicator of her busy and disorganized mind.

A car crash, perhaps, I reflect, is how Terri views life right now. Only, who's driving? I picture "L" plates in my mind.

Terri also pays people to touch her: an osteopath who re-aligns her spine and with quick, sharp movements cracks parts of her body that are twisted and ache; a masseuse who offers grateful pain to the well of her back, her glutes. She enjoys touch again and doesn't mind paying because she doesn't quite trust herself to be touched unless it's by those offering a pro-fessional service. Soon she will feel a stirring again, but not yet. For now, she must pause and explore her desire with "L" plates.

Kirsty eventually moves out and Terri finds herself walking as though there is glass beneath her feet. A chronic tiptoeing through her home that she barely recognizes. She pulls boxes of old photographs from the corners of her wardrobe, and watches them as if waiting for words to fall out of the mouths of her past selves. What would they say now, seeing her like this, unwashed and fearful? No longer the happy-go-lucky woman who loved work and parties and dancing and travel— who loved life? Appearances have been important for Terri, they've kept her at bay and distracted her from who she really is. *The false self,* I say.

A very busy false self, she nods.

Terri's complicated yet grateful pain, much like cathar-tic tears or a worked muscle, is perhaps in part connected to a surprise visit from her mother, who, when she eventu-ally hears about the cancellation of her daughter's wedding, arrives, masking her rage. A bottle of wine gripped and swing-ing in each hand. Terri feels too sad and vulnerable to deny her mother entry and instead plants two wiped-clean glasses on the kitchen table. Terri is wearing pajamas; soft, warm, and smelling. A three-day-old canned tomato soup stain absorbed on one of the cuffs. Her mother is wearing a neat navy blue dress with endless pleats. She reminds Terri of a lampshade, one she wishes she could switch off, leaving her in the dark as to what is *really* on her mother's mind: her endless rage and disappointment.

Much of what Terri's mother says is just white noise, and Terri's vision seems to go in and out, like a fading dream. She notices her mother's hands—slim turquoise veins and liver spots. How quick and sneaky they'd been for all those years, waiting for a moment to catch her daughter off-guard. A small body, hurt enough times, firstly goes into shock, then fear and denial, then fight or flight, and finally dissociation. We call these amnesic barriers. But with therapy and openness and determination the body starts to slowly remember—until eventually the body holds the score. It recalls the pain it has endured, the suffering it's survived. Body memory holds on to what the mind has disavowed. Terri chugs down her glass of wine and immediately pours another, leaving her mother's glass dry.

You need to pull yourself together and apologize, her mother barks. *I've no idea what's happened; Richard was very secretive when I called in on him, but you need to fix it.*

Fix it? Terri says, a red mist rising.

Yes, and soon!

I cannot fix who I am. I refuse to fix something that is not broken, or wrong. You are a terrible mother. Fix that.

The sight of her mother—her tight pink mouth, chest moving with great effort—unsteadies Terri's footing. She takes hold of the table's edge, grips it tightly. She is glad that both of her hands are occupied, otherwise what might they do?

You'll die alone, her mother spits in her papery voice. Her parting shot. A low blow. A slug to the gut. *A cruel, punishing mother is no mother at all,* Terri speaks out loud before her mother finally stands and leaves. Terri's chest is suddenly tight, her eyes overflowing, and she repeats, *A cruel, punishing mother is no mother at all,* heard by no one but herself. Terri breaks down at the kitchen table and takes an inventory of her fingernails that long to press down hard and into her skin. She soon stops herself, instead pulls down her pajama sleeve. The tomato soup stain still there, like a friend who has outstayed their welcome.

The long night stretching ahead—her mother denying her peace—suddenly feels unbearable for Terri. She places the two wineglasses in a sink full of hot, soapy water and quickly rescues the glass with her mother's lipstick attached. With her fingertips, Terri traces the impression, pink and small, and offers herself up like dust, like the world's smallest grain of sand, to the universe. *Help me get through this,* she cries.

More dreams. Terri buried alive. Her mother's hand shooting out from the dark like Thing in *The Addams Family* and strangling her throat, a violent tick in her tight jaw, her pink puckered mouth like the ass of a cat on repeat, *fix it, fix it, fix it*—

Night sweats; night delirium; night terrors—until finally, finally, morning arrives.

Terri awakes, surprisingly calm. Yesterday's visit from her mother falling to the back of her mind. She checks the clock on her side table—9:17 a.m.—and feels her appetite mildly returned. She pictures eggs, scrambled, crispy bacon, a pot of fragrant coffee. Without mania, she showers and dresses. Seeks out her suede boots and a clean pair of jeans. She spends a little more time in the bathroom too, deciding she will get her hair cut and brightened next week, her nails buffed and filed. A long glug of spearmint mouthwash is poured down her throat and the burn feels good, and clean. She decides on swallowing instead of a spit, thinking the liquid will cleanse her throat of the words vexed at her mother. Checks her work schedule and calls Kirsty to fix a time to meet up. Terri feels relief; her chest and hands are a little shaky, but she has spoken the bold and daring truth to her mother, finally, leaving her with a sense of pride, courage and autonomy that releases her from the belief that she *was all wrong*. Today her home, flooded with light, doesn't feel quite so foreign and precarious beneath her growing steady feet. Today she is sad but not depressed.

No feeling is final, she speaks out loud. The upward turn.

Do you know that scene in Dirty Dancing? *The one where Baby and Penny are dancing together, face-to-face in their leotards and silver dance shoes?* Terri asks.

The one where "Hungry Eyes" is playing? I offer.

That's it, she points, giddy that I know the exact scene. *Huuungry eeeyes,* she sings.

We laugh together. The upward turn.

That's when I knew I liked girls. The way they looked at each other, the way they moved. I just knew, she says.

A welcome memory? I play.

For sure, she smiles.

Dirty Dancing remains one of Terri's all-time favorite films.

Freud believed there were two basic drives that served to motivate thoughts, emotions and behavior—all human experience, actually—and, simply put, these were sex and aggression.

While patients reclined on his famous orange velveteen couch, Freud was seated behind and out of view, allowing his patients to free-associate, which involves the expression of one's consciousness without censorship. I occasionally wonder how intimate moments might have been shared between Freud and his patients. How possible connection and creative play like that of *Huuungry eeeyes* would spark with him out of view and out of gaze. Modern psychotherapy isn't as binary, or as

simple, as life and death. And perhaps the drama of Freud's siz-
zling interpretations and insightful moments are lost in today's
consulting room. Today's therapies tend to steer away from
mind-blowing insight or revelation. My aim as a relational
psychotherapist is to build a safe and meaningful relationship
so patients feel understood, and to grow intimacy in order to
explore some of the most profound questions about what it
means to be human. Psychoanalysis is an opportunity to think
clearly about what we want. With this comes a commitment to
understand women from diverse backgrounds, of different ages
and with different socioeconomic experiences who articulate
their needs in whichever way necessary: regretfully, fiercely,
resentfully, freely, intellectually, and, sometimes, apologetically.
Every woman shares her desires and experience of woman-
hood, however painful or liberating. We know what women
want.

Terri knows what she wants.

I know what Terri wants.

Terri wonders when it will be safe to visit bars again. She
misses them. She misses the fun, the connection with women,
the freedom and the way her body feels when she's cut loose
and dancing.

Why not take Kirsty? I ask.

Maybe, she says, voice softening further.

Terri is back at work and needs to have something in the
evenings to look forward to. She explores her desire—different
now that she's not sneaking around. The thrill's temperature
turned down, but craved nonetheless. She has started to read
again, swim again, paint and laugh and breathe again. Work at
Blaze becomes enjoyable—a possible filming trip that wouldn't
have been possible for her a year ago. There's also talk of a
new and upcoming series of fly-on-the-wall documentaries

exploring global hatred toward women's bodies, and I watch Terri talk about this with more animation and zeal than I've seen in her in months.

She also wonders whether to write to her mother at some point; this, another stage of the grief process, when a consideration of reconstruction and working through enters the framework. But she worries it may set her back. *Nothing has changed between us,* she says. *If we're to have any kind of relationship moving forward I need to be myself, no more hiding.*

I feel a glow of pride. Terri, the North Star—glowing. Seen in her entirety.

Shortly before Christmas she decides to give sport another try. Something about the rapid change of season, the cold, and needing to get her body moving again. *Yoga's great,* she shines, *but tying myself up like a pretzel doesn't quite cut it anymore. I want to feel my body's strength again, the push and pull. The burn.*

She fixes on cycling. A new bike: *Pashley, Bobbin, Roubaix Sport, Hybrid, Cannondale?* We spend considerable time poring over all the options. At one point Terri watches my eyes glaze over. *Okay, I get it, choose one already,* she snaps to herself, like I've rolled over and slipped into a catatonic sleep.

She settles for speed: a Roubaix Sport. And I confess to feeling mildly concerned about her safety in light of her previous risk-taking. I imagine gifting her a high-vis jacket, a helmet, many bike lights, noting my protection and care of her.

Do you have a helmet? I ask.

Sure, I've got everything. No point me doing all this work for me to go die on you now, is there?

I note her glib words and request that she *Pause. I wonder if it's painful for you to acknowledge how much work you've done, and continue to do. That I care about you. Jokes are an easy way to fend off well-earned change, and intimacy,* I offer.

Her preferred time to cycle is at night. Winter clouds; crisp, transparent air. She likes the lights and the freeze and the fresh wind as she flies across Waterloo, Westminster, and Southwark bridges. On a good night she makes it over to Battersea, her T-shirt drenched in sweat and suctioning her healing body. She cycles at least twice a week and every weekend. And she wears a high-vis and a helmet. And I am reassured.

The depression starts to lift as she cycles, and the upward turn has Terri gliding like a bird of prey through streets rarely ventured, prominent squares unremarked. She begins to view beautiful London differently, looking up—at balconies and cornices and cupolas and eaves never seen. It excites her to feel in control again, the lick of speed, the thrill of finding her shape and fully baptizing her body into it, orgasming into it. A shape she desires and wants.

She rides and rides and rides and rides until the insides of her thighs burn with a feeling she decides and promises to never put away again.

Her name is Beth. Not Elizabeth, not Bethany, simply—Beth.

Beth is the kind of woman who will hold Terri accountable for her feelings, and her word. She does not meet Beth in one of the bars she's been hanging out in, sometimes with Kirsty, sometimes alone. Instead, Beth glides in like a majestic swift, under her radar at first, hired to work as a freelance editor on the new series of documentaries about women's bodies.

Terri notices Beth's boots first, the sound of them. Not the usual carpet-swallowing footsteps of the rest of her colleagues. She arrives, her back to Terri at first, who continues with her email, skewering the production designer for a *major fuckup that will delay editing for at least a week*. But one eye is also fixed on Beth's shape, which appears statuesque, confident, and attractive. Terri discovers from her neighboring colleague that the woman is Beth, her new editor. Beth is right on time, Terri thinks.

When Beth turns around, Terri is greeted by a tall, beautiful human. Quick eyes, ridiculously high cheekbones, and a handsome jaw. Her hair is long and auburn, piled high. A pencil stabbed in to hold its sleek weight. She extends her hand for Terri to shake, her smile gummy and wide. *I'm Beth,* she chimes.

I'm Terri.

So we're going to be working together—fantastic. Beth smiles again.

For the next few months she and Beth are simply friends. And on the occasional night out after work Terri pieces together Beth's shape: forty-three years old, Irish mother, a fatherless girl. Beth likes dogs more than cats, preferring to be master not servant. Noted, Terri thinks. She listens to Radio 4 and jazz, is a nervous flyer, and reads everything on The Booker shortlist every year, without fail. Last year she read the longlist, too. She subscribes to *The New Yorker*, left-leaning dailies, and *Gardeners' World*. She lived in LA for three years working freelance as an investigative journalist, and two years in Budapest working on a series of off-beat cultural documentaries. Beth is an only child who has many friends, most of whom are women. She has a penchant for sleek stationery, figurative art, Hitchcock, and Obama. She tells Terri one drunken night after several rounds of karaoke that men and boys rarely desire fatherless women and girls, but she doesn't care, she says, *I prefer women.* Terri catches this thrilling piece of news and places it in her pocket for later, her ears pricked up like a spirited lynx. Terri attempts to calm herself, to stay cool and to meet Beth's shape with her own, which is longing and hopeful. *Me too,* Terri says, scrolling the karaoke index in search of Amy Winehouse.

The following day she springs into session, a shine in her eyes. Her limbs are reluctant to rest and be seated. *Can I just stand here for a while?* she asks, flicking her hands and ankles like she's about to do a sprint.

Sure, I answer.

We talk about her wanting to tell Beth how she feels. *Happy, longing, a desire for something more than friendship,* and *When I see you I want to hold you tightly, and kiss you on the mouth.*

Something is stopping you from saying these things? I ask.

I'm terrified, she replies, hands now resting on her hips.

Say a little more.

I fear her rejection for obvious reasons, but really, I think it's because she's the first person I've met and known who I can imagine loving and desiring.

I take a moment to acknowledge and honor Terri's growth and change. A connection to the parts of herself—fearful, secretive and wanting—that in the past had struggled to fuse love and desire. I recall how she'd compartmentalized her love for Richard but had preserved her desire for the women who came and went. Women whom she desired but didn't allow herself to love and be loved by. Now, with Beth, she is able to merge both love and desire perhaps for the first time since her teenage years when she'd known Rebecca. Years spent alone, negotiating feelings of longing that were split off, denied, and ordered to melt to keep her safe. We lock eyes. A follow-up smile. Terri rests her limbs and lowers herself to the chair.

Greenlight your desire, I offer. *It's worth the risk. Not only do you desire Beth, but you're experiencing, for the first time, the possibility of loving her, too. That's quite a shift—to have and feel both.*

There is only a month left until Beth's leaving party, when

her freelance contract is due to end. Terri knew the day would come when Beth had to leave but chose to ignore it. Denial protecting her from imminent hurt.

Something small and fun, Beth glints, while handing everyone in the office photocopied party invites. *Drinks, then dancing! Save the date,* she smiles.

Terri accepts, of course, and spends the next week planning what and when and where she'll gently and nervously tell Beth how she feels. How, when she gazes at her at work, she senses such a clear shape of them both together. She will share how strong and calm she feels circuiting her orbit, and that the room, any room, is just fine with Beth in it. Like she's totally got that space covered, no drama, just anchored ease. Terri wishes to stay there, with Beth, simply *with* Beth. She wants her.

You're right, shines Terri, *it is worth the risk. And it could be that Beth feels the same way too. Don't you think?*

Chances are she may already have a good idea of how she feels, I say, *particularly in light of how intimate you've become.*

Earlier in the week Terri had shared how, over lunch, she and Beth had talked about what it was like growing up. School, church, hobbies, friendships; Terri mentioning the time she was sent home from school with head lice, her mother forcing a tenner at her chest and ordering her to *fix it*. Kirsty had patiently dragged the small white comb and its tiny teeth through Terri's crawling hair. Terri wincing, yelling that she didn't mind the minuscule bugs nesting in her long red hair, they kept her company after all, and would never leave unless she were the one to kill them off by washing, disinfecting, and combing them out. *I must have had them for weeks,* she says, *but I didn't care if it meant someone, something, cared enough to stay, however itchy it felt.*

As Terri told the story, Beth had taken her hand, stroked it and smiled. Terri imagined herself saying: *I feel like I couldn't love you any more right now,* but instead smiled back, offering, *Shall we order coffee?*

Here's another early childhood memory: Terri's first crush. Not Penny or Baby in *Dirty Dancing,* but Ms. Appleby, her year eleven English teacher. Terri didn't know if Ms. Appleby was married, divorced, single, or just used *Ms.* because it took away any preconceptions and she liked that.

Ms. Appleby, whom Terri named in her secret world as *Ms. Apple Pie,* because that was the feeling she got whenever she saw her—the same as when she'd eaten apple pie, preferring it with custard over cream or ice cream. But sometimes the combination of all three worked, especially when she wanted to feel high on sugar and pleasure.

Ms. Appleby asked Terri to monitor the school library and she saw this as an invitation to acknowledge that she must be Ms. Appleby's favorite. On those days—Tuesdays and Thursdays after school—Terri wore her hair differently, usually up high in a topknot and secured with a delicate scarf, of which she had many. Terri was not sure if Ms. Appleby noticed her prepared hair, sprayed and scented, but she hoped that she did. *Because it meant the world to me that I was the one she had chosen.*

Acceptance and hope: Terri dares to entertain and mobilize herself through and toward the final stages of her grief.

The night of the leaving party finally arrives. Gently, tentatively, Terri shaves her legs, lathers her hair, her skin, and takes the time to notice her new body. New, in the sense that she barely recognizes the different feelings she has going on inside of her. The curves that have always been there, remain. The pop of her small belly, accepted. Feet large and slim, are good enough. Her legs feel stronger and more athletic though, which surely has something to do with all her cycling in the past eighteen months. She notices the tiny crystal dish next to the toothpaste and razors—no longer used to store her heavy engagement ring, it now holds soft cotton balls instead, nuzzled inside like baby chicks.

She climbs into black jeans, a cream silk blouse. Deciding on shoes or boots will be dependent on the weather—spring showers—just before she leaves. Her bed is left unmade, an indication of managing her expectations. Instead, Terri's hopes are just that—hopes.

She arrives at the bar, a slight tingle in her body. How distant past urgencies to get laid feel compared to tonight's joining the party. More lioness striding, less alley cat wild. Terri spots her huddle of work colleagues and walks toward them, Beth at the center, kidding around with the production designers who have made her a leaving gift, a work plaque that reads: *Turns out, I'm the real deal!* Terri couldn't agree more, she thinks, smiling inwardly.

During the night, their pinkies find each other and touch, then linger. Colleagues ask, *What's next?* And Beth answers: *I've got a few commissions, which I'm excited about, so I'm going to take a small break and then get back to it.* She glances at Terri, who says, *That sounds like a great idea.*

At the end of the night Beth walks Terri home. Their fingers laced together. Occasionally they catch a side glance, both turning their heads like owls, two shining faces. Terri slows their pace to stretch a night she wishes will never end. Above them, green leaves darkened with night; a street light of orange shining down; cold earth beneath their feet; warmth in their bodies. A journey that might have taken one hour, takes two. Finally, they pause at Terri's yellow door. Something holds them as they hold themselves: a soft embrace.

And finally; the kiss.

Terri kisses Beth for every girl, and every woman, she has ever not kissed on the mouth, the neck, the soft part behind her ear.

My bed is unmade, speaks Terri.

Then I'll say goodnight and wait for an invite, speaks Beth, *but don't leave it too long.*

Her relationship is by no means perfect. And Terri likes it this way. She likes that when Beth leaves town for work—for a week, even a month sometimes—she misses her and feels able to do so without acting out. She likes how Beth smells in the morning, the way she smiles in her mouth and says, *How's your day looking?*, then joins Terri in the shower, steals the soap and shares a towel to dry off. Simple pleasures. She likes Beth's friends, some more than others, and the ex-girlfriends who linger are a drag. But Terri knows she is beloved and cherished by Beth, and she takes every opportunity to remind herself of this whenever her mother's voice decides to tell her otherwise. She enjoys the *small, normal, everyday things. The fate of romance over time,* she says, *is not fatalistic, but ongoing, and that's okay with me.*

Terri doesn't like that it has taken her this long to find love, that so many years were spent codependently pleasing others, apologizing for who she was and hiding herself from the world and its corners. She doesn't like that she made her mother into her higher power; that displeasing her was a far greater risk than honoring her own desire.

Better late than never would be a glib and dismissive statement to speak, so I find instead the words, *Welcome, it's good to know you, to see you, to witness your desire.*

For a moment Terri is absorbed in what appears and feels to be peacefulness. *It's good to be here,* she smiles.

★

Terri had denied her desire because she was frightened. When we began the therapeutic process, she believed that compartmentalizing her feelings would protect her from the inevitable task of confronting and accepting what she wanted, and who she was. Coming out, honoring her true self, and letting go of oppressive and harmful behaviors that attempted to dismantle her identity didn't have to result in rejection when someone truly cared about her. Terri needed therapy that was containing and compassionate—a secure base offering connection—to feel more fully understood and accepted while she explored what she wanted, and needed. During our five years of working together, Terri taught me that dissociation and denial were both necessary as part of her survival against her mother's abuse and rejection, but came at the cost of suffering and a fractured identity. Years of hiding, of self-medicating, of secrets and lies had taken a toll.

What I was consistently struck by, and in admiration of, was Terri's commitment to understanding herself more deeply, and how lovable she was in the process. Terri believed she was *all wrong*, that she was *unlovable*, and that she had to *fix* herself if she were ever to be loved and celebrated. She showed me the weight and complexity of her pain; a direct result of her mother's and father's neglect and her struggles to attempt to honor her desire. In many ways, owning her desire placed Terri in great conflict and jeopardy because it meant losing first her mother and later Richard, hence why she had split off her feelings regarding her sexuality.

Denial, dissociation, and memory loss are powerful defense mechanisms. We all do it. Catching them, understanding them and their origins is only half the battle. It is knowing what we can do with these defenses that will determine how we choose to live our lives.

Eventually, Terri was able to feel, express and set in motion her desire and love for herself and Beth. It was heartbreakingly clear that what Terri wanted more than anything was the love of her mother. A mother who loved her unconditionally. Sadly that has not been Terri's experience, whose story of grieving the loss of a longed-for mother meant growth and change was only possible once she was able to acknowledge the neglect she survived as a child.

To desire is an action. When we respect and commit to our emotional experiences, desire is satisfied and we are faced with our fear and self-destructive efforts to protect ourselves from its risks. And what then? What will we do with it? What will happen when we cross the invisible threshold of our desire that makes us scared to want? What and how will we feel when we are empowered and embody self-love before claiming and experiencing what we want? With this in mind, it is perhaps not our desire that is dangerous but rather the possibility that our wanting *can* and *will* be realized. The possibilities are mind-blowingly awesome and they are endless. When we change the focus and imagine the possibilities of our wanting, we move toward radical self-love and inch closer to claiming our power. We radicalize our politics, make way for our children, and we connect, grow, and change with, and for, each other. My heart hurts for the little girl who was ridiculed, slapped, and turned away from when she offered her shape in the world as a girl who loved other girls; a woman who loved other women. The unloving spaces where Terri once was are gently melting, and in this I attempt to hold a light for where she is heading, for where she is today. *Beloved*, Terri.

What is this impulse in me to worship & crucify
anyone who leaves me—

Emily Skaja, *Brute: Poems* (2018)

My Father, the Jerk

Disappointment falls into the pit of her stomach. Any hope that sleep may have canceled out yesterday's feelings is suddenly killed when she opens her eyes, checks the clock on her bedside table—*6 a.m.*—and swivels her smooth legs to the side before standing.

She runs a bath of cold water, adds fistfuls of ice and shrugs out of her pale cotton dressing gown. Four weeks ago she researched the cost of an ice machine but discovered there was little point unless she went hardcore industrial with the purchase. And so the bother of carrying plastic bags filled with ice cubes every week remains, at least until she *works this anxiety thing out*. And that's where I came in—*the shrink. After all, that's what we do, right? Pay people to figure shit out,* Kitty had scoffed in our first session.

She lowers her naked body into the roll-top bath—fingers gripping the curves of steel—and waits for the anesthetizing freeze to take hold. A crippling anxiety still alive and reverberating in her body after yesterday's phone call with her father and an exhausting photo shoot for a glossy magazine. Her anxiety prevents her from thinking clearly, fear floating like a gigantic balloon and wreaking cool sweats. She waits for the cold water to numb her pain, feeling both relieved and resentful to be starting therapy in a couple of hours' time.

Kitty much prefers the catwalk. She feels more at home stomping it out on the slim line of runway with its swooning onlookers and their fashionable clothes and oversized sunglasses. But with fashion week only showing twice a year in the four capitals, Kitty fills the rest of her time with advertising campaigns, editorials, and occasional DJ-ing at private parties. Yesterday's shoot for the glossy magazine had required a full day of compliance from her face and body. *More eyes; ease your shoulder toward me; extend your neck; lean into the shot—long legs, strong legs; head back,* the photographer ordered. Kitty's body achieved all of the above but her mind was somewhere else, gently adrift. A tiny, distant sailboat. The realization of how desperately alone and disconnected she felt making its way to her horizon. While she offered her smoky eyes and full mouth, Kitty wished she'd taken Vincent, *my annoying brother,* up on his offer of a yoga retreat in California, *a couple of weeks to kick back and chill, sis.* But here she was again, *the busy fool, fueling my insecurity, convinced that work and looking pretty will solve everything.*

Kitty crams her nights and days full with shopping, hours on her PS5, endless parties, and sex, where she can get her freak on so she will forget how terrifically blue she feels. She believes a pause in her life might cause a total breakdown. She is fearful of the feelings that will surface should she breathe, relax, and be still.

The truth: it takes approximately four minutes for Kitty's body to turn numb in the ice-cold bathwater. She closes her eyes and waits for the twist in her stomach to disappear, the clamp in her throat to ease, and for the thump in her chest to stop. *Stop thumping. Please, stop thumping.* And her frantic brain; that slows down too as she calls back images of soft, sleeping animals and knitting tutorials stored in an album titled *"Happy"* on her mobile phone.

Feelings of loneliness will not destroy you, Kitty, I will say to her soon enough. *No feeling is final,* and she will answer: *Are you sure? Are you certain? I'm scared.*

★

8 a.m. I am met with a swipe of red lipstick and legs for days. A smile so contagious that I find myself mirroring the expression without a second thought. From her lean, six-foot frame hangs an oversized white cotton shirt, masses of punk chains and a tiny leather skirt. Her ankle boots, black leather with three buckles and tiny gold studs, are scuffed just enough to hint at nonchalance and rock 'n' roll. Chloé, I think to myself, having seen them on the pages of various fashion magazines. *Hi, I'm Katherine*, she smiles, offering her hand, tanned, fixed, and steady, *but I much prefer Kitty.*

I'm immediately reassured by Kitty's candor, *much prefer*, an ability to name her desire to an almost perfect stranger. Kitty, I think, is far more befitting than Katherine. It suits her feline stretch and confident entry. One that might be expected from a catwalk model, a private education, and years of international travel.

Please, come in, I offer. *Take a seat.*

She scans the room, dumps her rucksack on the floor and squeezes the leather arm of her assigned seat before perching on the edge. Kitty is a striking young woman. I can imagine keeping my eyes on her for a long time without my interest waning. She takes a deep breath, another quick flash of the room with keen eyes, and runs her fingers through her hair: blond, straight, and waist-length.

Outside, winter clouds have erupted; crisp luminous air. *And we're off,* I find myself thinking, and wonder about this involuntary idea of an airplane, a race. A competitive starter pistol. Atmosphere charged with all the anticipation of an initial consultation, I wait to see how Kitty will begin. Which words she will choose to start her therapy.

My father, the jerk. He's the reason I'm here, she says, *and quite frankly I resent it. The cost. The time. So, fuck him.*

I feel the base of my back clench as it so often does when faced with unprocessed rage.

Sometimes I fucking hate men, she says. *Can I smoke?*

Before I have time to answer, she reaches into her leather rucksack, retrieves a pack of Marlboro Lights, taps them on the arm of her chair. I stare at Kitty. There are hot coals in her mouth. A desire to burn down the patriarchy and her father's house while she sets hers in order.

I'm afraid not, I answer.

Kitty rolls her eyes and tosses the cigarettes back into her rucksack, resting at her feet. She looks at me resentfully, thinks about what I've said, and eventually resigns herself and shrugs, *Your rules, I guess.*

She leans back in the chair, arm bent at the elbow, and guides her pale hair across her shoulder. Her shape has all the ease and confidence of a queen: regal, focused, and high-born. Crossing her legs, she mimics smoking a cigarette and laughs, revealing blaring white teeth. "Well, I'll smoke anyway," I imagine her thinking.

Quite the performer, I say, wondering if I should offer her an imaginary ashtray.

She throws me a half smile and leans forward. *So how does this work? You, me, therapy?*

A fair question, I think, and one I've been asked many times by patients during the course of my working life. *How do we do this?* patients have inquired. *How long will it take? Can you help me? How do I know if it's working? Will it hurt?*

That a person arrives at my small office to talk about their most intimate and troubling thoughts and feelings is confronting and daring, to say the least. The first crucial step in psychotherapy is the patient taking responsibility for their life predicament and the realization that they will, during the therapeutic process, become conscious architects of their actions and choices. Sometimes patients resist assuming responsibility, and one of my challenges as their therapist is to encourage them to think and analyze. Our sessions are a time for them to act upon and respond to their struggles. This takes time, mostly because trust must be built, as well as recognition of the reasons that bring a patient to therapy. Uncertainty, however, especially in the beginning of treatment, is a prerequisite for psychotherapy. Together, therapist and patient embark on a journey, not knowing fully what the shape or outcome will be. And it is the therapist's task to not be deterred or rattled, but to hold her nerve and find comfort in the discomfort of not always knowing.

In answering Kitty's question I offer the only thing I know of the unknown process, by saying, *It requires you commit to fifty-minute sessions each week to discuss what's on your mind. I have a couch but I'd encourage you to sit here, opposite me. And as we begin to talk I can assess how I can help you.*

She leans back. Nods. Drops her pretend smoking hand into her lap.

I feel anxious all the time, she begins. *Then I do whatever I can to avoid feeling anxious. Then I feel guilty, ashamed, or sometimes dead inside, depending on what it is I've done to avoid feeling anxious, which is mostly bad behavior, or sex stuff. I do this thing where I trick my body into feeling certain things. Quite often I immerse my body into cold water and trick it into feeling numb.*

This helps? I ask.

She nods.

How long have you been doing this?

Since boarding school, she says.

Kitty was eleven years old when she was sent to boarding school while her mother and father disappeared to Asia.

Her father, who worked in gas and oil as a reservoir engineer, had insisted *Katherine remain in the UK*, while her mother *wept buckets*. Vincent, Kitty's brother, who is one year older, also left with their parents. Kitty suddenly found herself without her family and terribly homesick. *I'm still so resentful and furious that they took Vincent and left me.*

Being away from her family had been a terrific shock. Kitty was understandably distressed, and as an attachment-based psychotherapist I confess to a similar collection of feelings from other patients who have been full-time boarders.

Kitty wrote to her mother most weekends begging her to *please fetch me, I'm so sad and lonely. I don't fit in, the other girls hate me*. Replies came by way of gifts: lavish hampers full of delicious cakes and sweets that were rarely eaten; new dresses, scarves, dolls, and stiff teddy bears. Sometimes there was a handwritten note attached: *Stay strong darling, we love you, Mummy xxx*

I didn't want sweets and dolls, Kitty says.

I nod and encourage her to elaborate further by widening my eyes.

I wanted to come home, Kitty continues. *She always does what Daddy tells her to do.*

Your mother had no say in whether you went to Asia with the rest of your family?

Kitty stares out of the window. *My mother had no say in whether I went to Asia with the rest of my family,* she repeats, adrift. Someplace else.

I note Kitty's preoccupation and robotic reply. An acceptance that her mother was powerless against her father's wishes, however homesick her daughter had been.

Have you talked to your mother and father about how painful it was for you?

It's not the done thing in our family, she says. *We don't discuss feelings.*

I see. That sounds painful in and of itself, I offer.

For real. Feelings are frowned upon, weak. Boarding school taught me a stiff upper lip was best all round.

Boarding school is not a world I am familiar with, I say, *and I can only imagine how terribly lonely this must have felt. You said your mother wept buckets. Was she more conflicted about you leaving?* I ask.

Perhaps, yes. I'd hoped she might protect me. Fetch me. But she didn't. Maybe it's more upsetting to think that a mother, my mother, could take one child and not the other.

This felt—

—Like a betrayal, she finishes my sentence for me.

A betrayal, I repeat.

Exactly. It feels like a bigger betrayal by my mother. It's easy to be angry with my father. I somehow might expect this from him, but a mother? I'll never send my children to boarding school.

Every morning Kitty prayed that her mother would change her mind and rush in like the maternal cavalry and rescue her from *boarding hell.* Kitty walked around the school grounds in a daze, and to her recollection only saw her family once at Christmastime during her first year away from home. But what exactly was home now? she'd wondered.

What will happen to Lettuce? Kitty had asked her mother, lip quivering, the week before leaving for boarding school.

Lettuce, she'd been assured by her mother, would be flown to Asia where she'd wait for Kitty to visit. When Christmas finally arrived, however, Kitty discovered her beloved Lettuce had gone to *rabbit heaven. Just be grateful she didn't suffer, Katherine,* said her father. Kitty wasn't grateful. She was heartbroken. She suspected her mother and father had been lying to her all along. Vincent looked away, painfully silent.

I wasn't grateful, I was furious and bereft, Kitty says.

Painful matters of the heart were better left unspoken, Kitty's House Parent had said, encouraging her to *cheer up,* or *Come along now, best not to talk about such things. It will only upset you.*

Kitty struggled to sleep, like many of the girls in her dorm, listening at night to their chorus of tears. She still has nightmares about it now—unwanted pictures of her small body in the dark, cold and fearful of the night's shadows and strange murmurs from the archaic building as she risked a trip to the bathroom. Eating was also a struggle. The artificial environment of the school's canteen much like a coliseum, the girls watching and competing to see how much was eaten, or not. One time, after losing significant weight, Kitty remembers being forced to eat dried toast and honey by her House Parent—a plump, stern woman with a tight jaw. *Come along now, Katherine, eat up,* she'd insisted. Kitty did as she was told. The dark toast made bearable by the knowledge that it would later hit the toilet basin.

After a short stay at home with her parents due to concerns about her excruciatingly thin body, Kitty overheard her father speak. *She needs to go back after she's gained weight. Boarding school builds character.* Her mother remained silent.

Kitty clears her throat.

And it did, boarding school did build character, she says.

How so?

I learned how to survive and to stuff down my feelings. But I also decided I wouldn't become attached to anyone again.

We are silent. A feeling of deep sadness is alive in my stomach. It is heartbreaking to me that a twelve-year-old girl decides to disavow any kind of attachment when she most needs it.

I smile at Kitty. *Survival attempts to harden us against the world,* I say. *Sometimes this includes our attachment to people, or perhaps even how we feel. It seems stuffing down your feelings was a way to protect you from pain and disappointment. You learned to master separation rather than to grieve it. And you avoided becoming attached by avoiding or dissociating, perhaps?*

I did what was necessary to survive, she says.

I agree and understand, but perhaps at a great cost emotionally.

She strokes her leather skirt.

So right now I'm completely broke, penniless, she smiles shyly.

I return a smile, pleased to be in a therapeutic dance. A moment when connection, understanding, empathy, and playful humor have all aligned as Kitty and I take to the dance floor. A playful jive. I note her creativity, her quickness to engage with good humor—not by way of defense but as a way to connect. Metaphors and word play are helpful in building trust and I am momentarily hopeful. Some therapies have proved more challenging in terms of attunement and playfulness. I recall the time when a patient came for an assessment and shared with me her desire to find a boyfriend. *They're all in hiding,* she'd said. When I replied that I wouldn't be able to conjure a boyfriend from one of my office cupboards, but we could look at her desire to meet a boyfriend, she'd turned to me with all seriousness and said: *Don't be ridiculous. How could my new boyfriend fit in that cupboard?*

We both decided we wouldn't be the best fit for psychoanalytic inquiry.

Something Kitty had been grateful for, however, was her height. Age thirteen saw an awakening in her necessary survival to fit in at boarding school, and Kitty put this down to her height. *Something shifted; people began to see me differently. Which in turn meant they began to treat me differently. The first two years were an absolute hell. I was terribly lonely, but then I discovered I had some control—over what I ate, my learning, which incidentally turned obsessive, and sport. I was very good at hockey and my grades were good. I discovered being competitive gained me respect from the other girls, and I also found thwacking the crap out of a hockey ball very pleasing. On the mornings I felt anxious I'd wait until all the other girls had fin-ished showering, by which time most of the water had run cold. When I stepped into the cold showers I was immediately calmed.*

You discovered a way to freeze out your feelings, I offer, thinking my response rather obvious, clunky, too interpretive and ped-estrian, and so I try again: *The cold shower was perhaps a coping mechanism against your disappointment and loneliness?*

Exactly; but over the years it's become more extreme. Because as we get older, feelings get stronger, right?

Perhaps feelings evolve, hence the bags of ice cubes in the bath? I reply.

She nods. A pause.

You mentioned earlier your father, the jerk, I say.

Kitty sniggers into her hand. *It's funny hearing you say that,* she smiles. Her response, I note, feeling much younger than her twenty-three years.

Why is he a jerk? I ask.

He's threatening to cut my allowance now I'm working. I mean, money is the least he can offer after what he puts me through.

I gesture for Kitty to elaborate.

Take yesterday, she begins—

The day had started with a cool shower. Next, a phone call from her father—an insomniac—who said he was planning a special birthday party for Kitty's mother. *So you'll fly to Sarasota on Saturday,* he said. *I've booked your ticket. Bring something suitable to wear, nothing too tight, or too short.*

She'd eyed a short, tight dress hanging in her custom-built wardrobe and felt a flicker, a thrill of "fuck you, control freak."

Sure, Daddy, she smiled down the telephone.

Kitty's parents, who were now retired, spent most of the year in *the sunny place for shady people, only they're the squarest people you'll ever meet,* Kitty says.

Control over how she looked at her mother's birthday party was to be expected, but news of her allowance being significantly cut *because you and Vincent are both earning well and capable of standing on your own two feet now,* was not. Kitty saw red.

I have to go now, she said, a rush of heat causing her chest to rise and fall at terrific speed; *I have a shoot in an hour.* On replacing the handset, Kitty thought about running a cold bath, but realizing she only had an hour before she was needed in southwest London, poured herself two fingers of vodka instead. On her way to the shoot she called Vincent, who was less impacted by the news. *He's got a point.* Kitty again saw red and ended the call.

He's such a pussy, she says, a look of disdain.

At the photo shoot Kitty was preoccupied and overwhelmed with indignation. Who did her father think he was slashing her allowance without warning? *Such a jerk.* How she hated the control he had over her, still. The speed at which he could deny her and Vincent of their allowance that was *both needed and relied on.* She seethed quietly while awaiting instructions for the day's shoot, unimpressed by the studio's offering of a yogurt and tiny segments of fruit that had been fanned out into pretty exhibitions. She wanted a big fat pastry instead. *Do you have any pastries, croissants, carbs?* she'd asked rather firmly, and was met with disguised irritation from the photographer's assistant. Later, she felt annoyed at how long hair and makeup was taking, shooing away their busy hands. *Can you hold your head still? Turn; close your eyes,* they'd directed. Kitty scoffed down her pain au chocolat, encouraging the pale flakes of pastry to live in her mouth. She was suddenly struck by how small and powerless she felt, *like I was eleven years old again,* she says. *Alone and defenseless.*

Vexed with their demands, Kitty decided on a bathroom break, the lingering conversation earlier with her father still preoccupying her thoughts.

Why are people always telling me what to do? she asks.

You're a model, right? I say.

Yes.

Am I missing something?

No. Touché.

I reach for a sip of water.

In the bathroom she'd scrolled her mobile phone for pictures of bichon frise puppies and fluffy white kittens, the "*Happy*" album storing at least two thousand images of cute, tiny animals. She'd checked her watch and decided hair and makeup wouldn't mind if she sat awhile longer and watched a short tutorial on how to knit a particular style of winter scarf and hat with oversized pom-poms. *I have a tummy ache,* she'd lied, which hair and makeup would presume was code for *I've eaten a pastry and now I need to throw up.* But they would be wrong. Kitty simply wanted to be left alone to watch and listen to the clicking of knitting needles, the purring of kittens. Both sounds helping to soothe her sad and lonely heart.

I note my desire to balm Kitty's pain, her crippling aloneness. Her previous bravado of pretend smoking and strong language suddenly making clinical sense while she defends against her anxiety. I picture her perched in the bathroom cubicle, hiding, attempting to self-regulate watching her mobile phone. I wonder what other survival mechanisms have been nurtured and honed to calm her living angst.

During the shoot Kitty felt as though she'd left her body. *It was as if I was floating, like I was on autopilot. I just did what the photographer told me to do.* Just moments before, she'd pictured herself on a calm beach and suddenly felt an overwhelming wave of aloneness and regret for not having taken Vincent up on his offer of a warm holiday.

Your body did as it was told? I inquire.

Exactly. I couldn't feel a thing.

We all dissociate, to some degree. Take, for example, the times when we double-book and find ourselves meeting a friend for lunch having made an appointment at the dentist at the exact same time. Another example of mild dissociation is when we might walk into a room with no recollection of what it is we are going in there to do. At the other end of this continuum is where complex trauma-related disorders are characterized by a division of the personality into different "alters," each with its own response to the trauma that the patient has survived. This is what is now known as dissociative identity disorder, previously known as multiple personality disorder. Often when a person experiences dissociation they will feel detached or disconnected from their body and/or their feelings. This is sometimes described as feeling numb, unreal, or as if one is an outside observer of their own life, which can manifest into having out-of-body experiences. There can also be experiences of "the unreal" that patients have previously described in session as *living in a fog,* or *a haze.* I was interested to explore further Kitty's possible dissociation, and whether this was a regular occurrence in her life.

I think you may be describing what is known as dissociation, I offer.

I do it quite a lot, she says.

With her body *on autopilot, a puppet on a string,* Kitty's mind turned vague, blank almost. The photographer with his sad mouth and ordinary eyes ordering her to *ease your shoulder toward me; extend your neck; lean into the shot—long legs, strong legs; head back.* Kitty's body did as it was told for the desired shot, her thoughts adrift and convincing her that she had the easiest, most glamorous job in the world. *Who wouldn't want my life,* she thought, all the while picturing bichon frises, fluffy white kittens, and knitted pom-poms.

Submission is commonplace in my life, she says, and I listen.

The first time Kitty slept with a man who suggested cuffs with no keys, it felt like a tiny skylight had opened up inside her. She wasn't sure if it was the way she'd forced him down on the couch or the sight of her heels that had gotten him so roused, but the invitation and possibility had thrilled her.

He'd put his hands above his head and pressed his wrists into the velvet cushions to give her an idea of what he wanted. *Over there, in the top drawer,* he nodded. Kitty stared over her shoulder in the direction of a sleek lacquered cupboard and ordered him, *Stay where you are.*

She spent no longer than a few seconds searching for the tiny key that would later unlock his leather cuffs, but quickly decided this was not her problem, cuffed him and made herself a cup of tea. His kitchen cupboards, she noticed, were rather empty but his selection of glamorous teas was abundant, superb even. She liked the vast choice of boxes he'd stacked like a game of Tetris and settled on licorice and fennel. *Stop moving,* she ordered from the rectangle of his kitchen door, slowly sipping her tea from a bone china cup. This was the first time she'd found herself *as a potential Dom,* a dominatrix, but it seemed to come rather naturally, she thought. The tiny skylight offering a multitude of possibilities, explorations and, more importantly, *freedom.*

Later, they moved their bodies into his bedroom. A clinical, Muji-esque showroom with a low wooden bed, rubber plants, and lots of blaring white by way of cushions, bed linen, and curtains. Kitty noted how clean and fresh-smelling the room was and immediately felt the urge to spoil and disrupt the order of things. *A desire to rip it all up and cause chaos.*

The man lay on his bed. Arms again stretched above his head, stiff with pleasure. Kitty recognized his thrill and felt a sleek rush of her own between her legs. A flutter in her chest alive as she held her breath for amplified bliss. She wanted him to want her. She wanted him to submit to her so entirely that she possessed his desires and could know him so completely that he never had to ask for a thing. She straddled him, pushed his wrists deeper into his immaculate mattress and cotton bedsheets and with her free hand, held his throat.

Tell me what you want, she asked.

He sighed. *I want—*

She quickly moved her hand from his throat to his mouth, whispering, *Shhhh, I don't care what you want.*

The man rolled his eyes back in his head. *What do you want?* he attempted to speak beneath Kitty's fixed palm.

She looked at him and closed her eyes. *I want,* she began, then stopped herself. She knew what he wanted her to say, and refused him. Dirty words, words whispering shock and filth so he felt utterly desired. But what she really wanted was to burst him open, to have him submit to her entirely, body and mind, and to see and feel what was at the core of him like a ripened peach.

You strange, beautiful thing, the man said with clenched teeth.

Kitty didn't like the reference to *a thing, an it. An object.*

Her next move was surprising.

I'm leaving you now, she said, reclaiming her slim leather belt on the way out. The man's skin turning magenta from several of its lashes.

On her way home she stopped for a slice of pizza and couldn't stop smiling.

Kitty looks at me. *I know this might sound strange to someone like you,* she says, *but I've struggled to feel that intimate with anybody else, since.*

Someone like me? I inquire.

Normal, she says.

After the photo shoot had ended Kitty thanked the photographer and the team of stylists and apologized for her earlier mood. She also thanked the photographer's assistant for her pastry, and hair and makeup for their patience. *Let's have a drink some time,* she suggested, knowing nothing would ever come of it.

I'm curious why you offered to meet them knowing nothing would ever come of it, I inquire.

She shrugs. *It's just habit,* she says, *it's polite.*

Kitty hailed a black cab and headed across town to her friend Lavinnia's house, her face perfectly painted, hair back-combed into a coiffed French plait. Ethan, her *annoyingly keen* boyfriend, was already there waiting for her and had called several times to check where Kitty was. *I'm working, Ethan,* she'd barked down the phone. *I'll be there when I'm finished.*

The cabdriver checked his mirror.

Going somewhere nice?

A friend's house.

Busy day?

Yep. Working, she smiled.

What do you do?

I'm a dog walker.

My daughter likes animals, she wants to be a vet. Ever thought about being a vet?

Nope.

You're never alone if you have pets.

Kitty plugged in her headphones. There were several

voicemails on her mobile phone. One from Ethan checking if she'd left the studio and one from her father with suggestions of birthday gifts for her mother: *a watch, new luggage, something from Hermès, perhaps.* Kitty listened and deleted his voice and texted back: *I've already got mummy's gift, but thanks for suggesting. Speak soon xx.* A reply was sent seconds later: *What type of gift?*

Kitty hadn't in fact bought her mother's gift yet, but she didn't care for his suggestions and replied, *It's a surprise! xx*

Your mother doesn't like surprises, he texted back.

FUCK YOU, she wrote and deleted. *Call you later, daddy xx,* she wrote instead.

What prevents you from speaking your truth? I ask, one eye on the competitive nature of the father-daughter exchange, aggression played out from both sides of the pond.

It's just easier that way.

Easier?

Kitty looks away.

You're uncomfortable with potential conflict? I ask.

Perhaps. But not really. Maybe it's just with my father.

Why do you think that is?

A pause.

If I'm honest, she speaks gently, and I note that what she's about to speak pains her, *I just want him to love me. To see me. He sees Vincent, but not me. He sent me away and kept Vincent.*

She cries and her shoulders tremble. I catch her eyes in mine. Suddenly Kitty's work as a model makes perfect sense.

Kept Vincent, I think, is a curious detail, and one that might be used to describe a pet. I recall Kitty's earlier disappointment and how her beloved Lettuce was most likely left, abandoned. Kitty's pain locates itself in my stomach and collapses inside me. My body aches with Kitty's loss and separation. I acknowledge her earlier rage against her father *the jerk* as defense against her psychic pain and wonder how much of Kitty's early childhood suffering has been internalized in her body.

I sense there are feelings Kitty wants to avoid, feelings that perhaps are too painful to even think about. It seems I am having these feelings on her behalf. My countertransference an indicator of what she does not allow herself to feel. I am holding these feelings that Kitty understandably chooses to disavow in order to protect herself.

My countertransference is strong and insistent. While transference deals with feelings that the patient transfers onto the therapist and is often founded on earlier relationships, countertransference is the reverse: that is, similar, sometimes irrational feelings that I, as the therapist, have toward my patients. Occasionally, countertransference can make the work deeply uncomfortable, sometimes impossible. Imagine, for example, a psychotherapist of color treating a patient charged with racist attacks, or a victim of domestic violence treating a manic abuser, where the therapist is drawn into a reenactment of the racism and violence she has survived, and potentially spent considerable time in psychotherapy attempting to heal. What is reexperienced, albeit under different circumstances, is felt as secondary retraumatization. Understandably, the therapist may feel the injustice and pain is too great. The anger too outraging—especially if the patient is unable to feel remorse or hold themselves accountable for the crimes they have committed. I have in mind a consultation with a woman in her early forties during my first year of clinical practice. She'd contacted me because she was frequently finding herself *in scrapes with the police, do you have any free space?* What came to light during the consultation was that these *scrapes* involved her having racially attacked several men and women while in bars and nightclubs. One of her victims had been hospitalized. Another piece of information the potential patient chose to disclose was that her girlfriend had given her an ultimatum, *Get some help or we're over*. A red flag is raised for me when someone comes to therapy by way of ultimatum from a partner rather than wanting to begin therapy for themselves; I declined. But the biggest flag was when she told me, *Chinese are all right, they keep themselves to themselves. In fact I've had a couple of Chiney girlfriends*. A rookie therapist at the time, I'd struggled to contain my devastation and outrage. I think I may have even stuttered and stammered my way through what felt like a very, very long consultation. My common sense and countertransference were protecting me, warning me to pass the referral to a more experienced psychotherapist. Twenty years later, would I do things differently? Perhaps. But one thing's for sure—the stammer has gone.

But in milder form, countertransference can also be one of a therapist's most reliable tools, and without doubt one of the most effective. When a patient is unable to access her feelings—is perhaps dissociated, in denial or guarded against certain events—I often sense these feelings and hold on to them, processing when it might be a good time to reflect them back to her with ruminations such as, *I'm aware of feeling (angry, sad, bewildered, disappointed, and many more such adjectives) when I hear you say this. I'm wondering where you are, and how you feel?*

Kitty's shoulders begin to settle. Her breathing is more regular. She risks a smile and wipes her eyes with the back of her hand. The heavy chains on her wrist rattle like keys.

I'm sorry your parents sent you away, I say.

Thank you, she speaks quietly. *I felt so abandoned.*

Initial consultations are important for understanding what is at the heart of a patient's desire for therapeutic healing. At the end of any first meeting, the patient and I assess whether we can, and want, to work together—whether there's been a meeting of minds, hearts, and intention. More often than not, I'll feel my way through our conversation by asking if I like the patient and can imagine us working together. I'll inquire of myself whether I can be effective and have enough interest in the issues she's raised and would like to address. Usually, I have a fair sense of whether we're a good enough fit. And while I may have particular insight, knowledge, and experience of the psychotherapy framework, I also assess whether we might work collaboratively and if the unearthing of growth, intention, and inquiry are possible. If enough connection has been made during this first session and if the circumstances and logistics are workable regarding times and fees, our collaboration can begin. *After all, that's what we do, right. Pay people to figure shit out,* Kitty had said.

Have a pleasant flight, the flight attendant smiles. She walks Kitty to business class; plush, spacious seats. Her lean height matching Kitty's lean height. Kitty doesn't like that the pretty attendant appears perky and fresh and immaculate, and feels a wave of competitiveness rush through her body. *There's no such thing as a pleasant flight,* Kitty remarks. *I'd like a blanket, please.*

The flight attendant senses Kitty's coolness. *Can I get you anything else?* she asks, reaching for a blanket in the overhead locker.

A large gin and tonic, thank you.

Kitty hates flying. *Pleasant flight, pfft,* she scoffs again. Right now, she'd settle for a tolerable flight made less intolerable by the cushion of alcohol, distracting movies, and a couple of sleeping pills.

She slips her pedicured feet into cashmere slippers and swipes a fix of cute animals on her mobile phone, knowing she'll soon be ordered to *turn off all portable electronic devices during takeoff.* Recently, she's taken a shine to sausage dogs wearing bow ties

and cute, tiny outfits. *Fashionista dogs.* She likes their choc-
olatey eyes, kindness imbued in their delicate little faces. Kitty
wonders whether she might feel happier were she to have a
companion, a sausage. The flight attendant returns with Kitty's gin and tonic.

Thank you, Kitty smiles, softened by the scrolling of sausage
dogs. *I'm thinking about getting a dog,* she says, turning her phone
screen to face the flight attendant.

How cute, the attendant smiles with perfect teeth.

Kitty chugs down her drink. *Keep them coming,* she says.

She suddenly remembers Lettuce and her family's suspicious
cover-up. A prick of tears is forced away as she pops two sleeping pills, no liquid, the tight lodge of the pills forced down
with a harsh swallow. Eyes closed, she reflects on her first therapy session and then changes the diary on her mobile phone to
accommodate our next appointment, via Skype. Having just
one session before her trip was not ideal, we had both acknowledged, but necessary. Kitty wonders how old I am. Where I
live. If I'm happily married, single, a mother perhaps. She wonders if I like her.

A year or so into her therapy Kitty will ask me these questions, and I will answer some—not all—of her curiosities with
caution.

Kitty buckles up and imagines herself in the cockpit, hands
on the steering wheel. Destination: Sarasota for her mother's
special birthday party. She quickly looks up what a steering
wheel is called on an airplane and discovers it's called a yoke,
alternatively known as a control wheel or a control column.
Kitty knows she is distracting herself from her feelings. Just
seconds ago she was back in touch with how *cruel and dismissive*
her family are, how *when they left me I felt so much rejection it was
as if I no longer existed. Like I'd completely disappeared.*

She feels her chest tighten and wonders if she's about to have a panic attack, searches for the customary paper sick bag to breathe into. The flight attendant returns with her second gin and tonic. *I'm a nervous flyer,* she admits. The attendant squats down beside her and rests her hand on the arm of Kitty's seat. *Would you like me to sit with you for a while?*

No, I'll be fine, Kitty says, unable to accept her professional kindness. The flight attendant stands and leaves.

Please turn off all portable electronic devices is announced into the ether of the airplane. Kitty closes her eyes again, feeling both dejected and comforted by the flight attendant's orders. She wishes she didn't feel so satisfied and soothed by other people's commands.

Part of our therapeutic process will be concerned with Kitty's resistance to nurture and kindness. When people offer their love and support she struggles to believe and trust it. She suspects pity or domination rather than friendship or the cheer of having people who care. We will explore how this unkind-kindness reminds her of early deprivation while at boarding school, where she stuffed down her feelings for fear of total collapse. There, she discovered survival through competition, and this was effective, to a point. The behavior serving to protect her, but also making Kitty fearful of the bonds of love, dwarfed and thwarted by possible intimacy.

She drinks herself to sleep with the help of several tiny tins of tonic water and gin, and dreams that she is swaying in a garden hammock, warm air dancing across her cheeks. But the dream turns to one of menace: she is suddenly trapped in an overhead locker of an airplane. Kitty senses dampness beneath her. She realizes the claustrophobic locker is filling up with ice-cold water. She bangs on the locker door with her fists, her chest charged with anxiety. She cannot breathe. She screams. When Kitty finally wakes up she is breathless, disorientated, and frightened. She attempts to call back images of the garden hammock, but her mind refuses her this balm.

The flight attendant offers her a smile as Kitty disembarks.

Thank you, Kitty offers politely.

Her father is waiting for her at the airport's arrival lounge wearing a loud shirt and light-colored trousers. When he waves, Kitty feels conflicted with feelings of love and hatefulness. Tanned and smiling, he rests his hands in his pockets. His relaxed energy puts Kitty on edge. She is tired and groggy after her flight and wishes her mouth had a peppermint.

Hello Daddy, she says, leaning into his shirt that is soft and loud with botanical print.

You look thin, he says, *and pale.*

He wraps his thick arms around her and the moment Kitty's body accepts his holding of her, she sobs uncontrollably. For a moment she is the little girl returned to her family, homesick and exhausted after a year at boarding school. She allows her body his warmth.

Kitty doesn't show up for her appointment via Skype, as planned. Instead, she leaves an apology on my voicemail saying she wasn't able to find a safe place to talk. Her message is confusing and garbled. Her tone much younger than I recall from our first meeting. I wonder if she will return.

I use the session to reflect on our first meeting. I'm curious as to whether Kitty has had second thoughts; if she felt there had been enough connection between us. Maybe it is too big a risk for her to trust a therapist, a new person to share her thoughts and feelings with. Or perhaps she has decided therapy cannot help her after all. Listening to her telephone message and my experience of meeting her feels inconsistent and confusing. *Possible regression,* I write down in my notepad. I also write down: *Abandonment anxiety, Sibling rivalry, Dissociation, Submission, Rage at her father (the jerk?) Mother? Intimacy?*

I wonder if I'm overthinking things and note my discomfort. Perhaps my unease is a window into how Kitty felt when her parents left to live overseas. I sit with my confusion awhile longer and read an email Kitty had sent me after our first session that stated: *Please don't leave without giving me significant notice.*

I make a pot of tea, thoughts of separation alive in my mind as I watch the tiny peppermint leaves settle. After my second, third sip, an image of Kitty materializes in my mind: The lost child returned home for her mother's birthday party.

Angry rain falls behind her.

I'm sorry I didn't make my session last week, she begins. *It was difficult to find a quiet place. There were lots of people in the house and it didn't feel safe.*

How were the birthday celebrations? I inquire, noting I am pleased, mildly relieved even, that Kitty has returned to therapy.

The birthday had started with breakfast on the terrace. *Champagne and fruit,* Kitty says. She'd kissed her mother's cheek, *Happy birthday, Mummy,* and thrust a bouquet of pale pink roses at her chest. A lesson learned last year after a huge bouquet of blue hydrangeas was met with, *Oh darling, they won't match a thing!*

Vincent, already on his second glass of fizz, had invited and introduced his new girlfriend who he'd met in California on a yoga retreat the week before. Kitty liked her immediately, *she's so much more fun than his last girlfriend.*

Later, gifts were offered and opened—Kitty having selected a new handbag and a carefully curated photo album from which she was missing for the first few pages. Her mother was thrilled.

Look how cute you both were, her mother giggled, pointing at a fading square memory of Kitty and Vincent eating ice cream one summertime in the UK, though where the photograph was taken escaped her. Cornwall? St. Ives? She couldn't remember. Memory loss: the cure for all things horrid, I think to myself.

Her father gifted his wife of thirty years a new watch, and Vincent happened across a Hermès scarf. Kitty's mother couldn't have been happier.

Later, at the party, Kitty drifted from room to room, dipping quail's eggs into celery salt while catching up with old and new friends of her parents. She glanced at her mother, glamorous, animated, and flush with birthday happiness. Her father was adoring, the observer. Kitty's dress was black and knee-length, not too tight, and her father congratulated her on this. *You look pretty,* he said, *very elegant.* Kitty thanked him and felt a rush of acknowledgment, albeit the dress was to his taste and not hers. *Can we talk about my allowance?* she asked. *Not tonight, Katherine, it's a party. Go help your mother with the shrimp.*

He shooed me away like I was a stray pet, Kitty says.

Later, Kitty had sex on the beach. The act, like the drink, was delicious, fruity, a pleasant kick to it. Kitty enjoyed how connected she felt to the man and his body. His arms were thick, hands not as keen as she'd hoped but firm nonetheless, chest smelling of limes. A small party had gathered and as Kitty walked barefoot along the pale sand he'd casually approached and invited her to join their intimate group and campfire. Afterward they drank vodka, neat, and talked about her made-up life and the latest series on Netflix. She told the man her name was Deborah and that she was over visiting friends for a couple of days. He'd asked for her phone number. *Sure,* she said, writing down numbers on his hand, purposefully missing a digit at the end. She wanted to see if he'd try to work it out. How committed he was to find and reach her. She liked the man from the beach.

I can't open my heart to anybody but strangers, she tells me, crestfallen.

When Kitty returned to her parents' house, a very drunk Vincent let slip a hurtful secret: *Lettuce never made it to Asia.* He gasped and placed his palm over his mouth. *Please don't let them know you know, I swore I'd never tell,* he smirked. His new girl-friend fixed an enquiring eye on her new boyfriend, suspicious perhaps of the intention behind his disclosure. Kitty waited, mindful not to appear vengeful, but when the time was right her fragility turned into a bomb, and she let slip, *Mummy and Daddy took you to Asia because they knew you wouldn't cope without them.* She gasped and placed her palm over her mouth. *Please don't let them know I told you. I swore I'd never tell.* Kitty smiled. *What was your nickname again?* She paused. *Weakling.*

The following evening Kitty drove all five of them along the west coast in search of a good seafood restaurant. *That one,* her mother pointed.

Inside, Vincent asked for a table overlooking the beach. *I'm afraid we're fully booked, sir,* said the maître d'.

No tables, Vincent shrugged, turning to face his family.

Oh, that's weakling talk, Kitty spat, pushing past her brother while glancing at her father for approval. *Leave it to me.*

Five minutes later they were shown to their table overlook-ing the beach. *You're too kind,* Kitty smiled at the maître d', her mother and father both notably impressed.

It pays to be insistent, Vincent, Kitty said.

Throughout the visit neither of Kitty's parents offered any real interest in her life. Each went about their days, golf mainly, and shopping appointments. Her mother insisting that Kitty relax and sunbathe. *You're so pale, darling. Rest up.*

On the final day of her trip Kitty decided to download pictures of herself from her most recent modeling shoots. Her favorite was a close-up for a beauty editorial. She liked the way her eyelashes were curled, the blue of her eyes enhanced to appear like vast, open lakes.

Why are there no pictures of me here? Kitty asked her mother, scanning the room. She didn't say that she'd counted no less than five framed portraits of Vincent in various rooms of the house. *What do you mean, darling? Don't be silly.* Kitty's mother led her to the hallway and downstairs bathroom. *See!* Her mother pointed at a magazine cover hanging next to several light jackets and coats. *And here,* she said again, pointing at a photograph of Kitty in her teens, turquoise dress, a wide smile, hanging next to the bathroom sink and perfumed hand soap. *I love this photograph of you,* she said. *Daddy loves it, too.*

Kitty leans toward me in her chair. *It's really lovely having your photo hanging where people piss and hang their coats.* She leans back, quiet. Thinking, I suppose.

I can see how much this has upset you, I say.

Not really, she shrugs, *I'm used to it.*

I note how quick she is to dismiss my empathy and care.

I'm not convinced of this, I challenge. *Getting used to feeling hurt is not something I'd encourage.*

But it is what it is, she spits.

Sounds a little defeatist, I add.

She fumbles for a counterargument and cannot find it.

You don't need to suppress, deny, or feel shame here, I say. *We can study your emotions. Here, we can figure them out as we proceed.*

She nods weakly.

Thank you, she says.

Kitty explains how out of place she'd felt during the trip. How she'd felt much younger than her years, a little girl, a teen. Her grown-up self left behind in London. *I left a woman and arrived a little girl,* she laughs. A lunatic smile.

There is a problem with your joking around, I say. *While we've talked about the issues that troubled you, such as your photograph hanging in the toilet, the five photographs of Vincent, leaving a woman and arriving a girl, we haven't dealt with your hurt. You avoid your pain with defensive humor.*

Kitty casts a look south at her feet. *If I don't make a joke out of it I'll feel sad the whole time. That, or complete rage.*

But do you see that in not feeling sadness or rage you avoid the opportunity to understand yourself and your situation more fully. Humor may help for a short time but it doesn't help to heal the wounded girl inside, or your parents' behavior toward you now as a woman.

I understand, she says.

Silence.

The man on the beach didn't call. Whether he tried to figure out the missing number, we'll never know. *His loss, for real,* Kitty says, a tinge of disappointment in her voice.

I didn't have the conversation about my allowance, either, she says, her mood turning low. *When Daddy's made up his mind, there's no changing it.*

I imagine that can feel very frustrating, I say.

Frustrating, like I'm a child.

You mean infantalizing? I ask.

Yes. Anyway, money can't replace what I lost as a girl. I do know that.

I'm relieved to hear you say this.

Are you? I'm not, Kitty says. *It hurts like hell.*

I take a deep breath and clear my throat.

We often hurt before we heal.

The therapeutic encounter is, in essence, a human event. A moment of intimate meeting between two people that explores some of the most profound questions about what it means to be human: *Who am I?* a patient might ask, and, *What do I really want? Who will love me? Am I lovable? And can I love in return? Am I holding on to something that I need to let go of? When do I get to choose? How do I respond to someone in a position of power? Is there a God? What is home? What's the point? How can I best contribute to my community and fulfill my own desires and interests? How do I do this? Will it hurt? Will I ever be free . . . ?*

And from the therapist: *What do you want? What do you need? Are you safe? When you pause, what happens? What would you do differently if no one was around to judge you? Are you doing enough about loving your person? How do you connect but remain an individual? When you fell down as a child, who picked you up? Do you trust yourself? What small act of kindness do you remember? What does desire taste, look, and feel like? What would feel empowering for you, right now? How might you liberate yourself? If not now, when?*

For the next twelve weeks Kitty arrives for her sessions with keen inquiry. She brings a notepad and pen and asks for recommendations to support our work—books, texts, and podcasts—and expresses a desire to increase her once weekly session to twice weekly. She talks about Ethan, her *on-off boyfriend*. A carpenter who works with large chunks of wood and creates beautiful chairs—*works of art*—their seats hollowed out after hours of care and commitment. *Try it out. Is it comfortable?* Ethan asks. Ethan's chairs are always comfortable.

Kitty tells me she feels safe in his predictability and homeyness. What she previously read as *annoyingly keen* has morphed into a pleasurable, tender relationship, Kitty delighting in their nightly intimacies; sweet zealous communion. This shift in her attitude feeds my soul. That he isn't too possessive is attractive to Kitty and allows her the opportunity to have passionate, yet brief attachments with new men. *We agreed some time ago to have an open relationship,* she says, piling her hair high before stabbing a pencil in to hold its weight.

This works for you both? I inquire.

Sure. Well— She pauses and glances at the ceiling. *I think Ethan would prefer it if we were a couple, exclusive, but I can't.*

Can't?

Won't, she adds quickly.

Say a little more.

I fear his abandonment, she says. *It terrifies me.*

Words are not events. They represent events. If one continues to let a word terrify and inform life choices it will feel as if you are in a time loop of repeating the past, staring once again at the primal wound which in Kitty's case was early childhood abandonment.

I understand, I say, *but if you allow the abandonment to frighten you, it will always feel as if you're still back there, the eleven-year-old girl who was left while her family set up home in a different country. Do you see?*

I do, she nods.

The effort it takes to distract or avoid, be it work, sex, or ice-cold baths is exhausting. You and I need to reframe what separation and abandonment mean to you, otherwise it is possible you will continue to feel trapped and caged by your avoidance to heal.

How do I do this?

The way to, let's say, neutralize the pain associated with a particular feeling is to try your best to be with it, to lean into it knowing it will only hold power as long as you are guarded against it. I believe that no feeling, such as your fear of abandonment, or the imagining of it, can hurt you more than the act of avoiding it.

A pause.

Got it, she whispers.

Kitty also explores, with playfulness, alternative careers:

shop owner, writer, designer, florist, photographer, nutrition-
ist, dog walker/trainer, cook.

How did you come to be a model? I ask.

I just fell into it, she says, checking her nails. *I was scouted one
weekend when I was in Top Shop trying on jeans. I was only seventeen. It helped that I could ski, ride a horse, and snowboard. Modeling
agencies like athletic models who can actually do something other than
look pretty.*

She settles on the idea of exploring further her love of cooking and nutrition and talks about kombucha with such passion
that I find myself buying several bottles the following week
from Whole Foods while on my lunch break. *What's scoby?* I
ask, wanting to mirror her enthusiasm.

It stands for "symbiotic culture of bacteria and yeast."

None the wiser, I ask her to educate me and she does this
with energy and spirit.

The following week Kitty brings me a bottle of homemade
strawberry kombucha. A charming label attached that she has
taken the time to adorn with tiny strawberry stickers.

I'm not sure if I'm allowed to give you this, she says, lowering
her eyes with shyness, *but I thought you might like to try it. I made
it myself.*

There is much discussion among psychotherapists regarding
the offer of gifts from patients. Some therapists claim the eroti-
cization of gift-giving is meaningful because of its connection
to the libido; that often the gift represents love and affection
that is not always verbalized in the room. Over the years I have
been offered gifts from my patients. Some I have graciously
declined and others I have gratefully accepted. Acceptance is
based on feeling, clinical understanding, and connection, and
my preference is that patients find words to acknowledge and
express their feelings rather than offering gifts.

Thank you, I say, receiving Kitty's kombucha, *I love straw-berries. And look at this cute label you've taken the time to create.*

I hope you enjoy it, Kitty smiles, and for a moment I am faced with her younger self. Keen for intimacy, bold in her attempt to connect.

We also discuss coping strategies for her anxiety and I encourage Kitty to reflect on her struggle to be present in her everyday life, *in the here and now.* I explain how preoccupation with the future by constantly planning, keeping extremely busy and avoiding feelings will increase the likelihood of her ongoing anxiety. We also talk about the other end of the continuum, when one is preoccupied with the past, and that is where depression awaits. *This is a rather simplistic explanation,* I say, but my hope is that by encouraging Kitty to be more present she will be able to address her fear of feeling.

Kitty whips out her phone like a handgun from its holster and downloads one of the many apps made available for meditation and mindfulness. I note the urgency of her desire, agency alive and potent, and this pleases me.

When the app has finished downloading she turns her phone to face me. *There, done,* she affirms.

Very good, I say, sensing validation and acknowledgment is important. While Kitty is a responsive and receptive patient, I wonder whether, in appreciating her willingness and therapeutic progress, I'm embodying a type of collusion. Am I reenacting what others before me have done by way of affirming "the good student"? I will have to wait and see.

During our time together Kitty has talked of her desire and craving for external validation, and what she calls *The warm gaze.* This makes her feel wanted, accepted, and seen. It began at home with her parents; later, her House Parent and the other girls at boarding school when they championed her talents for hockey. Later still, teachers, professors, boyfriends, lovers, modeling agents, and photographers. Kitty would bask in their attention, their gaze; her child within longing to belong and be seen. And although I'm keen for Kitty to ignite this validation within herself rather than having external opinions rule over her, I'm mindful that growing self-love and acceptance takes time and discipline.

Kitty swipes her phone again and stares at its screen. She is quiet. Eyes fixed.

Do you remember me telling you about my "Happy" album? she asks softly.

I do.

I have other albums, too.

Oh? I inquire.

Pictures that thrill me, sadden me, shock and excite me. Sometimes when I space out, what I now understand as dissociation, say on a modeling job where I need to feel and perform, I tap on my phone to look at the images. I forget sometimes what funny, excited, sexy, or calm feels like, but when I see a cat dressed as a superhero or aquatic fish swimming in the ocean it helps me to get in touch with my emotions.

I see, it helps to have a reference point? The image accesses feelings that might not occur without these pictures?

Exactly, she says.

A pause.

I catch her damp eyes in mine.

There's another album, she adds tentatively, a veil of quiet tears. *They're mainly pictures of me.*

Of you? I say, curious with inquiry.

She nods. *I call this album, "Lonely."*

Knowledge is liberation. Self-knowledge is emotional liberation. In owning this visual record and understanding of herself, Kitty has allowed me to witness her vulnerability.

Issues of how a patient can trust, how betrayal can make us fearful of intimacy, what desire and sexuality mean to the individual, how abandonment and disappointment can impact on self-worth, and how we risk opening ourselves up again through healing are all present in the psychotherapeutic process. The intimate relationship in the consulting room becomes a witness to, an advocation for, and a participant in a unique moment of emotional liberation.

Thank you for sharing this with me, I say.

I'm conflicted, she says. *Part of me feels seen and wants to trust you, but part of me is also thinking about when I can leave therapy. Because if I get attached, you could leave me.*

I imagine trusting somebody is a great risk, I say, *but one that is perhaps worth taking?*

I'm ambivalent, she says. *I want my family, especially my father, to see me. But at what cost?*

Good question, I say. *Perhaps being seen for "you" rather than for all your achievements is a good place for us to start. I like to call it the "Inside-Out."*

Inside-Out?

If we address challenging feelings here, inside your therapy, it's possible you'll feel more assured and safer about challenging feelings outside in the world. It strikes me that you didn't have a home in which to safely explore your emotions while you were at boarding school. Instead, you turned to cold showers, competition, and controlled eating. I'd like us to try something different, here: a secure base, potentially.

I'd like that, she risks.

We are silent.

I wonder if another album might be added to your phone? I say.

She leans forward in her chair. *Yes?*

"Connected," I smile.

★

After six months of working together Kitty and I hit our first rupture. In an attempt to honor her request of *considerable notice before leaving,* I let her know three weeks in advance of my forthcoming holiday but am met with hostility and defense.

Kitty is late for her sessions and cancels two, calling on previous survival strategies by way of dismissal, denial, and competitiveness.

I think a break from therapy will be good for me, she spits. *Out of sight, out of mind; I'll be away for two weeks when you return;* and, *I completely forgot you're on holiday next week.*

Perhaps it's difficult to acknowledge my leaving for a holiday, I say.

I don't remember a time when I needed a holiday, she scoffs. *But I guess doing what you do must be tiring.*

I take the bitter sideswipe, offering, *Holidays are of no interest to you?*

Until recently, holidays were just an opportunity to be where I should have always been: with my family. Just as I'd start to feel settled, it was time to leave again. So holidays were not pleasant. They were a reminder that I was alone.

I take the opportunity to show her how past events shape current feelings, and say, *I wonder if my going on holiday triggers that same feeling. That when I leave, you will be alone, again.*

She looks away, tears forming in her eyes.

Your leaving feels like a mini death, she says.

Kitty recalls the time when she and her family had taken a holiday in Cornwall. *I must have been nine, no, maybe ten years old,* she says, surprising herself with the memory that, until now, had been understandably forgotten, dissociated from.

I remember when you were celebrating your mother's birthday, you mentioning a photograph, I say, *one with you and Vincent eating ice cream. I seem to recall you saying how your mother thought how cute you both were.*

I did? says Kitty, confused. A pause— *Ohhh—yeeeah, I did,* she says slowly, eyes narrowing, head nodding, *I forgot about that.*

Memory loss, I say, *the cure for all things horrid.*

It was the last holiday we took together as a family before I was sent to boarding school, she recalls. *I remember we'd all walked down to the beach after eating our ice creams. Vincent and I decided to go swimming in the sea. But Vincent panicked. I thought he was messing around, so I ignored his attempts to let me know he was out of his depth. When I swam back to the beach I turned around and he was gone. Lifeguards were called. Mummy and Daddy were furious with me. He'd ended up further along the coastline and when he staggered back to us he was hysterical. It was my fault, apparently. A stronger swimmer, I was expected to keep him safe. The following day they told me I was going to boarding school. I couldn't help but think it was punishment for what happened to Vincent.*

This may sound like an obvious question, I say, *but is it possible you associate separation and abandonment with doing something "wrong," the expectation that you should have kept Vincent safe, for example?*

Yes, that's why I try to put things right by being polite, or apologizing. I'm terrified of being rejected.

Like the time at the photo shoot? I ask.

She nods.

I'm always expected to be the strong one, she adds. *It's exhausting.*

Of course, it must be. It's a very binary position. You are strong and Vincent is vulnerable—or so the story goes. You have mentioned that your parents believed Vincent wouldn't cope without them. Then came the rather challenging description of the weakling, I say.

Whose side are you on? she barks.

I don't believe in sides, I speak calmly. Her aggression is quick to rise, and for a moment I catch a glimpse of how defensive and frightened she is. *But I do believe in exploring how one's past shapes future behavior and beliefs. While our past doesn't define us, it has a habit of repeating itself until understood. I think part of you likes to believe Vincent is a weakling because it helps protect you from the hurt that your parents took him and left you.*

Yes, she admits, *I don't mean to be cruel. He was vulnerable, not a weakling.*

Kitty continues to describe our separations as *mini deaths.*

But I do know you will come back now, she smiles.

There is a period of deep depression at approximately one year into our work when Kitty lives and leans into her feelings of aloneness. She tells me, *The drugs don't work anymore,* meaning previous survival strategies such as sex, shopping, excessive working hours, and days on her PS5 no longer help her escape her crippling solitariness. Her baths, however, are no longer iced. Instead, they are drawn at night before bedtime and enjoyed, not endured—sweet-smelling tubs of warmth. For the past year she has even added various tinctures: bubble bath, lavender oil, salts, and enjoys the warming balm they offer. Often, she sits in the bath for hours at a time, topping up the cool water with hot, which she experiences as a *warm hug.* Here she reads, listens to podcasts, plays chess with Ethan, and even considers moving in a television before realizing this *probably isn't the safest of decisions.*

Sometimes I think I'll always feel like I'm alone, she says.

There's a difference between the feeling of being alone and the reality of aloneness, I offer.

Ethan wants us to move in together, she says.

Oh?

Do you think I should? she asks.

Do you want to move in with Ethan?

Part of me does. But part of me feels scared. If he moves in and then leaves, I'll be even lonelier.

Feelings of loneliness will not destroy you, Kitty, I say, *and no feeling is final. But if we live life fearful of the "what ifs," we wouldn't change a thing. Do you see?*

Kitty stares me square in the eye.

Are you sure? Are you certain? I'm scared.

Intimacy and attachment can feel scary, I offer, *but if you avoid these feelings it's possible you will make life choices based on fear, and not liberation.*

Words are not events, she says.

Exactly.

Three months later, Ethan moves into her apartment. They decide to paint the walls a different color—*elephant's breath*—and add soft, pastel furnishings. Art is chosen, paid for, and later hung. Ethan also makes two chairs and Kitty enjoys it when they settle at night beside one another before she eventually climbs onto his lap where she curls herself, fetal, content, *a sleeping pussycat.*

Finally, I feel like I have a home.

Home is not the house, but the people who occupy it, I offer.

So true.

In working with Kitty for just over three years we have explored and gained insight into the power and pain of her anxiety. *Home is where we start from,* the pediatrician and psychoanalyst Donald Winnicott told me once, and with this in mind I was curious and determined to explore with Kitty her rage and powerlessness toward her father, no longer *the jerk,* and with whom she has developed, alongside her mother, a different kind of relationship—less as the compliant, dutiful, and successful daughter, and more as the strong, sensitive, and also vulnerable adult woman who is not defined by her past but who is healing from it.

Woven into the archaic tapestry of middle and upper-middle class British culture is the experience and acceptance of early separation from one's parents at boarding school. A blueprint of painful separation. Kitty experienced this separation as *abandonment* that was enhanced by her feeling rejected after her parents decided to take her brother with them to Asia. Much of Kitty's earlier life was spent in the mastering of her hurt rather than the grieving of it. Children taken from their homes at such an early age are encouraged to *be brave* and, in some cases, grateful even. They are also encouraged to convert this loss into believing *it will be good for them*, a belief that *boarding school builds character*. For Kitty, separation from her family was traumatic on many levels. She internalized and experienced feelings of being "less than." A story developing in her mind that she was unloved, unwanted, and that she must, at all costs, be high achieving and successful in order to be seen. But Kitty did not feel seen, and never more so than when she was modeling.

To be in a foreign community with only a photograph and teddy bear for comfort was very frightening and confusing for Kitty. Furthermore, she knew her brother was at home and that she would only visit her family once, possibly twice a year, and that her beloved pet rabbit had died. To have her parents explain that it was in Kitty's best interest to be sent to boarding school made no sense at all. It is heartbreaking.

While Kitty's parents focused on her academia and independence, there was little attempt to soothe, heal, or speak of Kitty's aloneness, her loss, trauma, and terror. So Kitty honed her survival skills. She became a fierce competitor in hockey matches, a straight-A student who rarely fell ill, a brave young woman whom her parents thought was driven and determined, a fearless traveler and travel companion, a passionate lover who *performed bedroom gymnastics worthy of a gold medal*, a much-in-demand fashion model, and, later, a highly committed and hardworking patient.

Later, Kitty's rage kept her hurting alive, and while she continued to exist through the surviving of it, healing was limited because she was repeating old behaviors. Her desire is now focused on strengthening her core self, where feelings are not numbed by iced water but are acknowledged, owned, and felt. She accepts that her feelings will not destroy her.

After a period of depression that lasted for eighteen months, Kitty was able to grieve the loss of her longed-for childhood and home. That her parents sent her to boarding school remains a painful reality. There is no escaping this truth, and while she acknowledges the suffering this caused, and the sibling rivalry it evoked, Kitty chooses to not let it define who she is and the life choices she now makes.

One year after her father reduced her allowance, Kitty wrote to him to say she no longer wished to receive this monthly allowance at all—a desire to have agency in facing that which she feared most: *control and rejection.* This had an immediate impact on Kitty, the decision experienced much like an expansive freedom—a radical liberation—where she no longer felt beholden or frightened that something could once again be withheld or taken away from her. And at the close of her therapy Kitty's relationship with Ethan remained. As they edged closer to monogamy, Kitty continued to jostle with the ambivalent push and pull of *just the two of us,* but she no longer experienced his affection and commitment as *annoyingly keen. On the contrary,* she said, *he loves me, and I love him—for real.*

Anger as soon as fed is dead—
'Tis starving makes it fat.

Emily Dickinson (1890)

My Body, My Rules

She was once a girl who played with plush, primary-colored Care Bears. A girl in a ra-ra skirt who loved nothing more than collecting novelty erasers, Cabbage Patch Kids, and Duran Duran posters, and who dreamed of one day becoming a hairdresser. But shortly after her ninth birthday this rainbow was ruined, her childhood fell on quicksand; a stepfather arrived and settled, who, she tells me, *hurt me and took pleasure in watching me cry.*

She turned to food. A thread of shame pulling her toward the balm of a fridge, kitchen cupboards, and the pantry. She loved sweet things the most. Sweet and small so she could stuff them in whole and chew really fast and make the hurt disappear. Focusing on the bite, chew, and swallow distracted her from her feelings and his hatefulness toward her. It gave her brain a chance to switch gear, where she faded misery by disavowing her pain. But part of her also mistrusted her food friends. *Fingers,* she told herself, *were an even better friend.* Fingers—fore and middle—were forced down her throat and rid her of her suffering that, given half a chance, would be digested and attest her dire reality.

We will call him Nick because she has requested I use the initial "N," which was the same as his. *But really what do I care,* she says, *he's dead now, anyway.* A heart attack when she was seventeen years old and he was fifty-two. *His death was over too quickly,* she spits. And then shares how she'd wished for something slower, tormenting, psychologically menacing.

Something that had him suffering the way she had suffered. We will revisit her desire for revenge later, but for now I will introduce her as Ruth.

She was reserved and awkward when she telephoned for an initial consultation. I had a waiting list and no regular appointment slots free, but there was something about her slow, quiet voice and tentative approach that gently pulled at me. I left a message on Ruth's mobile phone suggesting we meet the following week. *Do let me know if this time suits . . .*

Ruth receives my message, her appointment, while scanning a customer's groceries. The supermarket where she works doesn't allow employees the use of their mobile phones while on the shop floor, but she senses the tickling vibration against her thigh and thinks Eve, her younger sister, or Aaron, the guy she's been dating for just under a year, must be leaving her a message. It's only when Ruth asks the customer she is serving to key his card number into the small plastic machine that she wonders if the therapist she contacted yesterday might have returned her call. Ruth is not used to people getting back to her or even noticing she exists. Sometimes she believes that were she to disappear entirely, no one would even notice.

Ruth feels calm when she stares down the line of supermarket workers all wearing loose cotton overalls. She likes the way that everyone looks the same, albeit with different hairstyles. Sitting behind the till offers Ruth anonymity and an opportunity to hide her body, a body that when standing in front of a mirror morphs and expands and swells. *Mirrors,* she will tell me in our first session, *are traitors. They lie the whole time. I don't trust them one bit.*

The ritual of scanning supermarket goods is something that Ruth does trust and enjoy. There is certainty to it—a repetitive neatness of beginning, middle, and end. Sometimes she makes conversation with her customers about the weather or a certain food item she's not seen before, or the various holidays that bring about special and particular purchases. The customers tend to not look at Ruth, not really. She is, after all, *a middle-aged woman not particularly blessed with good looks or charm,* she will speak shyly in one of her sessions. They are too busy unpacking their baskets ready for scanning, and Ruth likes it this way, a destitute gaze upon her. *I like it this way,* she will shrug.

Sometimes, I will soon learn, Ruth feels envious of the shoppers who pile up their baskets and trolleys with expensive foods, toiletries, and wine—the price displayed in front of them luxuriously ignored. She watches them add two, three, and sometimes more of the same item, which she'd only be *able to afford once a month, if that.* She wishes she had their freedom, and that she didn't have to visit the discount fridge at the end of the day, shame leaking into her fingertips as she sifts through strange and unwanted foods.

Often, when she has not eaten, she is triggered by the delicious sweet foods placed on the rolling rubber conveyor belt of the checkout line. She scans these items swiftly and tries to pay them no mind as they gently slide toward the bagging area. Having her stomach empty when she does this, she says, is experienced as respect and remembrance of her struggles. *If I fill my tummy I will get fat and forget how angry I am,* she will explain later. And I am incredibly sad and moved by her insight.

While on her lunch break Ruth checks her mobile phone and reads my message. After a few minutes or so she connects with a cluster of feelings: relief, fear, and disbelief that someone she doesn't know has actually bothered to reply to her message. She reaches inside the pocket of her cotton overalls and pulls out a bar of chocolate, thick and dark, tears off its crackly foil and stuffs it violently into her mouth. Less than a minute passes before the chewed brown sugar lands in the toilet basin. After her stomach is *unburdened* she takes out her phone, a voice in her head insisting she is weak while another accepts she needs help. *Hi Maxine,* she texts, *thank you for your message, I look forward to seeing you next Friday at 7.30, Ruth xxx.* And then another message shortly after: *Ps . . . Sorry I put kisses on my last message. I'm probably not meant to do this, Ruth.*

7:30 a.m.

She arrives—a petite, waiflike woman in her late-forties with a bulging rucksack, her large brown eyes cast down at the ground. I invite her to remove the hefty paraphernalia, imagining it must be heavy, while offering her a seat. It is almost as if I see the rucksack before I see her, but perhaps this is what she intends. Ruth doesn't remove the rucksack as I suppose she might, and I note my discomfort and irritation. *Why would she do that? I think to myself. Carry and sit with such unnecessary weight?* This question, I will soon discover, is integral for the work ahead, but in this moment I am struck by the awkwardness in Ruth's posture as she marshals her body to the edge of her seat.

Thank you for finding time to see me, she begins.

I note Ruth's in-turn of feet. Clothes, big and lifeless, like they're disguising or perhaps hiding her from the world. She quickly takes out her purse—small and tan with a gold clasp—held tightly in both hands. *Do I pay you now?* she asks. *I've only had therapy on the NHS and that was free. It lasted for ten weeks.*

Whatever you feel comfortable with, I offer, explaining that I work with a sliding scale and adjust my fees accordingly. We settle on a fee.

Okay, thank you, she smiles, allowing her shy body to set free the heavy rucksack before easing back into the chair.

I'm interested to know more about why you'd like to start therapy again, I say.

She rests her purse in her lap. *I need help,* she says. Ruth also shares how she wants to get better, feel better, about herself and her body because she's met a man who she *really, really likes and possibly even loves, and I don't want to mess it up, not now, not ever. I met him in my local pub about a year ago, his name's Aaron.*

And you mention the possibility of love, I say.

She nods, *Yeah,* she says, staring down at her rucksack. *But like I said, I'm worried I'm going to do something that will—*

She looks at me.

Mess it up? I answer, letting her know that I am listening.

Yes.

How so? I inquire.

She sighs. *I have so many problems, I don't know where to begin.* Ruth believes that being thin will solve everything: her likability, her lovability, and her ability to fit in. She believes that *mirrors are traitors. They lie the whole time. I don't trust them one bit*; that social media fuels depression. So why now, when she's hit her target weight, *do I feel the unhappiest I've ever been?* She tells me that her insecurity makes her *fly off the handle,* that she *gets all crazy* if Aaron doesn't respond to her calls. *I seem to be getting worse,* she cries. *I just want to be normal.*

I observe how young Ruth appears and feels, her forty or so years not quite matching, in my mind, the woman sitting in front of me. I note again her clothes, disheveled and too large for her slight frame. A combination of flared jeans, trainers, and a tie-dyed hoodie, something that perhaps a teenager might wear.

What is your vision of normal? I ask.

Someone who doesn't freak out when her boyfriend makes a new friend or doesn't call her back straight away. Someone who can be herself.

She talks about the mask she wears at work that is different to the one worn when she is with Aaron. When she is with her sister, Ruth wears another mask, and another when she goes online in the dark and talks to strangers with kinks.

And what about here? I ask. *Or perhaps it's too early to say.*

Yeah, she says, eyes narrowed and fixed, *I'm still sussing you out.*

I take a moment to remember the tentative woman who spoke to my voice mail last week, the apologetic text message and the shy woman who arrived earlier, but the woman sitting with me now, I note, has teeth.

I'm interested in your sussing me out, I say. *This keeps you safe?*

I guess.

What do you believe you're protecting yourself from? I ask.

She shrugs off my question. *I don't know, I just don't trust people easily.*

Trust takes time, we agree.

I don't make friends easily, she begins. *I've been burnt a few times. And I have major food issues. So as you might guess, I'm secretive. I also think Aaron will leave me. I don't sleep well. My only surviving family member—Eve, my younger sister—and me don't really get along. A lot of the time I feel paranoid and my neighbor is a complete dick.*

I am struck by the list. It is an interesting one. I am also fascinated by Ruth's candor and the clarity of her desire for seeking therapy, and how, even though she doesn't trust people easily, she has voiced her struggles and named her skill for secrecy.

She looks about the room. *But I guess what I really want to talk about is my eating—*

A pause.

I've never been to the doctors or been diagnosed with an eating disorder. But I've always had issues with food.

Can you say a little more? I ask.

It's usually all or nothing.

You eat and purge? I ask.

She nods. *And sometimes I don't eat at all.*

How long has this been happening? I ask again.

A long time.

Since you were a child?

A teenager, she says. *So, on and off for*—a pause—*maybe thirty-odd years.*

The first time Ruth made herself sick was on her thirteenth birthday, in spring 1986; *part of me saw it coming.* She was familiar with the balm of confectionery, of long-lasting tastes in her mouth as she popped in hard candies, sherbets, and cake, while her body, she tells me, *started to fill out, to grow up. I didn't like it.* Her mother had asked what type of cake she'd like for her birthday. Ruth had answered: *Chocolate! With chocolate sprinkles and chocolate icing!* Her mother had kissed her on the head. *Chocolate it is,* she'd smiled.

On dark days, Ruth suspects her mother was trying to fatten her up so she was less desirable, and on lighter days, when her unquiet mind is still, slow, and steady, she allows this thought to take shape as a question rather than a statement. There are other days when Ruth wonders if her mother ever sensed Nick's wandering eyes and creepy stares. Did she know and choose to ignore his inappropriate leering, his constant threats and dark cruelty? *How could her need for him be more important than my safety and sanity? Why didn't she protect me? Did she even care?* Ruth asks, so many unwanted images accompanying her questions: a teaspoon dipped in boiling water and pressed against her skin; secret and bizarre inventions of early morning rituals and tortures; a bar of soap forced into her mouth; fists tugging at her waist, the threat of sexual violence forever a possibility but thankfully never realized; his hand forced through the stair banister and chopping at her ankles; her hand pinned down to the kitchen table as he took a knife and jabbed it hard and at speed between her small, trembling fingers.

Breathe, I whisper inwardly.

On the day of her birthday Ruth asked herself whether Nick did these things because she was not his child and a constant reminder of the man before him, her father—who Nick knew. She worried his hate would *get worse because he might think turning thirteen meant I was a teenager* and therefore equipped and *woman enough* to withstand his spite and cruelty. Ruth could see no way out. Her dad was long gone, remarried, another wife, another family, another life somewhere in the north of England, miles away. As Nick liked to remind her, *You're all alone, your dad's gone, he left you and your mum to make another family. Your mum loves me now. Mess me around or say anything to your mum and I'll . . .*

Nick never finished the sentence. *Not once, not ever. And somehow,* Ruth tells me, *it felt more terrifying than knowing what he would do to me. My imagination went to all kinds of places. Did my mum not see what he was like, that he was cruel, controlling, and tormenting me? Was she really so blind to his vile and sadistic ways?*

In asking these questions Ruth attempts to make sense of her past and her suffering. Inquiry means she hasn't forgotten what he did to her. *I can't help myself,* she says, inquiring further: *Did he do these cruel things because he hated me? Or was it simply because he could?* What had been his story as a child, as a boy? Ruth has also wondered. *Did he ever feel remorse for what he did? Guilt? Shame? Disdain for the man he was?*

Ruth knows these questions will never be answered—*Not now, not ever*—her mother and Nick now long dead. She imagines him in hell, or in limbo if he ever held himself accountable after he worked his destruction. And as she learned the news of his quick death, aged seventeen, had wanted to make sure it was true, but also felt rage that he hadn't spoken: I'm sorry for what I did, Ruthie. I'm so sorry. Can you forgive me?

Would he have thought about what he'd done if his death was slow? she also asks. What if he'd had cancer, kidney failure, or Parkinson's disease—*would he have said sorry then as I sat beside his bed waiting for him to die?*

After Ruth's first session I take notes and reflect. I observe my heavy heart and close my eyes. My outward breath takes in the breadth of her struggles. Her request: *But I guess what I really want to talk about is my eating*—which I suspect is our starting point, a leap of faith and commitment and one of the many symptoms caused by the heinous acts of cruelty and violence she has survived at the hands of her now dead stepfather.

A desire felt deeply within me to support Ruth, I listen and observe my countertransference. There is hunger and wild stirrings in my stomach alive to her early childhood trauma and the impact it continues to have on her life. I write the words: *regulation, containment, consistency, care,* then, *What else does Ruth need?*, suspecting the rage and suffering she is turning upon herself needs to be directed toward the source of her pain: Nick.

I recognize, also, that building a secure base so Ruth can reflect and think clearly about the cruelty that was inflicted on her is crucial. That she was a victim and has survived needs to be named, felt, and realized. It needs to be embodied. It needs to be taken hold of and set free, I tell myself. And this, for sure, will take time.

In six months' time, Ruth and I spend time imagining what an apology might look like from the man who inflicted so much pain, fear, and suffering, and Ruth writes a letter to her younger self with the hope of expelling the power he continues to hold over her. *I've read a few books and magazine articles about people who've done this,* she says, *how they talk and care for their inner child. It sounded like a good idea.*

She holds the letter in a tight fist. *I wish my mum was here to read it,* she says, and asks if she can read it aloud, hoping that somehow in the ether, her mother will hear her words, her truth.

Some years following Nick's death, there were many times when Ruth wanted desperately to talk to her mum about Nick's cruelty. She'd even purchased and written in a diary after he'd died and left it on her bedside table hoping her mum would one day be curious enough to snoop. *How does a mother not want to read her daughter's diary?* says Ruth. *How?*

Perhaps she was respecting your privacy, I offer.

Pfft. More like she didn't want to know. Once you see and know something, you can't unsee it, right?

Right, I say. *You mentioned your mother died ten years after Nick's heart attack?*

Yes, cancer. She was only fifty-six.

You never had a conversation with her about Nick, and how he tormented you?

No, not really. After he died she could see no wrong in him. Me and Eve used to call him Saint Nick. If we ever tried to talk about how vile he was, Mum would change the subject and say how lucky we were that he stuck around, which, she'd say, was more than my dad did.

It must be incredibly painful, not having had the opportunity to address how cruel Nick was. This is why you want to read aloud what Nick did, with the hope that your mother will somehow hear you?

Yes, I didn't want to destroy her pipe dream, rob her of what she thought was love. We rarely spent time alone together, Nick or Eve or their friends were always there, hanging around, and then when he died she completely fell apart. A few years later she was diagnosed with cancer and it just felt too cruel, too selfish, to tell her what he did. There never seemed to be the right time to talk to her.

Silence.

I'd like to read my letter now, she says. *You don't need to say anything—just listen, please.*

Eight months or so into her therapy, Ruth tells me she has a memory she needs to share. *Can you listen? It's related to the letter I wrote to my younger self,* she says.

Again, I listen. Mindful of Ruth's keen desire to be heard, witnessed and understood. The power and transformation of her healing brims with agency, her silence changed into language and action; her memories and responses fully present.

Spring, 1986.

Happy birthday, Ruthie, ta-dah! her mother sings. A chocolate cake held up and glowing with thirteen slim candles, a halo of warm orange light.

Nick is leaning against the kitchen door, watching, waiting. Suddenly Ruth's three-year-old sister Eve appears with her wooden walker and crashes into his leg and laughs. *Monkey!* he says, picking her up and tickling her tummy. Eve jiggles and wriggles her small body, happy to be picked up, happy to be held. *Happy birthday to you,* they begin singing, *happy birthday to you,* her mother makes her way to the kitchen table, *happy birthday dear Ruthie,* settles the cake on the kitchen table, *happy birthday to you!* They applaud. Ruth leans in to blow. But just as she moves closer, Nick rushes in and blows out the candles and laughs.

Nick! her mother shouts.

Don't blame me, she did it! he laughs again, pointing at Eve.

The moment of celebration is killed. Ruth starts to cry.

Oh baby, come on, I'll light them again, her mother says, scrambling, searching for the matches.

Don't bother, Ruth snaps.

Hey, points Nick with his free hand, *don't speak to your mum like that.* He plops Eve on the kitchen table who, fascinated with the smoke escaping like a genie, takes a swipe of the cake and stuffs it in her mouth.

Oh Eve, stop that, her mother pleads, trying her best to patch and smooth over Eve's chocolate carnage. *Nick, why did you do that, where are the matches?*

Not sure, he says. *Where did you put them?*

Right here. They can't have just vanished—

Ruth knows exactly where they are. They're in his trouser pocket. She wipes away her tears and imagines forcing the knife about to cut the cake into his body, his chest. She's seen it done in films, in the horror movies Nick watches at night with a six-pack of Carlsberg and a packet of Salt & Shake crisps.

Anyway, I'd better be off to work or I'll be late, says Nick, locking eyes with Ruth. *I'll give you your present later, Ruthie. Have fun!*

The image of the knife is suddenly eclipsed with terror.

Nick puts on his hat. *See you later,* he calls.

Not if I see you first, her mother calls back, vexed and nodding her head.

Don't worry, love. Here, pass me the knife, her mother says, lifting Eve down from the kitchen table. *I'll make us a nice cup of tea and, look, it's your favorite—chocolate cake.*

Ruth makes her way to the living room, slides back the curtains to check Nick is leaving, and is momentarily soothed when his police car pulls away. The ache in her tummy is momentarily eased. But then she remembers she is thirteen today—*I'll give you your present later, Ruthie,* and the terror reappears once again, making her tummy flip and cramp. Ruth walks back to the kitchen and slices a large piece of chocolate cake, taking big bites and chewing, the calming, pacifying effect of the sweet delicious chocolate a balm for her fear-sensing tummy. *Hey, go easy,* her mother says, eyeing the speed of Ruth's devouring, *no one's going to take it away from you.*

But somebody already has, Ruth thinks; he has. Nick's taken away our happy home, my mother, and now his daughter thinks she can just ruin my birthday cake. I hate him, I hate living here, I hate that I'm frightened all the time, I hate that you married him and have another daughter—with him; I hate it, I hate it, I hate it. This was the first day Ruth made herself sick; *part of me saw it coming.*

She turns up the volume. A quick blast of Queen before applying turquoise eye shadow and a curl of mascara. Before swiping her lips with gloss, Ruth takes a large gulp of wine, then another. She piles her almost waist-length hair into a high ponytail, leans into the mirror thinking her roots need some love, and pouts. Last month she bought a kit from Superdrug but the color match was nowhere near the picture on the box so she'd worn her hair tied up, in a bun, hoping no one would see the *mistake* she'd made. *I felt exposed,* her face no longer hidden by hair and a beacon to the world—*I know this sounds weird, but I felt like an open target. I just kept looking away or down at the floor, avoiding any eye contact.*

Another glug of wine. Ruth notes yet another of her plants is wilting. The rubber plant's leaves curling, sad-looking and brown. She tends to kill most of her plants by overwatering them or completely forgetting they exist. It had been the same as a teenager when she'd won a bag of goldfish at the fairground, later killed by her overfeeding or ignoring them entirely. These extremes of all or nothing behaviors also cast their net to work, friendships, and boyfriends. A compulsion with the binary where she devoured and purged on work by throwing herself in completely, which she later resented due to her exhaustion, before eventually giving up. It had been the same with her friendships. Ruth made people her best friend almost immediately and was shocked and disappointed when they described her as *full-on and controlling* as she attempted to fill her diary, and theirs, before they eventually fell away, ceasing contact. *I just wanted us to have fun but now I think it was because I was lonely. When I manically organized nights out it stopped me feeling alone and unlovable.*

Boyfriends only stuck around for a short time, too. Until the *bedroom gymnastics had settled down* to something that Ruth longed for which was more loving and connected. But then she was accused of being *frigid, of losing interest, a fake*, and *of not making an effort*. Ruth managed these cruel abandonments with order. Her counting of things, objects, calming her angst and disappointment. In counting, she regained a type of ataractic control that she didn't have at work or with friends and boyfriends, avoiding odd numbers, especially single digits—*it was the only way I could cope*. If a single tin of baked beans was left in her kitchen cupboard, Ruth would rush to the supermarket and buy another one or three. Kitchens, for many years, were a double bind. The constant checking of the gas hob and the oven was a source of exhaustion—her preoccupation and negotiations only made better by speaking out loud: *The oven hob is turned off, the oven is turned off, it is eleven o'clock*. Then, several photographs would be taken with her phone so that when she left her flat she was able to soothe herself with the pictures, knowing her home was safe. This continued for many years, the symptoms causing an obsessive compulsion that kept her caged and frustrated but at the same time calmed. The double bind, she reflected, *is similar to the way I feel about my sister, Eve. It's complicated because I love my sister but she's also the daughter of a man who hurt me.*

Ruth checks her watch. Aaron will be here any minute, she thinks, and sprays her throat with perfume—his favorite. She hopes he feels as excited as she is and senses a swell of pride for having made it to a year, *even with all my baggage.* She'd booked a table two weeks ago at their local Italian, *Ciao, Ciao,* knowing how busy it gets on the weekends, a live pianist who *plays like a madman and serenades anyone who's willing* adopting a following of local people as well as city dwellers. Aaron loves the tiramisu. And the spaghetti vongole, vitello al limone, gnocchi, and scaloppa villanese. She watches in amazement at his capacity for spontaneity, how he can simply choose a dish that he fancies, a dish that will feed his mood or hunger. Ruth always chooses the spaghetti carbonara. She has deprived herself all week so she can order the spaghetti with its *eggy, creamy, bacony, cheesy* flavor that she savors and takes her time to chew. Each mouthful is like fairies tiptoeing on her tongue, and if she refuses pudding she won't have to purge. She really doesn't want to purge tonight because it's a celebration. *Why not try something else, something different?* Aaron will say, smiling. And Ruth will reply as she always does, *But why? When I like the carbonara so much?* She suspects he will stop asking soon. All her other boyfriends did.

They arrive at the restaurant and Aaron takes her waist as they enter. *Ruth! Aaron!* the waiter sings, and Ruth feels an immediate swell of warmth for his friendly and familiar welcome. She also likes that he has spoken her name first, not Aaron's, but then slides away her competitive streak, especially tonight because it's a celebration.

They are shown to their seats.

I understand we're celebrating tonight, says the waiter.

Aaron smiles. *It's our one-year anniversary.*

Ruth feels a smile dance across her lips.

Aaron orders scaloppa villanese. *I'd like the spaghetti carbonara,* says Ruth, happy, joyous, afloat. They drink red wine, chat, touch hands, and talk about the time when they met in their local pub and how Aaron *had my eye on you all night.* He laughs and reaches beneath their table and strokes the soft part of Ruth's leg and winks.

Did you now? she flirts back.

When their plates are cleared, Aaron excuses himself to the bathroom. Ruth notes he is gone for a long time but amuses herself by watching the other diners and smiles at a few. She orders more wine.

Sorry, says Aaron, *I bumped into an old friend.*

Who was that? asks Ruth.

A woman I used to know: Cassie. She's over there with her boyfriend and her family.

Ruth already dislikes Cassie. She has no reason to, but her brown eyes have turned green. Envy descends and snakes around her shoulders.

Let's order dessert, shall we? says Aaron.

I'm fine, but you go ahead.

Aaron looks again at the menu but as he searches for the waiter to order, Cassie appears at their table. *Oh, hey,* says Aaron, *Ruth, this is Cassie.*

Hi, nice to meet you, says Cassie. Her intention, Ruth thinks, is to disarm by glowing. *We're sitting over there. I thought I'd just come over and say hi.*

And you did, now do one! Ruth thinks.

Hello, says Ruth, smiling and watching Cassie's beauty, her perfect figure, blond hair, and tiny animal teeth.

We love it here, don't you? shines Cassie. *It's our go-to place,* a flick of hair. *We're waiting for the pianist. It's my mum and dad's anniversary.*

Oh, it's our anniversary, too, says Ruth, making a note to find an alternate restaurant in the future.

Happy anniversary, smiles Cassie. *Can I get you a drink to celebrate?*

We're fine, but thanks, says Ruth.

Okay then, well, she smiles again, this time bigger, more teeth, *lovely to meet you. See you later, Aaron.*

Aaron smiles.

Silence.

Really? A friend? asks Ruth, eyes fixed on her wineglass.

We dated for a while, but not for long.

So why did you say she was a friend?

I didn't want to upset you. It's our anniversary.

She looks away from him.

Ruthie, come on—

Don't call me Ruthie.

Ruth, come on—

Liar, she does not speak, anger beneath her silence and ready to explode.

The waiter appears. *Dessert?* he asks.

I'll have the tiramisu, says Aaron.

Me too, snaps Ruth.

Later, she tries her best to shake her green eyes but any attempt Aaron makes to soothe, reassure, or calm is rebuffed. Ruth wants to fight. She wants to scream. While searching her handbag for her house keys, a voice in her head tells her to relax, it's all right, calm down. But then the screaming fighter reappears, repeating the words, Liar! Why did he lie? People only lie if they've got something to hide. Then: Who can blame him for not saying she was an ex-girlfriend on our anniversary? He was probably trying to be thoughtful, considerate. Stop. She wants the voices to stop. She wants to cry.

Maybe I should go home, says Aaron. *I don't want to upset you anymore. I'm sorry I lied. I thought I was doing the right thing. I made a mistake. It won't happen again.*

Ruth doesn't know if it's his apology or her fear of his leaving that softens her, but for a moment the screaming fighter within her ceases.

She turns her house key, takes a breath, and opens the door. *I'm sorry too,* she says, relieved not to have completely *messed things up*. Aaron takes her coat, kisses her tenderly and their night resumes, more wine, more touching, kissing, albeit slightly dampened by *my jealous insecurity*. But as the night progresses Ruth is unable to shake her intrusive thoughts and excuses herself from Aaron's caresses on the sofa. She visits the bathroom and purges. A voice in her head once again reminding her: people only lie if they've got something to hide. A wave of upset follows the purge and she is reminded of her thirteenth birthday, which she suspects is down to her therapy. She is disappointed that she feels so paranoid tonight, that she's purged, because it was meant to be a celebration.

Leaning against the bathroom sink, Ruth recalls how her stomach had formed knots in waiting, restlessly, for Nick's irregular return home from work. This, adding further anxiety to Ruth's not knowing when and what cruelty would be acted out and presented as her birthday gift. The memory unsettles her further. That Nick worked for the police force, a supposed enforcer of the law and defender of the public, adds further concern in his heinous acts of abuse. We are to believe that our police force will protect us from harm, but as Ruth shared with me in one of her sessions, *He used his position and power as a policeman to terrorize me.*

How so? I asked.

He'd threaten me, say no one would believe me. That they'd think I was silly, stupid. Jealous of his relationship with my mum. He said everyone would believe him because he worked for the police.

And your mum? I asked.

Ruth shrugged. *I think she felt safe, protected by his so-called power. She used to say how hard he worked, the good he did. Deluded. But then again, all his rage was turned on me, the other man's daughter. If he had one outlet he didn't need to hurt her.*

I had in mind the many women hurt and killed by men who are or have been in the police force. Sarah Everard, the thirty-three-year-old woman who was killed while walking home from her friend's house in South London. I remember my bone-shaking rage and heartbreak on hearing the news of these crimes. Like Nick, these premeditated acts of cruelty and violence were inflicted on those who were too scared to speak out, or perhaps even trusted their perpetrators. I dared to think how utterly terrified Ruth and Claire Howarth, 31 (2009); Josephine Lamb, 58 (2009); Samantha Day, 38 (2011); Heather Cooper, 33 (2011); Janet Methven, 80 (2012); Natalie Esack, 33 (2012); Victoria Rose, 58 (2013); Emma Siswick, 37 (2014); Jill Goldsmith, 49 (2015); Leanne McKie, 39 (2017); Avis Addison, 88 (2017); Bernadette Green, 88 (2018); Alice Farquharson, 56 (2019); Luz Margory Isaza Villegas, 50 (2019); Claire Parry, 41 (2020); and Sarah Everard, 33 (2021) must have been. How utterly alone. Ruth survived, but the sixteen women named here did not. They were killed by former or currently serving police officers. I cried, felt sick to the gut. Called friends and colleagues. We were shocked, and struggled to accept what Couzens and the other police officers had done, but we were not surprised because this was one of many, many killings, corruptions, and abuses of power by those who had pledged to protect and serve us.

What's wrong, Ruthie? her mother had asked, sensing her jittery and unsettled behavior throughout the day of her thirteenth birthday. *Have you eaten too much sugar?* No, I just vomited it all up, she did not say. I'm frightened and I hate the man you love, she did not say. He hates me and hurts me when you're not looking, she did not say.

His punishment didn't happen on her birthday as she'd suspected. It came much later, six months in fact, when Ruth was caught off guard and least expecting it. Instead, Nick had gifted her a gold pen and a pretty diary with buttercups along its spine. Maybe he's regretting how awful he's been to me, Ruth had hoped. Perhaps he's changed, or maybe Mum's had a word. Ruth wasn't to know that Nick's gift would later be used against her to make everyone in her family mistrust and dislike her. The diary was a trap.

3 a.m. Ruth wakes up, a vision of Cassie—confident, beautiful, glowing—falling at the front of her mind. Wide awake now, she reaches for her mobile phone and attempts to *track my nemesis down.* Twitter, Facebook, Instagram: she checks them all for proof of Aaron's affair. Convinced that they kissed when he went to the bathroom, Ruth feels her chest start to rise and fall at speed. What had they talked about? *He was gone for a really long time* when he *"accidentally" bumped into her?* And didn't he seem nervy when Cassie came over to say hello, or is she imagining this? Wasn't he unusually quiet while they ate dessert? Or is she imagining this? And the way he looked at her, *he never looks at me that way.* Or is she imagining this? Now she needs to pee.

Dazed and upset, Ruth feels her way to the bathroom, pulls

on the dangling cord—the overhead lights dazzling and causing her to squint. She stares at herself in the mirror, lifts her
vest and watches her stomach bulge and her breasts shrink.
She grabs a fistful of flesh from her thighs, believing she's put
on significant weight in the last twenty-four hours. When she
turns away from her reflection and cries, a sudden stab of aloneness engulfs her. *Back to bed,* she tells herself, reaching quickly
for the cord once again.

She climbs back into bed and tracks Cassie down on Instagram: 1,287 followers. Most of the pictures are of Cassie with
her friends, family, and boyfriend on holidays and walks, in
restaurants and bars. Last month she ran a marathon for cancer
research. The month before she helped community fundraise
for her local primary school. *Goody Two-shoes,* Ruth whispers
under her breath, and then checks Aaron is still sleeping. More
investigation: Cassie works as a corporate events manager. She
has a cocker spaniel called Rufus. She clearly likes cake. Ruth
watches on repeat a reel of Cassie, just hours before, celebrating
her parents' wedding anniversary in *Ciao, Ciao,* her boyfriend
sat beside her. Ruth checks to see if Aaron has liked or com-
mented on the post. He hasn't. And Ruth is mildly calmed when
she sees how happy Cassie and her boyfriend are together—his
arm wrapped gently around her bronzed shoulders and kissing
her cheek. Calm down, says a voice in her head. The screaming fighter falls back to sleep.

I can't help it, she cries, *I get so crazy paranoid.*
Ruth explains that it had taken her *a while to fall back to sleep.
I just kept picturing them together, even though I knew I was being a
complete and utter madwoman. Even when I told myself, over and over,
she has a boyfriend and Aaron loves me, I was convinced he was lying,
having an affair or just waiting for an opportunity to leave me.*

I am curious about Ruth's turns of phrase: *crazy paranoid, complete and utter madwoman*. I want to understand more fully not only what this felt like but also whether these words were used out of familiarity. I imagine Ruth's words have the potential to dismiss, shame, and cage an understanding of herself, but they are also windows into her oppression. How long have these unhelpful labels existed in her mind, I wonder? When and where had she heard and learned of them? What did they serve? I reflected on a few occasions when Ruth had talked about how she'd been called crazy and paranoid by an ex-boyfriend when she'd questioned his whereabouts late one night after she'd called, spontaneously, at his home. Two months later she'd caught him in a lie, a month later in bed with another woman. When Ruth, filled with rage, demanded that the said ex-boyfriend admit and tell her how long the affair had been going on, he'd turned to Ruth, matching her rage, screaming, *Get out, how dare you, you mad cow!*

A lucky escape, Ruth told me.

Lucky, and painful, I said.

There was also the time when Ruth tried to tell her mother that someone had been in her bedroom, moved and hidden her things, a lipstick found at the bottom of her laundry basket, earrings under her pillow, underwear stuffed behind a set of drawers. *They must have fallen down there,* her mother said. *No they didn't,* insisted Ruth, *someone's been in my room.* Her mother shook her head. *You're being silly and paranoid. Who'd want to go in your room, Ruthie?*

It was Nick, said Ruth in one of her sessions, *he was trying to fuck with me. Let me know in no uncertain terms he could come into my bedroom any time.*

Ruth reaches into her rucksack, pulls out a bottle of water. Takes a sip.

I'm interested in the crazy paranoid and madwoman you experienced, I say. *Even though part of you knew and knows Aaron loves you, she seemed to take center stage and sabotage what you knew to be true. She convinced you that he's waiting for an opportunity to leave you or have an affair.*

That's exactly how it felt. Like I was turning into a madwoman. My mind runs away with itself and before I know it I've imagined and pictured all sorts of hurt and catastrophe.

Do you think yourself mad because you can imagine how painful your ending with Aaron would be? Are you crazy if your awareness is heightened? I'm not sure that you're either, I say. *Rather, I think you're very attuned to your feelings, your fears.*

No. I'm a madwoman, she spits.

Madwoman or emotionally engaged, I try again.

She does not answer.

I can see we have our work cut out and make a note to explore further, but not wanting to lose momentum I instead offer a suggestion: *I'd like us to reimagine last night.*

Okay, she agrees.

When you were in bed and Cassie's face appeared in your mind—

Yes—

—and you reached for your phone with the hope of finding clues to affirm their affair—

Yes—

If you imagine pausing and not reaching for your phone, what do you suppose you might have felt?

Ruth pauses. *Frightened,* she says. *Scared that she's going to take Aaron away from me.*

Right, I say. *So let's just stay with your feelings for a while longer. What next?*

She closes her eyes. *Still frightened,* she says. *I feel like he'll leave me because Cassie is more beautiful and fun and friendly. All the things I am not.*

Anything else?

Insecure. Angry that he lied. And jealous of Cassie. She seemed so light and fun and happy. Blah, blah, blah...

Right, I say. *Stay with me, what do you feel now?*

Upset, like I want to cry. She cries.

A pause.

There, I say, *you were feeling frightened, scared, insecure, angry, jealous, and upset. Can we acknowledge how many feelings you just had. Picking up your phone was a distraction from these feelings. It's understandable that you wanted to avoid them but it's important that you give yourself the opportunity to have them. Part of our work will be about acknowledging your feelings and digesting them so you can make choices about how you want to respond, rather than react, to certain situations. The feelings will eventually pass, no feeling is final.*

But that's the thing, she says, *I know I'll get all crazy and flip out so I guess I look for distractions to avoid what I might do.*

There's that word again: *crazy.*

And what will you do? I ask.

Ruth looks at me and nods her head.

It feels frightening to say it?

She nods yes.

I wait.

I'm scared I'll be violent. Break something. Destroy something special, she cries.

So instead you turn this violence upon yourself?

I guess, yes, she says. *It feels safer that way. I can control it and I don't hurt anyone. I can decide what and how much to eat and then I can decide to purge or not. Maybe I should end it with Aaron before he does. That way I can leave with some self-respect. Not like when I was a kid.*

I am struck by the power of Ruth's internalized anger. Her

decision to order dessert—food, a fleeting balm—knowing she could purge, was a way for her to lose control and later regain it as she had as a child and teenager. This, I imagine, was a reenactment of her earlier years when she'd felt frightened and powerless and turned to food and number counting by way of internalizing her rage. I wonder what shape her violence might take if she were to allow herself the full extent of her feelings. And how we might channel and understand this rage rather than acting on it. It is possible that if Ruth had felt able to articulate her fear and anger at discovering Aaron's lie, she might not have felt the need to purge. I also note Ruth's desire to leave Aaron before he leaves her—a desire to assert agency amid her fear of abandonment in an attempt to mobilize her feelings of powerlessness. I am curious to explore how deep Ruth's anger runs, her fight or flight responses most likely related to the violence inflicted on her as a teenager.

So this is an attempt to do something different from your childhood when you couldn't leave?

I guess. Crazy, right?

I'm not sure it is crazy, I say. *But more like a symptom of your past. Do before you are done to, so to speak. But there's also the possibility that your inner saboteur is at work.*

Makes sense, she spits. *Fuck him.*

Aaron? I ask.

No, Nick—fuck Nick. He made me like this.

There it is. Ownership of her primal wound. The source of her pain. Her anger arrow aimed and fired and spearing the bull's-eye of Nick's attempt to destroy her soul.

I'm crazy and bad because of him, she says.

You are not bad and you are not crazy, Ruth. Bad things were done to you. Terrible things. And rather than feel your pain and rage for fear of what you might do, you have turned this suffering inwards, which understandably makes you feel very frightened and alone.

I watch Ruth take in what we have both spoken. She clears her throat. Wipes her face. *Thank you,* she says, *no one's ever put it like that before. No one's taken the time to understand.*

What about when you were younger? I ask. *Did anyone understand then?*

To a point, says Ruth. *I used to keep a diary to try to make sense of things for myself, but then he got ahold of it and that was it. People, well, my mum mainly, stopped trying to understand. She took his side, which was his aim all along.*

I am struck by the premeditated act of Nick's hate. His buying Ruth a diary that he later used as a sharp weapon against her friends and family. A steely chill runs through me. I shudder. I am well practiced and knowledgeable enough to know that this was a man who was an expert in breaking people, the word "sadistic" forming and lodging at the back of my throat.

He had waited six months to gather his evidence, bookmarking the pages by turning their corners, and read aloud Ruth's most intimate thoughts. Words that spoke of her *mother's neglect and weakness to be with such a monster,* how she wished he and Eve didn't exist, while leaving out the part that spoke of Ruth missing her loving, safe home—her mum and dad. He read, a fake lump in his throat, of how Ruth wished him dead. How on the day when he'd gifted her a gold pen and a pretty diary, she had wanted to drive a knife through his chest because he'd played a silly joke by blowing out her birthday candles. Later, she wrote about the time when he'd forced her hand onto the kitchen table and jabbed a knife hard and fast between her small, trembling fingers. *Lies, all lies,* Nick shouted. He read more, and flicked to the page where he'd forced a bar of soap into her mouth. *More lies,* he said, *you're a complete fantasist. We have to deal with people like you at work,* he said, waving the diary in front of Ruth's face. He turned to Ruth's mother. *I suppose she's referring to the time when I told her to wash her face because she'd gone to school with a face full of makeup, do you remember?*

Ruth's mother looked at the floor. *I do,* she said.

I'm wondering if we need to contact social services, Nick said, like butter wouldn't melt. *I mean, what kind of dad would I be if anything was to happen to poor Eve? And what kind of husband would I be if I didn't raise concerns about my wife's safety, and my own?*

Oh, he was good. He was slick. And they fell for his lies. Ruth watched on in complete disbelief and awe at his conviction. His commitment to bring her down. How could they *not* believe him? He was the father and husband—*the bastard who brought home the bacon.* They needed Nick. Nick was a good man who had taken on another man's child. Ruth was the reason there was unhappiness and danger in the home. Ruth was the one with murderous rage. A fantasist. Ruth was jealous and bitter and mean and had brought shame and upset upon this peaceful, loving family. Ruth was a madwoman. Ruth was crazy.

Dearest Ruth, you were just thirteen years old.

What have you got to say for yourself, Nick demanded.

Nothing, I have nothing to say, said Ruth. Her mother burst into tears and it would be many years after Nick's death before Ruth was able to explain why she had thought the things she had, written the things she had. Many years until she could speak her truth about the diary, the kitchen knife, the soap ... remembering the time he'd stolen and manipulated her words. The time he attempted to destroy her soul—

Ruth searches everywhere. Where is it? She lifts up her mattress again. *It's gone,* she speaks out loud. She checks her bookshelf, her wardrobe and her wash basket, knowing it won't be there but the act helps calm her frenzied heart, racing like a prized racehorse. She shoves aside her schoolbooks, checks the wastepaper basket under her desk. Again, her bookshelf, wardrobe, and wash basket and back to the mattress. It is gone.

Fear takes hold. Where is it? Who's taken it? But part of her already knows the answer. She is drowning. Ruth counts the posters on her wall; the cuddly toys lined up on her bed; the bangles on her dressing table. *There are eleven bangles on my dressing table,* she says.

Ahem.

Someone clearing their throat behind her.

When she turns, Nick is leaning against the frame of her open bedroom door. *Oh dear, oh dear,* he says, shaking his head, smirking and holding up the pretty diary with buttercups along its spine. *Looking for this?*

She is drowning, frozen to the spot. Ruth can neither fight nor take flight.

There are seven posters on my bedroom wall; there are nine cuddly toys on my bed, she speaks quietly.

Nick tucks the diary in his back pocket, turns on his heel. He is gone.

Ruth reaches for the box of tissues and stares at me. *Tell me we're nearly at time,* she says. *I want to go now, I'm really tired.*

As she makes her way to work, Ruth buys an extra large coffee and four chocolate bars and walks very slowly to the bus stop. She chugs the coffee, hoping it will wake her up. She doesn't know how she will make it through the day and decides to text Aaron. *Really tough therapy session. Call me later, please xxx*

Now that the can is open, she wonders if she can slap it closed again. The worms forced back inside. Why did she think this was going to help, unearthing all her memories, all the pain? Everyone knows talking about abuse with a therapist gets worse before it gets better. But then a small voice tells her how well she's doing and that *Maxine seems like a nice, helpful woman.* She sips the remains of her coffee and tosses the polystyrene cup on top of the already overflowing rubbish bin next to the bus stop and takes out one of the chocolate bars from her jacket pocket. But then she realizes this will leave her with an odd three and decides to unwrap two chocolate bars instead.

A text arrives from Aaron. *Hey babe, I'm sorry it was a difficult session—I'm so proud of you. I'm free now until 9 if you wanna chat? I love you xxx*

She takes a moment to feel Aaron's love and stares at the two chocolate bars starting to melt in her palm. I have a choice, Ruth thinks, and reads Aaron's text again, and throws the two chocolate bars in the rubbish bin next to the bus stop. She licks her hand and looks around to see if anyone is watching, just in case she decides to retrieve the chocolate bars, but then forces them down deeper, deeper into the rubbish. Now comes anxiety. Ruth understands she has thrown away her chocolate fix. *No feeling is final,* she whispers to herself, and counts the cars driving past. When she reaches twenty-two she is relieved that her anxiety has eased. She takes out her phone: *Thank you,* she writes. *I love you, too xxx*

Was Nick *a monster.* A heartless, bloodless, diabolical committer of soul destruction. Note I have not put a question mark after the sentence. Shall we allow space for the man with an aching, broken, and vengeful heart. Should we be concerned, does it even matter? Certainly not in terms of the pain and cruelty and suffering he inflicted on Ruth's mind and body. But I fear my rage is getting the better of me and so I pause, I wait. Stay with the anger, I tell myself. Stay with it.

I reflect again on what Ruth needs in her therapy. It is possible that growth and change are mobilized by a current catastrophe, longing, or fear—an event or a collection of events that forces one into crisis, or even collapse. Was Ruth in crisis now? Was she close to collapse? *Why now when I've hit my target weight do I feel the unhappiest I've ever been?* she'd asked. I wonder if her desire for a specific weight had been a distraction from her early childhood trauma. A goal to help keep her away from painful memories and a way to stay in control amid a pain that I can only imagine was, is, too much to bear. That she remains discontent has perhaps caused more distress because in theory her controlled eating and counting no longer serves the magnitude of what she has survived— *the drugs don't work*.

Those who have been accused of lying about their suffering, beaten up and down, manipulated, punished, frightened by caregivers whose narcissism triumphs over their care, and who are made to feel worthless, "crazy," and a "madperson," will understandably turn to whatever coping strategies are necessary to survive. Nick worked daily to diminish Ruth's self-worth, to break her will and her capacity for survival. He had known she was a sensitive and thoughtful child who liked nothing more than playing with her soft, cuddly toys, collecting novelty erasers, and listening to pop music. Perhaps he sensed this innocent vulnerability and hated how it made him feel. Perhaps he hated that she was not his child. Perhaps his making Ruth *wrong* and *crazy* and *bad, a liar,* was an attempt to not feel alone with his own diabolical behavior, his own lies. The truth was, Ruth believed herself to be someone who hadn't ever wanted to lie. Lies were not something she had even entertained or was capable of. But told enough times, she began to question whether she was in fact a liar, and that perhaps she was *truly bad and evil to the core*. Nick's gaslighting smothered Ruth's truth. Isn't this the unjust story of so many surviving patients, I think to myself;

isn't this the wrongful story of so much history that I listen to and witness in my consulting room. Those in power who create lies do it in order to serve one purpose and that is almost always self-serving. Nick devoted hours, months, years of his premeditated time and cruelty to the endeavor of breaking Ruth's spirit. And a most chilling reality to me is that in convincing Ruth's mother, sister, and Ruth herself that she was *wrong* and *crazy*, he had all three of them believing that this was the truth.

Today Ruth wants to talk about *revenge, and my sister, Eve.* We have been working together for eight months.

She tells me how unjust it feels that, as an adult, she is unable to stare Nick in the face and tell him exactly the type of monster he is, that he is a heinous human not worth an ounce of respect or compassion. *You took my childhood and made it a hell,* she wants to scream. *I hate that you still make loving Eve so painful, I hate that you made me and Mum drift apart, I hate everything about you and if you were not dead I would wish that you were.*

Ruth's anger is potent. I sit up in my chair and listen. She continues: *I want my body back, healed. And I want you to know that if there is an afterlife and any sense of justice that you will be cast out from any love or care or respect just as I was. I want an apology from you, you complete and utter bastard.*

She breaks down.

We commit to silence, broken only momentarily by Ruth's sobs, deep animal pain.

I internally negotiate how long to leave Ruth with her grief, not wanting to puncture her feelings but at the same time not wanting her to feel alone with her suffering. I wait.

No feeling is final, she finally speaks, *right?*

Right, I say. *Small steps.*

I'd really like your help with Eve, she says, wiping her damp face with both hands.

I nod. *How can I help?* I ask.

I think a lot of my insecurity is tied up with our relationship. I'm so jealous of her, still. Even when she was a baby I envied her. I wasn't as loving as I should have been.

What did Eve represent for you? I ask.

That I was on my way out. That she'd take Mum away from me. I felt very lonely. Dad had gone. Mum had a new boyfriend and a new daughter. I felt like I wasn't part of their family. Nick made sure of that.

It must have been very upsetting dealing with so much loss and change, I offer, *and very difficult to be loving toward your baby sister whom you believed held so much power—especially when her father was so determined to cast you out and pit you against one another.*

It was. I wanted to be loving, she says, *I really did.*

A small suburb on the edge of southeast London, the winter sun setting low in the sky. Ruth grabbed her ski jacket, knowing her baby brother or sister was on the way. It was Christmas and decorations had been tacked and hung limp behind closed windows, fake snow sprayed across garage doors. Santa was either lit up, cut out, or bobbing his head in the homes on Brenfield Drive. Ruth's mother collected her small overnight bag and waited for her new boyfriend to warm the car and push the seat back. *Fetch my fags, Ruthie,* her mother said, and Ruth did as she was told. Then spun and held up the lighter as she'd been taught before placing it in the back pocket of her denim jeans.

As her mother waddled, a pained expression stretched across her swollen face, Ruth realized she would soon no longer be the only child and thought she'd make the most of it by nuzzling into her mother's fixed body, like a fridge. *I love you, Mum,* she said. She was ten years old.

Ruth held her mother's hand stiffly, protectively, and was respectful to the frozen path laid with ice that was black and hidden by December's freeze. Carefully, she guided her to the passenger seat of their Ford Cortina and watched the gathering of neighbors: kids in ski jackets similar to her own, exhausted mothers. *Good luck,* they called.

Eve was born the following morning—*Christmas Eve*—weighing seven pounds and six ounces, a tiny upturned nose. Her head sprouted a mass of alabaster curls, her eyes as turquoise as a polished gemstone. Ruth stared into the cot, smiled at her baby sister, stroked the peach fuzz of her cheek and said, *She's perfect, isn't she?*

She is, said Nick, *now step back, Ruthie, you're crowding her. All we need now is a little baby boy and we'll be all set.* Ruth's mother shot him a dark look, took hold of his collar and yanked down hard—*Dream on, stud.* They both laughed but Ruth didn't get the joke. The only studs she knew of were the gold ones in her ears, so instead she watched the look on her mother's face, enchanted, possessed and spellbound with the allure of love. *She is the most perfect little baby I have ever seen,* her mother shined.

Ruth quickly became *Li'l Momma* to Eve's every whim. She learned how to change a nappy at miraculous speed, warm a bottle, apply diaper cream, and cradle and soothe and dress her sister like a *show pony, a peachy princess with curly white hair. Everyone on the street thought she was perfect, too. Everyone wanted to hold her, touch her, kiss her face*—they couldn't help themselves.

During that first year Ruth felt a rising dread inside her that she didn't recognize or have a name for, but as it started to swell and build like a rumbling volcano, she realized she didn't like what it made her do. It made her pull a mean face, *my so-so face became even less pretty,* and have mean thoughts. She began imagining all manner of mean things that she wanted to do to her precious and perfect and adored baby sister. *One time when Mum trusted me to change her nappy, I imagined leaving her damp for a whole day, but I couldn't, even though part of me wanted to.*

Aren't you helpful, Mummy's little helper, spoke her mother. *Just watch her while I dry my hair.* Ruth dreaded the request. She didn't trust herself to not do *something bad. Something wrong.* In those moments she swaddled and nestled Eve on the couch between the crack of beige cushions. That way, she wouldn't roll or fall off the couch. *I didn't want to hurt her, I really didn't,* she says.

Nick, Ruth suspects, sensed her now known and named jealousy. He encouraged it by *pulling my mum and Eve even closer. And when I tried to join in with their playing happy families, I was pushed away and ordered to stop being jealous, go play with your toys.*

Moments before her mother returned with dry hair, Ruth scooped Eve from the couch and at once appeared like a perfect picture of big sister pride, rocking her, singing, stroking her curls. *Good girl, Ruthie,* her mother praised.

On her eleventh birthday Ruth was given a pale, plastic dolly and a secondhand pram. *Now Li'l Mama has her own baby,* her mother clapped.

I wanted a bike, Ruth dared.

Nick stepped forward. *Ungrateful little—*

Bikes are expensive, her mother intervened, *and anyway, you like babies more,* she insisted, while pointing a disposable camera. *Smile!*

Ruth smiled. Then killed any desire for a bike and instead placed Eve in the pram. When her mother wasn't looking, Ruth gave her sister *the ride of her life.* Eve enjoyed it when her big sister rolled her down the hill, Ruth told herself. The quick jolt of a brake as she reversed up at the corner shop, stuffing the pram with crisps, sherbet dabs, penny sweets, and shortbread.

I'd go home and stuff my face and just for a moment, forget I was disappearing.

Ruth reaches inside her rucksack and takes out a photograph of her and Eve. *I brought this in to show you,* she says.

I look at the photograph, thinking how, amid all of Ruth's pain, that her holding of Eve is incredibly tender. She passes me another two pictures, one of Eve aged around three or four years old, and another where I imagine Ruth, at Halloween, is in her late teens. I can see Ruth's distress in both photographs, her gaunt face with wide, harrowing eyes. *I can see how deeply unhappy you were here,* I say, pointing at Ruth and Eve in their Halloween costumes, *and in this one I sense the distancing between you both.*

That one was taken just after the birthday cake incident, Ruth replies, *when I made myself sick. I was so unhappy and lost. That's the chocolate cake mum made for me—when all my issues with food began, speaking of which . . .*

She looks to me to ask the question. *How is your eating at the moment?* I say, feeling lightly cajoled.

Mildly improved, she says. *I'm not bingeing as much.*

Good. Why do you think that is? I ask.

I guess I'm starting to feel less angry, she says, then corrects herself. *I mean, I'm starting to feel less scared of being angry.*

You have a lot to be angry about, I say, *I understand.*

I know. I thought that holding my anger in would mean no one would get hurt.

Apart from you, I add.

Apart from me, she says. *Thing is, I still like having the control. It's all I've known.*

I understand, I say, *yet continuing to harm your body with purging keeps the under-story of your abuse alive.*

Old behaviors are so tough to change.

Small steps, I say. We're just getting started. We have a lot of work to do, for sure. Your body, your rules. Only this time we have a clearer idea of how to respond rather than react. You have choices through your understanding.

Ruth moves forward in her chair.

My body, my rules.

I bumped into Cassie last night at the pub, says Aaron. *Turns out her boyfriend used to date Connor's sister.* Connor is one of Aaron's work colleagues. *I just wanted to tell you in case you thought I was hiding anything.*

Ruth catches her feelings, an attempt from old stories to mist and cloud her response. She wonders if his telling her this isn't overkill in terms of trust, or maybe, she thinks, he's telling me this so it looks like he's being a good guy when really he's up to no good. She asks him how Cassie was, then says, *I just felt jealous when I heard you say her name but I'm trying my best not to let it upset me, and us.*

I know, says Aaron. A kiss.

I don't want to feel jealous, she admits. *I sometimes feel insecure and scared because of my past but I want to do something different with you, Aaron. I really do.*

Ruth pictures herself in my small office, the box of tissues. *Small steps.*

We imagine what his apology might look like, the shape it might take; the smell, the taste, and the feelings it might evoke were Nick still alive and able to own his heinous acts of violence against her. Ruth and I sit with the reality that this will never happen—because the man who inflicted so much pain on her emotionally, physically, and psychically is now dead. The clarity of this reckoning is agonizing.

That he betrayed, lied, manipulated, abused physically and mentally, and gaslighted Ruth, Eve, and their mother is the under-story. Moving through and beyond these cruel and violent acts is where, with painful healing, one might envision how to be free. Free, without forgetting. Here, the curtailing of behavior can transcend and evolve into a changing behavior. Ruth tells me that were she to imagine his apology—and this she highly doubts—Nick would have to look inside himself and question what it means to be human. *He killed my trust in others for a long time,* she says. But he has not won. *Not yet.* Even after he stripped Ruth of a family life, of her mother's and sister's love. Of a safe and nurturing home where she could play freely and without fear of punishment. *Not yet.* Of days at school, reading, listening, and learning when she was too distracted and too frightened to concentrate. *Not yet.* Of friendships—boys and girls—because Ruth didn't trust anyone, especially not the teachers, and how could she when those at home, also adults, were meant to love, protect, and care for her. *Not yet.* When she gorged and gorged on food to balm her complete despair and crippling aloneness. *Not yet, not while I can love Aaron, work, come to therapy, and want to improve my relationship with Eve. Not while I can daydream for something else, something new. Today I am holding on to small slivers of trust. Itsy-bitsy shards of trust. And even though I've drunk myself stupid, had dangerous and frightening sex, swallowed pills, hurt myself, and eaten and vomited for most of my life—*

I am here. Healing. Not yet.

In witnessing Ruth's life journey for two years and ongoing, I honor her courage, determination, and healing sovereign self. My capacity to feel love in our work is my capacity for change. As with many of my patients, Ruth has taught me, shown me, and reminded me that humans are extraordinarily and heart-wrenchingly adaptive. With respect, connection, and a desire for deeper understanding from both patient and therapist, healing is possible for the most abominable and heinous beginnings in one's life. In inviting Ruth's rage to the consulting room for inquiry, she was able to discover and learn of her resilience and to withstand it as well as witness another's tolerance of it. This in turn enabled her to move her attention to finding language so she could express her feelings rather than reacting with rage. Over time, this resulted in the gentle easing away of her controlled eating crutch where other tools and resources instead were put into place. The fear of losing control was the very behavior that kept Ruth distanced from both love and trust. And in this, we, together, were able to explore her coping mechanisms for what had started out as an incredibly lonely and frightening existence.

Small steps, I remind myself. We're just getting started. There's work to be done for sure. Your body, your rules.

To want and not to have, sent all up her body a hardness,
a hollowness, a strain.
And then to want and not to have—to want and want—
how that wrung the heart, and wrung it again and again!

Virginia Woolf, To the Lighthouse (1927)

Baby, Sing the Blues

The man sitting next to her on the train is obviously aroused. He fidgets, smiles, attempts conversation, offers to collect a warm drink for her, a snack from the buffet cart, and on approaching Stevenage resorts—*what a creep*—to stealing glances at her chest.

He claims to know her from somewhere. *Maybe the telly; come on, I know you're famous. You look famous.* The man likes to watch his television while eating supper from a tray. It is how he spends most evenings now that his wife is dead. And this is the moment when Marianna feels momentarily sorry for the man and smiles. *Poor creep.*

Marianna is used to men gawping at her. Sometimes they say similar things to the man on the train. They believe they know her from somewhere, that she seems familiar. But she is by no means famous. Maybe acclaimed would be a more accurate description, or notable to many because Marianna is a singer. A beautiful, unfulfilled singer who people believe they recognize.

She turns her body away from the man, folds her arms across her chest, and stares out of the train's window in search of distraction. Marianna wishes she could move from her designated seat but instead remains where she is, frustrated and seat-bound.

When the train eventually draws up at Stevenage station, a young, frazzled mother with a babe in arms hauls a folded buggy into the baggage area. She relieves herself of a damp, bulging rucksack and wipes her forehead with her wrist, then sighs. The buggy fits neatly into a hole that looks as though it's been waiting to unburden the tired-looking woman and her grisly baby girl. Relieved on their behalf, Marianna offers to help lift the rucksack into the overhead luggage rack.

Thanks, I'm okay, says the mother, moving a bounce of curls away from her eyes with a manicured hand.

The train sets off again and the mother unwraps her baby girl from a red puffy coat, smiles and dots her on the nose. *Here we go, hold on tight,* she grins. The little girl does a full body jig and reaches for her mother's face with a chubby fist. Marianna notes how alike they appear, a duet of platinum curls, thick foreheads, and pale turquoise eyes. She quickly clears away her reusable water bottle, an empty sandwich box, and a copy of *Vogue* and enjoys how much closer she feels to the happy pair. If Marianna was to reach out her fingertips she could touch them both, but she doesn't. *Because that would be weird, right?* Instead, she looks down at her arms, empty. Her silk lap, empty. Her limbs, she notices, have nothing to do and are clothed in the season's fashion. What she'd do to hold a baby close to her empty body, to wipe away spit, exhausted after a full night of feeds. Marianna longs for a fat, toothless, talc-scented baby whom she can love, and whom she hopes will love her in return.

Bouncing on her mother's lap, the baby girl smiles while her mother leans in to peck noses. They clutch hands and mirror each other—a face duet. The baby girl giggles, dribbles, and a square of muslin is whipped out at speed to wipe away drool. A crippling aloneness alive in her chest, Marianna's eyes wobble wet with shine. She takes a guess at the baby girl's age—*twenty weeks*—noting the chub and concertina folds, like dinner rolls, around her wrists. She does the maths and calculates an approximate date of conception, then the breakdown of trimesters, first, second, and third, before finally settling on the birth date. She wonders how accurate she is.

She's so lovely, Marianna smiles.

Thank you, I think so too, the mother shines.

How old is she?

Nearly six months, another peck on the nose.

Marianna reworks the calculations in her head to accommodate the error and again stares out the window where sleek raindrops race across the moving train's window like tiny sperm. *Everywhere,* she thinks, *constant reminders that I'm childless and with a man who cheated on me.*

Outside, the rain has slowed to a pathetic drizzle. The big, restless sky a veil of blurry gray. I note the delicate tick of the clock resting on my desk and the pleasant temperature of the room painted white. I decide to wait another five minutes before calling her mobile phone. It is unlike her to be late and not call.

At 4:15 Marianna finally arrives, breathless. *Sorry I'm late,* she says, wiping her dank shoes across the coir mat beside the door. I see immediately that she's been crying and ask that she take a seat. *Damn trains,* she sighs, relieving herself of her caramel trench coat. The train from her parents' house, once her childhood home, Marianna explains, was delayed, *and I ran out of juice,* she adds, showing me her mobile phone, a blank dead face to it.

Next, she removes her scarf, tosses it into her leather tote.

We settle. Now into our work for just over three months, I ask, *How are you, Marianna?*

A deep intake of breath, she closes her eyes.

Not good, she begins. *Everywhere I look there's babies and happy couples.* The brittle control of her voice cracks and I listen. *Do you know how painful that is?*

Before I have the chance to answer, Marianna lets out a cry and attempts the impossible by trying to stop. She reaches for the square box of tissues resting on the wooden side table, dabs her eyes and replaces what she's lost by forcing her head back while liquid eye drops are plopped into thirsty green eyes.

It's important to allow yourself to cry, I offer.

I know, but I have to work tonight and you know how tired I get when I cry. I can't show up looking all puffy. Imagine that.

Last month she'd secured a rolling contract with the London hotel where she's worked for four years as their resident singer. There, she sings and smiles and performs three nights a week and every weekend. And while she has a fine time performing the ballads and big-hit crowd-pleasers to nicely dressed diners who rarely applaud, it is jazz that truly enchants her. Wild, loose, improvised jazz that thrills and enraptures her body; sweet harmony blues.

She has Ted, her father, to thank for this. To Marianna he was *Pops*; Edward to those with a formal acquaintance, and Teddy to friends he knew intimately. He'd splayed the immaculate squares of vinyl across the garage floor, a cold beer in his hand, thrilled to be sharing his lifelong passion with his only child.

Jazz is a right of passage, he'd said. *A pleasure that's felt, not learned. Reaching people, that's jazz.* He'd bent his waist and eased the turntable arm above his chosen record, dialed up the volume, and turned to her. *This right here: tolerance and freedom.*

She'd watched his passion—dramatic limbs, fixed, keen eyes—play out in the side garage next to their home, with "Cry Me a River" delivering the deepest pain and a high she's struggled to match since.

Can you feel it? he asked.

She had felt it. Deeply. Rhythmically. But her seventeen-year-old body was not enough. It was too young and half-baked for all the feelings that came with Fitzgerald's perfect pitch and epic scat. It didn't know what to do with itself apart from insist, *Pops, play it again, louder!* And the second time she closed her eyes, swayed her hips, took a chug on his chilled beer, and told herself to hold on to this moment because this was how she and Pops would bond. A moment created for them both to climb into and shine. He'd smiled; happy that she got it. Felt it.

Kiddo, you got jazz in your veins.

She blows her nose into a tissue.

Babies; happy couples; puffy eyes. Where to begin? I say.

Marianna clears her throat and glances at the clock. *Let's start with babies,* she says, taking a sip of something from a reusable bottle, *that's why I'm here, right?*

Sure. So, babies, I reply.

They're everywhere, she says. *On the train, restaurants, cafés, during my walk here. It's so upsetting. They're even in my mum's paintings. Big fat babies.*

She crosses her arms against her chest.

Have you thought any more about what we discussed?

She nods. *It's one of the reasons I went home. I wanted to talk to Mum about it.*

How did it go? I ask, knowing the delayed train has delivered her from a weekend with her mother. I make a note to discuss Marianna's longing for her mother's approval, but not today. Today I want to explore her desire.

Fine. She's doing okay, she says. *I tried talking to her but she thinks I should stick it out with Karl. She said it would be hard doing it alone, that I should wait until he's ready to start a family. Which could be never.*

He's no closer to wanting a family with you? I ask.

Not by a mile.

Even an inch would be an improvement, I say.

There was a mum and her baby on the train, sitting opposite me, Marianna continues. *They looked so happy and adorable. I wanted to reach out and touch them. But I didn't, because that would have been weird, right?*

Weird and inappropriate, I do not say, and instead offer, *I think you made the right decision not to touch a stranger and her baby. Though it would be helpful to explore your desire for a baby of your own.*

My mum thinks it would be a mistake to do it alone.

I check the clock to see if we have enough time to explore the complicated relationship she has with her mother and her current boyfriend. *Even though you're not happy with Karl?*

Marianna tried her absolute best to forgive Karl in early spring. He didn't say *I don't love you anymore,* or *I love her,* but after two years of what Marianna believed was love and commitment, his infidelity had rocked her to the core and sent her ricocheting out of control like a popcorn kernel.

She'd left a slurred message on my voicemail at 2 a.m. saying, *I maybe need to talk to someone, can you help?* Nighttime is so much heavier when alone, and forsaken.

Something in her stomach had grown gnarly. She'd suspected that Karl was sleeping with another woman. Yet the signs had felt too obvious, too pedestrian. That he'd changed his hair, his aftershave, increased his gym membership were surely signs of paranoia and insecurity on her part. Karl would never be such a cliché. But there it was, a misread of human behavior. Later, she turned nasty rhythmical voices upon herself. They claimed it was she who was the cliché, not Karl. *How could I be so stupid, and so blind?* she cried, intense green eyes holding mine. *Everyday I was sleepwalking, in denial of what he was up to.*

Psychotherapists call this a "defense mechanism," an unconscious attempt to protect and keep us detached from feelings within ourselves that are intolerable. Defense mechanisms, or survival mechanisms, are one of many ways in which the human psyche disavows self-knowledge.

We sometimes ignore the signs, however obvious, I say, perhaps because we fear the truth? The unknown known, as it were.

Denial is clever. And fearful. It attempts to keep us away from potential danger and hurting. It also acts as a way of preserving a relationship that a patient may wish to hold on to perhaps due to loneliness, fear of abandonment, or in Marianna's life because she so desperately wanted a baby to love. Marianna turned her denial inwards, telling herself, *You're overreacting; You're upset over nothing; You're so dramatic; You're so sensitive; Stop imagining things;* words that attempted to make less painful the truth of her situation. Reflecting back, she feels empathy for the part of her that couldn't accept Karl's cheating and duplicity. That she'd found receipts for intimate suppers she hadn't been a guest at, smelled perfume on his clothes, and sensed her bed free of desire, was quickly turned into: *stop imagining things.*

She also wondered if his blatant affair was laid so bare in the hope she'd find out and punish him, or whether, and this was more painful, he had simply ceased to love and respect her.

She shudders at the nerve, the gall of him, and then she punishes herself for being *so blind.*

She was twenty-three years old with small but pretty eyes and her name was Hen, short for Henrietta. She was petite, had a sharp mind, a sleek dress sense, a swish of black hair razored into a stylish bob, large breasts, *much bigger than mine,* and a talent for getting international clients to part with their money. Marianna has imagined, over and over, Karl resting his face between Hen's breasts, rustling her feathers, pecking at her neck. Pictured in the office late at night, papers are forced across the desk to make way for her tiny bum. She imagines them both high on cheating, Karl acting out some banal fantasy of boss and secretary being watched by office onlookers. This is what Marianna sees and it causes her pain.

She doesn't like to remember the *madwoman who lost her shit.* Her swollen body that took on the shape of a *fridge* after binging on wine and cake and pie—foods not usually acquainted with her lips. She is slow to acknowledge the trail of devastation left in the wake of his betrayal. The messy one-night stands, the lost nights at work, the shower she refused to clean and step into. She attempts to crush memories of the times at work when she was so laden with propranolol she hated to move, her singing voice expelling sounds that she barely recognized. And so she places the madwoman in a box and sends her careering out to sea. Destination: exile. There, the madwoman has no power to shame or remind her of his affair with Hen. The absolute suffering she endured and survived.

It took Karl six months to say sorry. *I've made a huge mistake, can you forgive me?* he said, armed with a cornet of white hydrangeas as he waited outside the hotel where Marianna works as a resident singer. She didn't reply and instead agreed to have a drink and made him hold the voluminous blooms while she walked along the Thames and listened. At the bar she felt disappointed with the part of herself that wanted Karl back, a longing in her chest with his name scrawled in blood. After the second glass of wine he'd moved a little closer to her, attempted to stroke the curve of her neck, but she'd held her nerve and pulled back. The scrawl of deceit still alive in her chest and unhealed.

Hadn't she earned his respect, comforted him after the death of his mother, which followed a messy breakup with his ex, Sam. *You broke my heart, Karl.* Hadn't she cared for him, built him back up, dropping all entanglements with keen men, and touched him in a way that felt healing, awakening—like love. Marianna had invited Karl into her life. *I chose him.* And yet somehow, she had been forgotten. Replaced. The magic and enchantment of a sales pitch and a fresh body had him absconded and Marianna turned into a *madwoman* who, as she lay on her bed, doubted her sanity, her desire, but worse still, who she was.

Karl ordered more wine.

I got scared and overwhelmed. But I'm ready now. I want us to make a fresh start, he said. *Let's move in together.*

And then came the kicker.

Let's make a baby.

It interests me how easily Karl was accepted back into Marianna's life. It troubles me that *Let's make a baby* is a carrot dangled on a mile-long stick. Recent weeks have seen him pull away again—not from her, but from making a baby together. His reasons: *I want it to be just me and you for a while, I've missed you, I love you,* are spoken in intimate moments, naked moments, and Marianna is suspicious but momentarily calmed. *I want some time to show you how sorry I am for what I did,* says Karl.

They continue to live in separate homes.

Karl is smooth.

A relationship after an affair, while changed, is by no means impossible or doomed. Why did Karl have the affair? I was curious if his affair with Hen was not so much an attempt to leave Marianna but to address something that wasn't quite right in their relationship. I wondered what this could be. I have, on occasion, witnessed relationships mildly improved after acts of infidelity—though this is rare. Trust is one of those ill-fated and commonly used words in discussions of relationships, and when it is broken what we experience is the fragility of one's trust toward the person who has hurt us. The healing that follows and the consequences for both people require painfully honest conversations about why the affair happened and whether it is likely to happen again. There is also an inquiry—once resentment, revenge, and hurt can be metabolized—into the debris of the relationship, the fractured foundations of trust.

Marianna did her best to query what her part might have been in Karl's infidelity. Had she been inattentive, preoccupied, or selfish? Had she pressured him about starting a family? Or was it because she wouldn't explore some of the kinks Karl was keen to try out?

You did nothing wrong, said Karl. *It was all me. The whole baby, dad thing—it scared me.*

Her answer is simple and direct when I ask about her readiness to accept Karl back into her life. *I'm getting older, I want a baby. I don't have the energy to start over with someone else. Maybe Karl's the one. Maybe this is it.*

I take the measure of what is occurring, the defensive tone of Marianna's voice, and consider her sharp inflection. *Maybe, but I worry I'd be colluding with you if we don't explore fear.*

Marianna leans forward. *Of course I'm scared. I'm thirty-eight. I'm running out of time.*

There's a sweet spot in Chet Baker's version of "My Funny Valentine" that slows down just at the point when his sweet, caramelly voice sings: *But don't change your hair for me, Not if you care for me, Stay little valentine—stay.* I always feel a pang of loss when the melancholic piano arrives after the second "*stay*." A gentle pleading for what Chet knows is already lost: his valentine. I wondered what would happen if Marianna and I slowed down the therapeutic process, if she didn't allow fear to inform her actions. What if we sat with her qualm and found a way to redirect what she believed was powerlessness, into freedom and choice.

With change comes loss. And pain is the agent of change. If our life is going well, if we are happy and content, there is rarely a desire to change anything. If one is fulfilled at work, we seldom look for alternate employment, and if we love and feel safe in our home, we rarely contemplate a move. But if we are unhappy, fearful, bored, distrustful, or anxious in our everyday life, that's when we go in search of change. Therapy helps to explore and navigate what is wrong. When someone has an affair, change is immediately imposed. And for the person who is "wronged"—in this case Marianna—the loss and pain is heightened, leaving a void in which she has to adapt to a different way of relating to the person who has acted unjustly.

How might Marianna trust Karl again? What would healing and trusting Karl require of her? Is her continuing distrust of Karl a way of remaining in the hurt and in the feelings of betrayal? I want to explore with Marianna whether her therapy is ostensibly about helping her to heal or end her relationship with Karl, to forgive Karl or perhaps to explore the discourse in their relationship in general. Now that Karl is in her life again, I turn the analytic gaze back toward Marianna.

What do you want? I ask.

I want a baby, a family, she speaks beneath a tissue.

This is meaningful for you.

Yes, right now it feels more important than my relationship with Karl. But I'm no sperm burglar, she snaps.

This is not a phrase I have heard before and the image catches me off-guard.

It's interesting you raise the idea of theft, of stealing, I say, attempting to concentrate. *But what's the robbery really about?*

She pauses, scrapes her hair back and secures her mass of curls with a band waiting on her wrist.

Me, she looks away momentarily, then quickly returns her gaze, *I'm robbing myself.*

How so?

I'm robbing myself of what I really want—to be a mother, to be happy.

I clear my throat.

So it would seem, I say.

There was a complex dilemma at play. Marianna desired a baby, yet the thought of leaving Karl and starting afresh with another person was overwhelming. As women we are painfully alive to the reality of our body clock, but I also wondered if there were other complications, histrionic struggles or re-enactments involved. What did wanting a baby and being a mother really mean for Marianna? I call back Chet Baker's sweet spot and write down my thoughts, underlining: *Sperm burglar??* And, *Slow down the process*. If Marianna's fear is paused, understood, and embodied, might she be able to understand and experience her longing differently? Might she discover there are alternative choices for herself, and her body?

I make a fresh pot of coffee and reflect on her mother's belief that it is better to stick it out with Karl and that *doing it alone will be hard*. I wonder about this—her preference for Marianna to be in a relationship but potentially unhappy rather than alone and with choices. What had happened to burn away belief in her daughter's desire? And how had these messages and beliefs come to be so impactful on Marianna?

She was wearing a gold, fishtailed dress when she first noticed Karl dressed in black. A simple brooch of diamanté was pinned to her breast, and her hair, wild and strawberry, bounced as she walked toward the stage. Marianna's five foot ten had been raised by three-inch heels and she liked how tall and statuesque she felt when she caught sight of him: also tall, hair sleeked back, and *a swagger that felt dangerous and exciting.*

In our short time together—less than a year—Marianna has expressed the importance, the absolute necessity of feeling sexually attracted to her boyfriends, past and present. And there are rules: *They must be funny, good-looking, exercise—fit body, loyal, charming, nice teeth, and kind.*

These rules, are they ever broken? I ask.

I don't know. I've never tried.

The bank where Karl worked as an investment analyst had sponsored the charity event. Marianna noticed his silk lemon handkerchief peek-a-booing from his jacket pocket and felt both thrilled and comforted by his old-world glamour. As she held his gaze and worked the microphone to accommodate her new height, Marianna wondered if he knew jazz.

The room slowly became a sea of black ties and floor-kissing dresses. Dozens of clear balloons filled with confetti had been tied to the backs of chairs with pale ribbons. Marianna reconsidered her set and turned to Leo the pianist who agreed, both of them settling on: "Spring Can Really Hang You Up the Most."

When she shared this with me in one of her sessions sometime in our second month of work, I smiled. A blank-faced therapist I am not. My face, I've been told on more than one occasion, hides nothing.

Do you know that song? Marianna asked.

I do.

It means something to you? she said, delighted, shifting her gaze with curious, narrowed eyes.

Disclosure in psychotherapy and the ethical dilemmas it poses is a much discussed and debated topic. Previously, the popular view of a psychotherapist generated from television, theater, and novels has been of a neutral, silent, and somewhat distant human who is mostly unaffected by a patient's questions and lively revelations. This, however, is not a method of practice I can use. My approach is relational and collaborative and my patients affect me, deeply. Where possible I attempt to create what John Bowlby, pioneer of attachment theory, cited as a "Secure Base." Here, the gradual building of a meaningful relationship between patient and psychotherapist can evolve. The patient begins to feel more fully seen and accepted. As trust matures, there is an emotional settling where truths can be shared and relational risks can be taken, much like asking the therapist questions—should the patient wish to.

My smile in response to Marianna's song choice was indicative that it had meant something to me. I found myself thinking about Fran, my late mother-in-law, who had written the lyrics to "Spring Can Really Hang You Up the Most," a name she neatly shrunk to "Spring!"

The first time Fran—*the godmother of hip*—played her song to me, I'd been sitting in her backyard thinking of ways to depart fully my career in journalism so I could concentrate on working full-time as a psychotherapist. As I sat eating Fran's signature dish of tuna bake topped with cornflakes, listening to Fitzgerald's version of "Spring!," I'd felt conflicted about the possible change in my life. I remember embodying the song's pain and sweetness, then turned to Fran and said, *I guess I need to let everything happen to me, beauty and terror.*

Sure, said Fran, *all the best decisions are made from that place.*

For psychotherapist and patient, part of what I believe makes for an effective psychotherapy is a collaborative journeying together. While it is the therapist's role to maintain boundaries, she also navigates and gauges from experience what to speak, how to speak it, or whether to speak it at all. On this occasion

I decided to answer Marianna's question and offered, *Yes, it means something to me. I first heard "Spring Can Really Hang You Up the Most" when I was thinking about becoming a psychotherapist.*

What did you do before?

I was an art director at a magazine.

Glad you're not anymore.

Had Marianna's question veered in a different direction, asking: *Who* played it to you? or *Where* did you hear it first? I perhaps might have elaborated further. Attempts for connectedness if responded to in a thoughtful way can encourage attachment and trust between therapist and patient while achieving something quite different from Freud's classical approach of the implacable listener. I noted that Marianna hadn't asked *Who* and *Where*, which gave me pause to consider the possibility of her not wishing to know such an answer. Her question, perhaps, confined to something she was able to hear about: my working life.

Thinking about one's therapist outside of the consulting room, I've been told over the course of nearly twenty years, can be a complex and sometimes deeply uncomfortable experience. Patients have shared various thoughts about me, and what they've imagined my life to be like outside of our fifty-minute sessions together. One patient pictured me driving a convertible sports car on the weekends; others have imagined me childless, motherless, a church attendee, queer, single, married, an expert in martial arts. Another patient supposed I never left my clinical practice and slept on the couch, which at nighttime transformed into a pull-out bed. Later, she was shocked and disappointed to discover the couch had no such talent, or mechanism, for this transformation. One patient also shared that she'd seen me shopping in a supermarket close to my clinic and had panicked, abandoning her shopping trolley

full of groceries because it had felt too overwhelming and dis-
orientating to see me outside the office where we met twice a
week. *Where do you imagine I might shop?* I'd asked.

In my world, you don't need to shop, or eat.

The classical Freudian view of one's therapist as a blank
screen has evolved greatly in the past century. That fewer and
fewer therapists work now as passive listeners perched at the
end of a couch with limited eye contact offering little or no
response is, I believe, necessary and welcome progress. Demys-
tifying therapy and therapists not only supports and heartens
conversations about psychotherapy but also encourages ways
to think and talk about emotional unrest, depression, trauma,
and healing. It is an opportunity to allow the desire for civic
life to take its rightful place beside work and love in the clinic.
Knowing that a therapist is not inhuman, or immune to feelings, subjectivity and therefore responses, that we eat, shop,
and breathe, are capable of love, desire, hope, fear, and unrest
like any other human, is important to grow intimacy, respect,
and recognition for each other. And in doing so the power of
healing is felt, shared, and experienced together.

So in sharing with Marianna that I had had a previous career,
that I knew the song she'd sung when she'd first met Karl,
was a point of contact. A moment of mutuality. And in this
exchange, this moment of meeting, we were able to acknowledge we each existed within and without the therapeutic space.

After Marianna had finished her set at the charity event, Karl
stood and applauded. Marianna felt her heart swell. Mimicking
a drink with his hand, Karl pointed at the empty chair beside
him. Marianna smiled, mouthing, *Yes, thank you.*

In joining him she'd sensed a particular sadness, even though
his conversation and glamorous clothes indicated otherwise.
Marianna learned that he liked jazz but hadn't experienced it

as *a right of passage,* though he was open to the journey if she'd kindly introduce him. Karl spoke about his role at the charity event, his own mother having recently passed away from breast cancer, and when he poured Marianna a glass of champagne she noticed his left hand was ring-free. Later, she discovered he lived relatively close to her home and enjoyed cricket and swing dancing. *Would you like to have dinner some time?* he asked.

Marianna made herself warm and scarlet by saying, *Yes, yes I would,* without pause. And he'd laughed in a playful way at her enthusiasm adding, *Good, good, I'm pleased.*

This is how they met.

They kiss on what would have been their second date. Scotch and warm peppermint tasted and shared from his lips. Marianna relaxed and kept her eyes closed after the kiss had ended, and when she opened them again, Karl was smiling. Delicate snow landed on her collar. The first planned date had been a non-starter, Karl arriving one hour late. Marianna had decided not to wait and instead walked home feeling hurt and abandoned while telling herself she didn't care. Apologies were sent. Later, phone calls. A note with a hand-tied bouquet of claret peonies was delivered and lowered in a turquoise vase onto Marianna's kitchen table.

Sorry. Can we try again? K xx the note read.

Marianna researched the meaning behind his choice of flowers, discovering shame and bashfulness had arrived. Or had she overestimated his commitment and attempt to please? Were the delicate red orbs, perfect and expensively out of season, simply chosen by the hand of a busy florist? Marianna waited for a week to pass. Careful not to be too reachable and just a little bit sulky, yet not so much that she appeared cheerless. Or mean.

Did your absence achieve the desired affect? I ask.

Of course, she smiles.

On arriving at the second restaurant, Marianna enjoyed the opulent paneled walls and intimate gold uplighters. Outside, the snow's thick fall landed on the pavement, an evenly spread shawl of pure white. She enjoyed the snow and touched the soft part of her neck that felt most cold. The chill it sent through her body made her shiver. The maître d', whose hair was also bespeckled with white, asked for a name and handed her a chip in exchange for her coat: black, vintage, and astrakhan. And there Marianna stood, fixed and pleased.

When the door suddenly opened, a thick chase of wind reared behind his back. Marianna felt the cold rectangle of night awaken her face and relaxed her broad shoulders.

Hello, said Karl, kissing her cheek. Marianna paid careful attention to his mouth, soft and keen. The sound it made as it withdrew from her skin and the sense it left, etched and silent.

Hello. I'm pleased you're on time, she teased.

I'm very sorry about that. I'll explain, he replied.

He made sure they were seated at the curved marble bar, exposed and center. She'd made sure to wear her new dress, black and slashed at the collar. Simple pearls resting on her pale skin like tiny animal teeth. Waiting for her knees to pivot, he paused before sitting beside her on a tall leather barstool. A strange negotiation of limbs feeling momentarily awkward, and ungainly.

What would you like to drink? Karl asked.

Something with fizz, she allowed.

Then let's have champagne, he'd replied, sweetly.

Their conversation turned to the charity event where they'd met three weeks earlier. Marianna's shoulders loosened as she tasted the collection of shellfish placed on tiers of shattered ice, a meaty lobster resting on top. Its claws were shiny, flush, and perfect. Eyes still intact and staring. She searched for the finger bowl that was late to arrive, picking delicately at each shrimp, cockle, and oyster. The temptation to lick felt necessary, like an itch, but Marianna worried she may appear uncouth or decidedly flirtatious were she to lick her mouth, her fingers.

Marianna and Karl did not talk about why he was an hour late for their first date, but later she will discover it was because he'd met Sam, his ex. Instead, they discussed work, the last holiday Marianna took in Valencia, friends, family—the usual first (second) date pleasantries. Nothing too heavy or opinionated.

Does your dad also live in Cambridge? Karl asked.

No, my Pops died last year.

Marianna suddenly realized she'd been talking about Pops as if he were still alive.

What do you understand of this, I ask, *talking as if your Pops were still alive?*

I hadn't accepted he was dead, she says. *Part of me still hasn't.*

After dinner they walked to his apartment in Kensington. Karl was energetic, eyes glassy with wine. Marianna was shy and watchful. Only her face was exposed to the cold—a rush felt when he removed a warm hand from his tan leather glove and gently stroked her cheek. Then the kiss; warm peppermint and scotch.

By midnight she'd smoked her second cigarette, naked, in his smart home, thinking she ought to have held out until she'd settled her other commitments. But the wait had felt pointless. Curbing. So she'd surrendered.

On her cab ride home Karl texted her a photo of his bed that she'd decided to leave at 3 a.m. because of an early singing lesson: *I miss you already, K xx*

He'd tried to convince her to *Please stay, won't you?* Had looked hurt, a touch bitter as she'd dressed and made her way to the door. She'd sensed a tinge of displeasure in his voice as he said, *Good night then, to be continued,* a flash of indignation at her leaving. On her way home Marianna wondered if he would punish her for this later.

And did he? I ask.

Punish me?

I nod yes.

Perhaps he's been punishing me ever since.

The following morning, Marianna wriggled beneath her bedclothes and pictured the night before. She'd enjoyed Karl's touch by his kitchen refrigerator that she suspected was filled with meat and lettuce, and the way his intelligent fingers knew to unhook her black dress. Pearls stranded on her naked skin, Marianna's collarbone acted as life raft for their stringed and delicate beauty. She remembered the way he'd taken her down to the cold kitchen tiles with him in one swift move. Bones and flesh pressing into the floor.

She wondered if Karl might be thinking about her too, and whether he'd forgiven her for leaving. She checked her watch and forced her bedclothes aside, glancing at her bag resting on the dresser. Inside: the pearls, which had been carefully placed and wrapped in bathroom tissue before she'd left his apartment; Karl's rough handling of her on the kitchen floor causing them to break. Marianna had felt a thrill of excitement as he covered her body with his great palms, his potent strength insisting that she kneel. The desire in his voice as he ordered her to do things to him made her feel high, almost drunk. Tomorrow she would take the broken necklace to the jewelers on St. John Street. Have them restrung. There, she would make some excuse about catching them on a zip or something. They'd been a special birthday gift, after all.

Four weeks into our work I'd asked Marianna, *Should I be*

concerned at this point? You mention getting off on being ordered to do things—this is a kink of yours?

I don't know, you're the therapist, she'd shrugged. *But yes, I sometimes enjoy risky sex.*

I took a moment to note her dismissiveness. *But it is you who is in the relationship, and I think you've come to me for help. Do we need to discuss the broken necklace?* I asked.

She stared at me, hard, and raised her chin. *No,* she said, *you don't need to be concerned. I just want you to listen. I enjoyed it.*

Okay then, I replied.

Later that evening in the hotel, Marianna dressed, applied a ribbon to her throat to cover the marks made by Karl's fingers, and again found herself thinking about him. He hadn't telephoned like most men did after she'd had sex with them and she wondered about this. A slight disappointment alive in her throat that she massaged and soothed with a cup of warm water. Marianna took out her bag, peeled open the bathroom tissue and stroked the loose pearls. She felt an affinity for their broken state. They rolled in her palm. Her fingers cupped their fall. Marianna wanted to carry a hint of their night together and placed the pearls in the pocket of her red gown. She imagined fingering the broken necklace while performing her songs that night. The smoothness of each pearl worked like a circle of prayer beads. Her disquiet momentarily eased.

Meeting boys is one thing, finding one you wanna spend time with is another, Marianna says, impersonating her Pops in a slow, deep voice.

Marianna sips water from a bottle she's brought with her and tells me that when she'd returned home after a date with a lad named Lix, she had flopped down on the faux leather couch with teenage drama, declaring: *That was the worst night of my life.*

Pops had been sleeping, an ashtray resting in his lap leach-
ing smoke and stinking. His eyes appeared shot and red, like
he hadn't slept in days, and she wondered if he'd been to work
that week, or whether the bar where he played piano had
finally decided to fire him. On the floor was a glass half full of
what looked like cola, but Marianna knew a slug of rum had
been added—even though her Pops had quit drinking again.
He'd promised to have a dry month. No drinking, no smoking pot. And the day before, she'd watched her mother hug
him in the kitchen while he prepared sandwiches. *It makes me
happy seeing you like this,* she'd said, *eating and sober.* Marianna
didn't have the nerve or heart to tell her mother that he'd
stashed several bottles of rum and tequila in the garage behind
the record player.

Come on, let's go for a drive, Pops said, striking up another cigarette and downing the remaining cola. Her mother was in bed.
She'll be fine, don't wake her, said Pops.

He'd driven Marianna to a bar on the edge of town. Outside
there was a covered eating area that served quick and easy food,
and a playground for the kids whose parents enjoyed dancing,
playing pool, and making merry inside. At the bar, she and
Pops sat side by side. He'd checked his pockets for a cigarette.
So what happened on the date? he asked.

She liked it when her Pops showed an interest and asked
questions. These moments were rare, fleeting, and she made
the most of them when they happened.

He's not interested. Turns out he's already got a girlfriend.

What a dog.

She tucked her chin into her chest and felt her lip quiver. *I
really liked him.*

Forget about him, what kind of name is Felix anyways? said Pops,
touching her lightly on the shoulder. Marianna can still feel

him there in moments of sadness. Like a ghost, an untouchable dream.

When she looked up, she spotted a pretty barwoman with a small waist. A belt cinching her mohair sweater. She brought her Pops a tumbler of cola with ice. Pops hadn't put in an order but she clearly knew what to pour. *And what about you, sweetheart?* she'd asked.

Malibu and orange, said Marianna.

She'll take a cola, too; or just the orange, said Pops.

Sure, Teddy, the barwoman smiled. Marianna noted she didn't call him Ted or Edward.

Party pooper. Who's she?

A friend.

Marianna kept secrets for her Pops. When he'd told her to lie because the truth would hurt her mother, she'd done as he'd asked. When he'd confided, *I'll never leave your mother, but I need my freedom, kiddo,* she'd decided to do as he'd requested because if he left, life would be hell—for her and her mother. She learned how to have a loose relationship with the truth.

Marianna tucks a wayward curl behind her ear. *So you see, Pops and me had the kind of relationship that was built on discretion.*

And your mother? I ask.

I kept her safe. I forgave him on her behalf.

And now she forgives Karl on your behalf, I say. *Only you know about Karl's infidelity, unlike your mother, who didn't know about your Pop's affairs.*

Or maybe she did.

How so?

Marianna takes another sip of water. *How couldn't she know about the other women? There were so many—she'd have had to be blind. Perhaps she wants me to stay with Karl because it makes her feel better. After all, leaving him would mean doing the opposite of what she did with Pops.*

I reflect on Marianna's "blindness" concerning Karl's affair. Had she got with a version of her father, and taken up her mother's role? *Have you ever talked to your mother about his affairs?* I ask.

No. But maybe it's time.

Time for . . . ?

Time for me to come off my contraceptive pill. Karl need never know.

Marianna looks at me without a trace of guilt or self-questioning.

A lie or betrayal can be shocking, distasteful, and awkward. This is one of those moments when my face, my expression, speaks on my behalf.

What? she spits, she challenges.

I feel my back straighten as I prepare for a bold, therapeutic exchange. A daring trial. The unpredictability of what I have just encountered has me alert and concerned. Do I comment on this potential entrapping, or invite Marianna to venture further? Or do I file the potential lie under: *further exploration needed?* The sharp right turn away from a possible conversation with her mother has veered so violently toward a lie that I wonder what Marianna's high-risk behavior is serving. Arrested development? Selfishness? Revenge? Or is intervention by another important for Marianna?

My confidence is suddenly shaken. *It's time,* I say, vexed that our fifty minutes are up. I observe that Marianna has dropped this bombshell of a potential lie at the end of the session with little time to challenge or explore. The abrupt disclosure of her having the final word leaving me curious, spinning. I wish I had longer to engage with the process. But I will have to wait another week.

I am interested in intervention. In the animal kingdom it might be said that human intervention is not the done thing. Darwinism believed that all species develop through the natural selection of small, inherited variations that increase the individual's ability to survive, produce, and compete. I have in mind the extraordinarily beautiful *My Octopus Teacher,* a documentary about the filmmaker Craig Foster who developed the most unlikely friendship with a wild common octopus. Every day for 376 days, Foster visited the octopus. In watching the documentary I felt incredibly moved by both the attachment formed between Foster and the octopus and how respectful Foster was toward their slow-growing and intimate relationship. A colleague who had also watched it said over lunch one day, *The octopus saved his life*. I disagreed. *Their relationship saved his life,* I said.

One day Foster witnessed a pajama shark attack and devour one of the octopus's tentacles. I had cried watching the octopus hide and quiver beneath rocks and algae with her severed tentacle, life slowly draining away from her pink body that gradually turned a ghostly pale gray. The life of a wild common octopus is a daily test of survival, a forever flowing assault course where she attempts to outwit, disguise, and hide from sea life predators. Why hadn't Foster tried to save her from the attacking sharks? *You realize there's a line that can't be crossed,* said Foster, as he swam to dry land. Why was the natural order of things so cruel? I felt angry, powerless. But mostly upset. I started thinking about my own vulnerability and limitations as a psychotherapist. Like Foster, my relationship with humans is forever changing and most days I am reminded that the process of psychotherapy is less than perfect. We are empathic beings who attune and feel for each other. Our success as the human species is rooted in our capacity to be aware of one another's needs, to notice another's pain or lack of safety, and to experience deep, emotional empathy. Something occurred to me as a baby tentacle began to slowly emerge from the octopus's wound. Perhaps modern psychotherapy is not so much about radical intervention but rather an attempt to reach the patient, to help her think more clearly, and to invite a relationship where she is not left to swim alone with her difficulties, be they lies or betrayals.

Psychotherapy is an endeavor of the heart and mind, where two people explore what it means to be human. As psychotherapists we might feel tempted to persuade a patient to do something differently to what they are currently doing—to not lie, for example. The method I have found to be useful, however, is not to coax, cajole, or convince, but rather to try to find a helpful question to ask about the lie or behavior. Understanding rather than persuading is where change breathes. It is where the patient can share her innermost fears, hopes, and dreads. Interventions, while necessary in cases of danger and self-harm, are complex, but perhaps denying the patient her experience of resilience and survival drowns out possibility. I would try to convey this to Marianna when we met for her next appointment.

News comes that one of her closest friends, Sienna, is three months pregnant. *We weren't actively trying but here we are,* Sienna glows, pointing at her belly. Marianna feels tears—sharp, prickly pins in her eyes—and quickly finds a way to disguise her envy by forcing a lunatic smile, broad and mildly shaky. *I'm so happy for you both,* she sings. They each order salad, no wine, and the assumptions begin: *What about you and Karl? Oh, I'm not sure we're quite ready. Really, but you've always talked about having a family? Well— Really? We've only just got back together. Sure, but don't leave it too long, tick-tock.*

Marianna excuses herself to the bathroom. She checks her bag for a beta-blocker. Recent weeks have seen an increase in the swallowing of these tiny blue pills that slow her aching heart, kill the shake in her hands, and prevent a line of sweat bubbling on her top lip. She stares into the mirror. The jet of her pupil expands and sets in the green of her eyes. She watches her panic melt away and speaks out loud to her reflection:

I am not happy
And something has to change.
And Karl need never know if I stop taking the pill.
And I can do this alone.
So what will it be?

4 p.m.
I'd like to start by revisiting your comment from last week, I begin.

Marianna's eyes widen and, just as she's about to speak, a look of defiance quickly turns to one of bashfulness.

I could tell you felt shocked and uncomfortable with my confession to come off the pill, she says, her shy gaze lowered to her feet.

Confession is an interesting word, I offer.

That's exactly what it was. A confession.

That you were the keeper of your Pops's indiscretions for so long, I can't help but wonder if sliding into similar behavior preserves your relationship with him?

So in a way, I become him? Yes, perhaps it keeps part of him alive to me. She pauses. *My poor mum,* she says.

Silence.

And then, *I don't know what to do.*

I point out to Marianna just how similar her relationship with Karl is to her parents' marriage. How she, like her mother, chooses denial over any evidence of infidelity.

It seems to me that in your confession, you were unconsciously communicating how painful and frustrated you felt as a child, I say.

A pause.

I hadn't realized how resentful I am.

My stillness leaves the crackling aliveness of her words vibrating in the room.

Marianna, too, holds her stillness.

Silence.

I recently watched a documentary, My Octopus Teacher, I begin again.

Yes, I know it. I haven't watched it yet, she puzzles.

There is a point to my diversion, I add.

I explain my experience of watching the octopus and how I'd felt incredibly protective of her. How I'd wanted Foster to intervene when the pajama sharks circled the rock under which she was hiding. *I was conflicted about his decision to not intervene, but I also believed his decision was respectful for the natural order of things.*

Like, don't mess with nature, you mean?

Yes. Therapy is much the same—and different, of course. I'm conflicted about intervention regarding your decision to come off the pill, but I also wonder if in telling me this you were trying to communicate that you need something else from me.

I want you to tell me what to do so I don't have to make the decision, she says.

I'd like to help you think more clearly for yourself, I say.

Her mood suddenly changes, the tissue in her hand quickly scrunched with a fist.

I was never unfaithful to him, she spits. *There were endless opportunities.*

I do not answer. It was true, she was not. She had loved Karl, deeply. And she believed that Karl had loved her too. It is important to this story to know that Marianna is beautiful. She is generous with her attention, her body, and her voice. When enthrallment rains and shines on Marianna she decides what she will do with it. And when rain fell from other men she warned it off with an umbrella of grace and wit. Letting their advances know she was happily in a relationship.

Marianna leans forward. *Do you remember when I told you about the time Karl and I were meant to take a trip to Antigua to see my auntie?*

I do.

She wanted to give me some of Pops's belongings after he died. Karl said he had to work, that I should still go. And all the while he was fucking Hen.

I also remember you saying how lonely and betrayed you felt, I say.

Utterly betrayed, she says, voice shaking at the edge.

Perhaps more than that, you are now faced with a choice, I say. *I'm sorry Karl betrayed you, and I'm sad for the young woman who had to keep her Pops's secrets. But our pain is not our destiny. What you claim is a confession, is really an act of revenge.*

I have listened to many patients fantasize about acts of revenge. Occasionally this offers agency with their suffering and feelings of powerlessness. It is helpful to talk and think about these dark desires so that feelings of shame, hurt, and humiliation are understood and acknowledged, rather than acted upon. A patient told me once of her desire to leave maggots under the carpets of a home she was forced to leave without notice from *a negligent, money-grabbing landlord*; another spoke of defacing the passport of a flatmate who'd slept with her boyfriend; sewing out-of-date food into the hem of a dress of her nemesis, a dancer, confessed another patient; while yet another shared how she would imagine planting drugs in a colleague's work locker. There were commonalities among the patients who wished to retaliate against their victims in all of these stories: hurt and betrayal.

Marianna often wonders why her mother never, to her knowledge, sought revenge against her Pops. *There's something far worse than revenge,* she says, *and that's indifference or canned self-pity.*

After her session Marianna heads straight to work for an early dress rehearsal, her outfit folded over her arm like a giant restaurant napkin. She can't escape her longing for revenge; neither does she want to. She wonders why indifference bothers her so.

Later, she turns to Leo the pianist—fixed pearls resting on her collarbone—and lets him know she's ready to begin singing. She notes her breath, deep and steady. The small pulse at her wrist, regular and sure. She smiles at a group of diners, seated with their triangular cocktails, an olive or two. She will also drink a martini after her set has finished, she decides. Marianna leans into what feels like a newly discovered freedom, closes her eyes and sings "At Last." Her voice is embodied, strong. She pictures Etta James, blond and pixie-faced, and finds herself smiling through each word, each blast of gospel. Blues and country like a blended dream, "At Last."

Marianna has choices, she is no longer the injured party. She has the upper hand, a whip hand, she thinks, and the capacity for revenge if Karl puts a foot wrong. The last couple of weeks have seen her test him, almost goading him to step out of line. When he's not able to drive over late at night because she wants to have sex, it is *noted*; if he doesn't return her calls immediately, it is *noted*; when he doesn't call her just to say *I love you,* it is *noted*; and when he orders a lazy takeout, *noted*.

So when do you think you'll be ready to start a family? she asks Karl, pincering slivers of black bean chicken.

Soon.

How soon?

I don't know, Marianna, soon. Noted.

That night she is tempted to stop swallowing her contraceptive pill and the idea both thrills and terrifies her. She and Karl have sex twice and make love a third time. She closes her eyes and imagines Leo between her legs—enthused and drunk on her body—Karl catching them both in the act. Later, she puts a cigarette hole in Karl's suit jacket hanging on the rear of his bedroom door. His favorite aftershave is accidently spilled in the bathroom sink. Revenge.

She feels both freed and a fiend. *I will decide how and when to get pregnant. Not Karl.* She has also *started researching sperm donors* should she decide on a different journey, and begins to explore the possibility of meeting someone else, should things not work out with Karl.

Are you talking with Karl, I ask, *does he know how you feel?*

She gazes out the window. *Kind of,* she barely speaks.

In a session when she arrives early one afternoon we talk about her simmering anger, a friend for her revenge, and revenge's enabler. *I imagine my predicament is quite common,* says Marianna. *You must see lots of women just like me. Women who want to be mothers, women who want a family.*

We sit in silence for a long time, neither of us speaking, and I think about our journey so far, still less than a year. I recall Marianna's very first message left on my voicemail at 2 a.m., the agony and suffering she'd survived after Karl's betrayal, the unresolved loss of her Pops, the depression, the ongoing disconnect with her mother. I picture her singing at the hotel, wishing she were at a jazz club instead. I imagine her as a single mother with a new partner, with Karl and their baby. I think about the possibility of adoption. I think about her without a child, so much planning, scheming, foreseeing without know-ing. I suddenly feel exhausted.

A knock at the door lifts me out of my reverie. *Excuse me one moment,* I say. It is the postman delivering a package that will not squeeze through the letter box. I sit back down in my chair and picture my son, remembering his birth, and my birth as a mother. I conjure his first birthday, his first steps, and his favorite plush toy. I am in touch with how rewarding mother-hood remains.

Marianna yawns and I ask her what she's been thinking about in the silence.

She looks me square in the eye.

Sperm donor or betrayal. Pick one, she says.

Pick one, her Pops says.

Marianna stares at the two sleeves of vinyl, knowing she is being tested. Get it wrong and she could find herself unloved at least until supper. Choose correctly and he will shine respect and adoration all of the day and all night.

She reaches out and touches Miles Davis's "So What." And her Pops grins, shimmies his shoulders and lifts the arm of his ancient record player before the simple, melodic bass and trum-pet slide in. He dials up the volume. Places Charlie Parker back in the box and sips slowly on his rum and Coke. Two chairs have been introduced to the garage. They are made of pale wicker with plump cushions to make more comfortable her Pops's aging body. The day after, they will celebrate his sixty-fifth birthday.

Hanging on the garage walls are her mother's paintings: impressions of Tuscan landscapes, seascapes, lovers, and fat sleep-ing babies. All the things Marianna desires and cannot have.

She thinks I'll forget her so she fills my garage with her artwork, says Pops.

I like them, it feels homey, Marianna smiles.

I don't want it to feel homey; this here is how I escape.

Marianna kicks off her pumps and tucks her legs beneath her. *Oh Pops, you're always sneaking off, always trying to escape. You're not going anywhere, we both know that.*

Pops laughs. *You're right. Forty years we've been together. Who am I kiddin'?*

Exactly.

What about you, kiddo? Anyone in your heart?

No, not really. There's Karl. But it's complicated.

Well, let me give you two pieces of advice, he says. *Always do what you need to do, to be happy, and second, learn how to forgive.*

The next day they listen to Charlie Parker and eat ginger cake.

This is the last day Marianna will spend with her Pops.

She arrives for her session, aflame and animated.

I think I might have found a suitable donor, she beams. *His name's Edward. How weird is that?*

Not that weird, I do not say, neither do I venture into Freud's Oedipal Complex, and instead wait for her to continue.

The good news is that he goes by Edward, not Teddy—phew, she says, swiping her forehead with the back of her hand while feigning relief. A roll of her eyes.

Nothing's set in stone. It's early days. But he's tall, athletic, and kind. I don't know how you feel about short and long profile donors, but he seems lovely, and suitable. Anyway, we talked and got along so we're going to meet for coffee next week.

And Karl? I ask.

She shrugs. *I haven't told him about Edward. I'm still undecided.*

I wonder whether we might explore your dilemma, and more importantly, what's driving your decision. I'm curious why you haven't discussed this with Karl.

Marianna pauses and I note her breath settle. I am relieved to see this. Her mania reminds me of our earlier work and my attempts to *slow down the process*. She clears her throat and leans forward in her chair. *I just want to feel like I have choices for a while longer.*

In a bid for freedom and before her swelling baby gets too big in her belly, Sienna organizes a long weekend away in Paris. *Come on, it'll be fun. Me, you, and Casey—just like old times,* says her happy, pregnant friend.

When Marianna returns to her flat after four days of French fun she has an overwhelming fear that she's been burgled. Instead of opening the door, she picks up her bags and heads out onto the street. There, she calls Sienna, no answer. Casey, no answer. Karl, no answer. She leaves a voicemail for each of them. Should I call the police? she wonders. Fear and paranoia consume her. She is shocked by the power of her paranoia, or is it paranoia? Are the burglars still in my flat? What are they stealing? She hopes they haven't found the one piece of jewelry she loves but never wears.

When she arrives for her session the following day, Marianna explains the terror she'd felt before being able to enter her flat. *It took nearly an hour before I could go indoors.*

One theory is that paranoia, or heightened awareness, allows us to ignore our anger, I say. *But there's also another theory I think you may be interested in. That is, paranoia is a response to the feeling that we are being treated with indifference.*

Marianna takes off her scarf and rests it across her knees like a blanket.

Karl didn't even bother to call while I was away, she says. *I left him a couple of messages. He texted back, but he didn't call.*

Paranoia is a defense, I add. *It protects us from feeling no one is holding us in mind. Perhaps the thought that someone had burgled your home protects you from a far more painful realization—that nobody cares. Or so you believe.*

She agrees by nodding. *I guess living alone doesn't help. Especially after Karl said we'd move in together.*

I take a sip of my tea. *Paranoia is also more likely if we're feeling alone or insecure. You're an only child,* I say, *what was that like for you?*

Nothing like how I feel now. Mum was always home, painting, and if she wasn't, Pops made sure that he was. I never came home to an empty house after school.

I gather her words and make them my thoughts. *So one might say that as a child you rarely felt alone. However, now, the paranoia of thinking you'd been burgled saved you from feeling alone. You asked me once what the robbery was really about. I guess the thought of someone stealing or seeking revenge is easier than being forgotten. Your paranoia protects you from feeling indifferent?* I say.

Yes. I feel very sad, Marianna speaks quietly. *Wanting a family suddenly makes perfect sense.*

The month of August sees a lot of psychotherapists vacate for the summer holidays so they can rest and play, an extended break much like mouthwash for the mind. Over the years, my holidays have been dependent on varying factors such as childcare, fatigue, and, more recently, writing projects. However, on this particular occasion I too had decided to take the month of August away from clinical practice, mostly to rest but also to spend some time with my son who needed a warm holiday after his end-of-year examinations.

Marianna was one of the few patients who expressed how

she was looking forward to a break from her therapy. *It's not that I won't miss coming to see you, but I can test out what I've learned,* she says in our final session before the summer break.

Test out seemed an interesting phrase and I wondered who and what she was testing, exactly. Herself, me, or both. *Noted.* I wondered if, when, and perhaps whether Marianna had lied to me, also.

She was still undecided about Karl, and although I'd suggested for the past few months that she try to experience her life by living more in the present and with feeling, Marianna had become increasingly preoccupied with planning her pregnancy, testing Karl and meeting Edward the potential sperm donor often for lunch. She was finding it difficult to move away from the position of *I just want to feel like I have choices for a while longer,* to one of honestly relating with Karl, Edward, and her mother. When I asked her about this, she replied, *Look, old habits die hard.* I noted how her defense mechanisms were still very much alive and unwell. Would she choose to be honest with Karl, or go ahead with Edward the sperm donor? Perhaps neither would achieve what she desired most: a family of her own. Five weeks is a long time, I thought, with no therapy when significant life choices are hammering at the door.

This powerful reenactment with me as Marianna and she as her Pops was frustratingly fixed and swelling. She kept the lies and duplicity alive and I was left to hold the secrets like she had as a girl and teenager.

It occurs to me, I say, *that the lies, the discretions as you call them, only stopped when your Pops passed away three years ago. But you still carry them around inside you. What do you think might happen if I were to say I no longer wished to collude with your confession?*

Marianna's eyes widen and turn glassy. *I'd be angry and then*

I'd worry you wouldn't return after the holidays, she whispers. *I'd think you didn't care.*

I pause for purpose, and take a breath.

But I do care, Marianna. Very much. It's important to break the pattern, I offer. *By keeping this story alive you make any previous hurt your destiny.*

Marianna is silent; she is thinking. She turns away, unable to hold my gaze, and collects her sweater from the arm of the chair, pulls it over her head and adjusts her shirt collar. The delicate ticking of the clock lets us know we're at time. The summer holidays await us both. Suddenly standing, I join her. Marianna collects her bag, clears her throat, and smiles. *There's something I want to tell you before I leave,* she says. *I'm pregnant.*

She leaves. I am in shock.

During our five-week summer break, my thoughts are drawn, like a moth toward light, to our parting session. Mindful that these visitations are more insistent than my other patients', I trust myself, and my journeying and experience as a therapist, enough to listen—to take note and observe. I find myself oscillating between irritation and confusion, vexation and curiosity that Marianna had absented herself with such a tantalizing and provocative parting shot. Why had she done this? Was it an attempt to feel she had control over our relationship as she had when she told me (again at the end of a session) that she was going to stop taking her contraceptive pill? That by leaving and dropping the baby bombshell I might experience, as she had with Karl, what it felt like to be tantalized and kept waiting.

I decide that her actions come from a place of fear and hurt, but they are experienced as cruel, like an acting out, and I am pained by this. I am also angry. And disappointed. I remind myself of the profession I am in, that Marianna's disclosure isn't personal, that a patient's behavior is a response to their struggle. But however "professional" I convince myself of being, I am human. And humans hurt and feel disappointed. They also welcome summer holidays. The reality of working with a patient so wanting of a baby, I think, so needing to be a mother, I realize, brings the whole question of desire into the center of my mind. I finally reach compassion. Marianna is trying, pretty successfully, to show me how hurtful waiting can feel. Surely there are easier, more pleasant ways of communicating one's frustration, I think.

September. Marianna is early for her first session. She appears calm when I open the door, eyes making contact. A glamorous smile. Her hair, I note, has been highlighted. Tiny shards of light bouncing off her curls.

I'll be with you shortly, Marianna, I say, showing her to the waiting room. I observe feeling mildly irritated for her being fifteen minutes early and close my office door and return to my notes from the previous session. But my concentration is interrupted, my reflections hard to call back. I decide on boiling the kettle and making tea while I wait. All the anticipation of discovering who Marianna is pregnant with felt in the pit of my stomach.

How are you, Marianna? I begin.

I'm well, thank you. You?

Good, I smile. *How was your summer?* I ask.

Nice, she shifts in her seat, *relaxing,* she fidgets.

Silence.

I realize I just left telling you I was pregnant before the summer. I shouldn't have done that, she says. *It was withholding. And mean. I'm sorry.*

I do not respond immediately. A pause. I want there to be adequate time for us to sit with the apology, which I welcome.

Thank you, I say. *I was shocked after our last session. Particularly because the topic of pregnancy has been such an important decision for you. I also wondered if you were trying to show me how painful waiting can feel. Especially as you've had to wait for Karl to commit to having a family with you. And of course, there's the matter of reenactments. I think you were trying to show me that holding secrets holds power. As you and your father had. And when I said that I didn't want to collude any longer this had disappointed you.*

Marianna nods. *You're right. I wanted to hold on to knowing I was pregnant without telling anyone for as long as I could. Something just for me and the baby. All my life I've kept secrets for others, waited for others, longed for others. I didn't even tell Edward until last week.*

So Edward is the father? I smile.

He is. I ended my relationship with Karl in the summer. I figured I was going to be happier doing it alone. Edward and I have become quite close. We've spent some time together during the holiday. I don't think Karl would have ever committed, and I don't know if I could completely trust him after his affair with Hen. I'll be twelve weeks pregnant next month, so I'll tell my mum and friends then. But for now it's just you and Edward who know. Marianna places her hand on her belly, looks to me and smiles. *I didn't want to bring my baby into the world through a lie. And that's what it would have been if I'd gotten pregnant with Karl. A lie.*

Marianna was childless when I met her six years ago. Now, Grace is in school and enjoys the company of other children, all things unicorn, and has a pet goldfish named Archie. Like Marianna, I also raised my only child alone. As dazzling as I experience and believe my son to be, those formative years were a struggle. And they were recurrently lonely. I was

often faced with a maternal awkwardness from other mothers and families at weekend playgroups; sometimes I was
quietly pitied, and I resented the straitjacket of conformity
that ill-afforded the idea of choice and creativity as a single
parent, but my desire and commitment, once rooted, blos-
somed quickly.

Like Marianna, I too feel an unconditional love for my child.
He is sensitive and kind, creative and curious, and the one person
in my life whom I choose to set (sometimes) before myself.
Marianna also talks of *this love, this unconditional love that is like no
other.* The words spoken almost like a song both lyrical and sweet,
her eyes half closed as she speaks them with deep maternal bliss.

Experiences of infidelity, repetition of family patterns
and the lies told in her relationships didn't taint, too harshly,
Marianna's heart. In understanding her desire along with
acknowledging potential family reenactments, Marianna made
her choices differently and autonomously from her mother
and what her mother had suggested. The knife edge of settling for a partner *she no longer respected and couldn't trust* proved
a challenge because, as Marianna often pointed out in session,
time was running out. How close she was to lying to Karl, to
acting out her revenge and becoming pregnant through a lie.
But what became clear as she swelled and grew larger by the
month, was how much she wanted to be a mother, and then
how devoted and loving and connected she had felt when
Grace eventually arrived.

How do you feel now? I ask. *Looking back at those times with Karl
and Edward?*

*Like I didn't know my own power. My own determination and
strength. I thought I needed a man, a partner or husband, for a family
to feel complete. And of course I'd have loved that, too. But this wasn't
to be—not for me, anyway.*

She takes a sip of water.

It took a long time for me to believe it was possible to have a child on my own. I wish more women spoke about this. Not having a family in such conventional ways, well, there's still such a lot of stigma, fear, and shame around it, a taboo even. But if that's what we really want, who's to say we can't or won't, Marianna says, leaning into the first and final words to make sure I've understood, and that I am right beside her.

And of course, I am.

I stop there, for who can tell me what beauty is?

Frantz Fanon, *Black Skin, White Masks* (1952)

White Noise

For example: the birthday party. She was nine years old and the only Black child seated at the precisely laid table. She smoothed down her party dress: velveteen and red. A large silk bow sewn at the collar that she'd fiddled with constantly. Her cousins, both girls, passed the bread rolls along the table and, when their hands were free, patted her hair with their pale, outstretched palms. *Why is it so spongy?* they asked. *Will it ever grow?*

She pulled away, answering that it was *spongy* because, like that of her beautiful mother, it was *different to white people's hair.*

Why not straighten it? Clare, the youngest cousin, asked.

I don't want to straighten it. I like it, the child smiled.

Still, Clare persisted, turning to her sister Emily. *But then you'd be more like us, wouldn't she, Emily?*

The child cast a hard glance at her parents, a silver fork stabbed and forced upright in a resting leg of lamb, a sea of minted peas. Her father looked away. But her mother leaned in, locked her bright eyes with her daughter's, uncertain. *Tia's hair is different to your hair,* she smiled, *and we like her curls, don't we, baby? Now eat up.*

Later, Tia and her cousins ventured outside into the garden where Tia made herself *play nicely,* an instruction given by her father after he'd witnessed her assert herself in an earlier game of doctors and nurses. Fueled by a desire to join in, she'd tried to show Clare and Emily how to use a red plastic stethoscope, but the trio of bickering quickly turned physical after a disagreement about where exactly the heart lived and could be heard. *It's here,* Clare insisted. *No, it's here,* Tia said, forcing her hand. *Ow, you did that on purpose!* screamed Clare.

Emily took her younger sister by the waist. *Come on, don't play with her,* she'd hissed, *she's not like us. She's mean.*

Mean and Black, is what they really meant to say.

Tia reaches for a tissue. *When you're "different,"* she continues, fingers mimicking inverted commas, *you do your best to fit in—especially when you're a child. You read the room and do your best at family gatherings. But my mother and I were always outnumbered.*

We were six months into Tia's therapy and there had been many stories like this one. Race tales. Stories of divide and structural racism. Examples of Tia and her mother having had their voices and confidence snatched away. The symptoms of racism had laid heavy on their souls and their bodies and Tia took her time to explain the struggles that ran deep and way beyond the skin. *I never felt pretty or beautiful as a child,* she told me. *It's as if I'd been shoehorned into a body that wasn't mine. A Black vessel that I just navigated from day to day but didn't really like, let alone care for.*

I had listened with defiance and a familiar sense of unease and agitation. Rage and grief, I was almost certain, making new lines on my face. I wondered about the work ahead, knowing from past experience that conversations concerning structural racism are both painful and challenging when they slam into the consulting room. I recalled the necessary healing through connection in my own therapy alongside those who have also survived racial attacks. Growth and change made possible when a joint connection is experienced by both therapist and patient. This connection is important because it allows both patient and therapist to explore and participate together in whatever struggle the patient brings, and also encourages the struggle to be named, felt and then hopefully explored. The patient begins to trust and grow a meaningful relationship with her therapist in which she feels more fully seen, accepted, less isolated, and where her pain can be shared and witnessed. This type of connection isn't just about listening or passively bearing witness to; it also evokes feelings, a felt and shared meeting of mind and body from both sides of the room. Here, compassion and deep recognition of the patient's suffering can be grappled with, a deep intimacy helping to heal whatever suffering she brings into session.

Tia tells me how she'd watch the note of confusion on the faces of new friends and acquaintances with their curious eyes, particularly when her mother was out of view. *Adopted? Fostered?* the friends wondered loud enough to hear. *Perhaps she's a little friend of Clare or Emily's?*

Later, Tia would see the penny drop on their puzzled faces. Baffled dots steadily joining up as her mother eventually appeared, like magic. A vision of soft skin, teeth, and red silk—her mother's favorite color. Earlier eyes were cast sideways, sly and raised. Voices turned to strained, trailing whispers.

Tia contacted me eighteen months after her mother's death—a shocking brain aneurism that Evelyn fought but sadly didn't survive. Tia was keen to work with a therapist of color, someone who could relate to her struggles, but had found the landscape and possibilities *rather barren.* Previously, she'd worked with a white therapist and together they'd engaged in important work, but as some of the issues she wished to address continued to involve her heritage and race, she felt it was important to find a therapist who *was not afraid to go there.*

In our very first session together, Tia disclosed the towering loss of her mother and talked about how she'd been *shook to the core. I'm still struggling to accept my mum is gone, forever. I suspect I'm depressed. My daughter Sophia thinks I need help.*

Evelyn—a hospital midwife for twenty-eight years—had been perfectly healthy, or so Tia thought. So when she received a phone call to say that her mother had suddenly been rushed into hospital, Tia had needed to steady her legs, her knees; her fall.

Tia talked about her inability to fully accept her mother's death and wondered if the significant loss was contributing to her increased stress levels at home and at work. A company lawyer, Tia was struggling to focus and engage with her work as she once had. Law cases similar to those she'd previously advocated and felt passionate about were slowly disappearing and instead offered to her younger, peppy, and more ambitious colleagues. Her days were experienced as if *wading through treacle,* one eye on the clock, a desire to leave the office and head home as soon as the hand hit six. Tia felt disconnected and ambivalent. *I have no energy or interest anymore. I hate the person I've become: lazy, uninterested.*

Tia also felt restless toward her daughter's jam with academia, and exhausted because of her own uncompromised judgment of those who *did not wish to be the best version of themselves—including myself.* I observed and felt my chest tighten. No perfect therapist here, I itched to say, but didn't. I wondered what early messages and beliefs had informed this desire for others to be "perfect," and anticipated the inevitable moment when I, too, would surely disappoint. Tia's expectations of herself and others, I suspected, would be helped by managing her expectations.

I suggested twice weekly psychotherapy.

I've always done everything on my own, Tia responded.

So therapy is quite a risk. A good risk, I offered, *but nonetheless, a risk.*

The room filled with a heavy silence. Tia looked with curiosity around my consulting room, taking in the bookshelves and the plants, the airborne orchid that I'd sprayed moments before her arrival, the piles of research papers and corner table polished and shining, fresh cut peonies resting on top. When her gaze finally landed on my face, she locked her eyes with mine.

There are two types of people—those who show up, and those who don't. Please don't be one of those people who disappoint me.

I took a moment to digest the weight of Tia's words. Her binary thinking and the seriousness of her request.

I'll do my best, I offered, *but I can't promise that I won't disappoint you. Managing expectations takes the sting out of potential disappointment. Perhaps we are all disappointing and disappointed sometimes?*

Tia blinked. *Not in my world.*

When a patient begins her therapy she will frequently arrive with hopes, ideas, and longings for whom she would like her therapist to be. She may hope and dare to imagine her therapist as compassionate, a good listener, open-hearted, and a good all-round human being—all of which makes the therapeutic alliance imaginable and possible for a patient to begin talking about what is troubling her. Both patient and therapist commit to a collaborative adventure, a voyage of heart and mind where no two patients or treatments are alike; yet while part of us engages each new person we meet with fresh, open eyes, another part of us also brings memories, blueprints, and encounters of previous relationships, family or otherwise, to the consulting room. Occasionally, a patient may be unable to see me as "me" because their vision is shaped by the emotional events she has already lived. I have in mind a young woman who came to therapy hoping to look at what she described as *envious mother-in-law syndrome* and whom I worked with for just under a year. Every time I spoke or offered my observations, she related my thoughts and reflections as something her own mother would say or do. *That's just what my mother would say*, she'd reply; or, *Say that again, you sound just like my mother*; and, *I can't believe it, it's as if she's right here sitting opposite me!* The comparisons and projections of me as mother continued for several weeks until one day I playfully spoke, *I've often wondered what it might be like to have a doppelganger*, to which she replied rather dryly, *You look nothing like my mother. She's much taller than you.*

Sessions were drenched in preoccupation—my patient fascinating, assuming, analyzing, and compulsively wondering what her mother was thinking, doing, or planning. The projection of me as mother was so powerful that I began to wonder how I might remain in my own body, my own skin. *My husband's obsessed with his mother!* she insisted one afternoon quite early on in our work, her palms offered like gifts to the sky. *He can't crap without consulting her first. He literally has a photograph of her in every room of our home.* Then she cried. The irony was extraordinary.

I wondered who and what had proved to be so disappointing for Tia. What had happened in her world that now didn't allow for even a sliver of disappointment? Her carrying the weight of mental unrest on her shoulders like Atlas, condemned to hold up the celestial sky and heavens. How would I possibly or impossibly live up to her expectations? *Not in my world*, she had spoken. *In anyone's world?* I asked myself.

Tia also emphasized that in the unlikely event that she ever be late, or not working hard enough in her therapy, she wished to be reminded, in no uncertain terms, that *lateness and laziness are character defects. I want a therapist*, she said, *not a mummy.*

★

Nine months later, Tia arrives for her weekly Wednesday session, gym bag swinging, briefcase in hand. It is 7 p.m.

Once seated, she quickly asks how my day has been before I have had the chance to ask her the same question. This is not unusual. I often need to jostle with the lively and inquiring lawyer who has rushed from work in her trainers to make her session on time. Initially, I'd wondered whether Tia was checking on my possible fatigue levels and capacity to be present for her at the end of both our working days. Or was she genuinely curious to know how my day had been? It was unclear, but if I were to trust my feelings, I sensed it was most likely the former.

I'm well, thank you, I say. *How are you, Tia?*

Tired. I have a pile of work to get through and Sophia has her exams next week. If she spent more time studying and less time on her damn phone we wouldn't be in such a fix.

What kind of fix? I inquire.

Last night we were up until 2 a.m. going through her history notes. She's so behind. I made her write out significant dates so she'll remember them.

Which period is she studying?

The American Dream. And the Tudors.

She's interested in these topics?

The Tudors—not so much. And then there's her English and art. I can't help her with her art, but English—maybe.

The American Dream part of her history curriculum, she enjoys this?

Tia shrugs, barely nods.

For the past few weeks Tia's tendency has been to focus on her daughter's *mishaps, inadequacies, laziness,* her struggles. She has spoken rarely of Sophia's victories, or the joy she experiences in her studies or friendships, and I wonder about this. While psychotherapy is an opportunity to reflect and think clearly about discourse, I believe it equally important to acknowledge moments of fulfillment and connectedness with oneself, others, and life interests. On further inquiry Tia shared that *Sophia is very happy when she is making art* and had recently been offered a place on a two-week summer school after submitting her paintings, most of them self-portraits. Tia, however, was unsure whether art was a path worth pursuing. *History and English will offer more possibilities, I worry a career in art will be limited.*

I appreciate Sophia's exams are next week, but maybe we can take a moment to acknowledge where she is thriving, too. Perhaps then we'll gain insight and have a balanced view of the situation. Is she still enjoying making art?

Tia reaches for her mobile phone and invites me to look at some of the photographs she has taken of Tia's paintings. *What do you think?*

She swipes, I gaze. We smile.

I think they're incredible, I say. *She's very talented.*

I watch a small, proud smile arrive on Tia's lips. *I don't really understand them,* she says, *especially this one. It looks nothing like her but it's interesting.*

Interesting, how? I ask. I am hungry for understanding, to make contact with Tia's thoughts and her sense regarding Sophia's creativity.

Well, it seems she's really studied her face. And she's not afraid to be bold with color. See here, Tia leans in closer, zooms in on Sophia's eyes, her forefinger and thumb stretching an image on the screen of her mobile phone. *Look at the detail, see?*

It's really striking, I say, smiling again, *she's certainly captured a moment and a real love of her face. There's commitment in her work, don't you think?*

We both stare at the bold portrait. A kaleidoscopic adventuring and expression of green and lemon hues. I note the confidence in Sophia's brushstrokes. Her fine attention to detail. The entire canvas is filled with Sophia's face, eyes fixed, shoulders straight—an abundance of strident color and recognition. I note my desire to reach through Tia's phone screen, take and hold up the portrait and mount it on my pale walls. I want to stare and admire its commitment and beauty.

We lean back in our chairs. A pause.

Now I'm interested in something, I say. *You mention the portrait looking nothing like Sophia.*

It doesn't.

I note the speed at which Tia comes back at me. Defense in her tone.

Even though the detail is good, she adds, *the proportions are all wrong. Also the colors: they're bold, but they're strange. Weird-looking.*

Perhaps it's not a like-for-like portrait in a classical way, I say, *but rather how Sophia wants to paint and express herself. Maybe she's attempting to communicate something through her use of color?*

Tia clears her throat and lowers her mobile phone into her handbag. I watch her mouth tighten, eyes turn low and narrow. Our earlier dance of smiles and pride has turned into something quite different—a brooding unease. Mood suddenly strained, I wait for Tia's response, realizing we are entering complex territory.

During the initial weeks of Tia's therapy, she had spoken, at great length, of a *painful regret. I feel ashamed to talk about it.*

In her early twenties Tia had undergone cosmetic surgery and shared how she'd *rejected my Black skin, my Black features, and my partly Jamaican heritage.*

The surgery had been a response to her crippling aloneness and the impact of structural racism, which she avoided by way of control and denouncement. I made an internal note to myself, my heart reaching for balm: *Reflect on oppression and Tia's protracted expectations—her aching to belong and connect. What had happened to qualify the rejection of her Jamaican heritage?*

Aged twenty-three, Tia had wanted to dismantle her appearance and be free of her mother's *unbroken gaze. My dad was my main caregiver and everyone we spent time with,* she paused, *was white. I realize his words had a great impact on my appearance. A devastating impact. I wanted to fit in, to belong. I wanted him to love me. I suspect if I'd been raised by my mother, or in my mother's country, life would have been very different for me.*

After the birth of her daughter, Tia had felt a stab of shame and disappointment for changing her appearance, and wished, wholeheartedly, that she could reverse those earlier decisions to *transform* her face. *A person of color will understand this need to belong, for friendship,* she says, lasering me straight in the eye, *but I hate myself for what I did back then. My mother never forgave me.*

Tia had changed her nose, relaxed and straightened her hair, and eclipsed her brown eyes with turquoise contact lenses. She had lightened her skin, transforming her body into what she explained was a *"browning": a lighter-skinned Black person. I was thirteen when my parents eventually separated. It was very difficult but, equally, I was relieved that they did. I lived with my dad and spent the weekends with my mum. Both demanded my loyalty and both had very strong opinions about who I was and who I should be. I found myself very split and very angry—a pawn in their game of chess.*

The analogy was painfully accurate. I pictured a chessboard, small carved pieces: a king, queen, and pawn. Busy fingers outwitting and removing parts of their competitor's life until... checkmate.

Who won? I asked.

Good question. Who won? she repeated, thinking and staring out of the window.

We were both very still, silent.

Though I'm not entirely convinced there are any winners, I offered. *Who wins when we don't speak truth to power?*

But in the end I guess there has to be a winner, said Tia.

Oh?

And that would be my dad.

A pause.

Perhaps it's time for another game? I said.

Tia leaned forward. *Shall we flip a coin to see who's Black and who's white?*

By another game, I mean, a different game. One that isn't focused on the binary, I said, alive to my own dual heritage mirroring that of Tia's. The trial and impossibility of being loyal to one culture alone.

Tia waited. Paused.

How about Snap?

Touché, I smiled.

Back in the present moment I check the clock: 19:20. Tia zips up her handbag, crosses her arms and legs, her body a sudden fortress, a moat surrounding her pain. I attempt to swim toward her, to meet and acknowledge the struggles she has been forced to reckon with.

It's painful to watch Sophia's confidence, says Tia—*how she accepts and expresses who she is. My daughter has such a fine sense of herself in the world but it acts as a reminder that I did not. I wish I'd been able to do that at her age. Life would have been very different if I had.*

Awake to the pain she might go through to have what she wants, I nod and wait for Tia's words to settle in my body.

It's important to acknowledge this loss, I say, *the oppression you've experienced and survived, and continue to realize. Our pain is not our destiny but our reason, and healing is as much about what we pass on to our children as it is about our own progress. Sophia has you as her mother,* I say. *You have taken what you've understood of your own journey and given her tools, guidance, and skills. Do you think it might be helpful to talk with Sophia about her art, to ask her what she's thinking and feeling when she paints?*

I already did.

And?

She told me she paints what she feels, not what she sees.

Words of a true artist, I say.

Tia smiles. *Thank you. She's incredible.*

As are you, I offer.

Tears fall from Tia's wide eyes. *Thank you,* she smiles, shyly.

I wait for her to wipe her eyes, balled tissues stuffed up the sleeve of her silk blouse. *I wish I'd been closer to my mother,* she says, voice shaking at the edge. *I miss her. It was a complicated relationship. There are so many things I'd do differently now.*

What kind of things?

I'd look after her—cherish her. I wouldn't mistake care for control. I realize I was trying to escape her. My dad was forever telling me that I looked just like her, acted just like her. I wanted to be free of that. I wanted to be my own person.

I remember you saying there were other complications, I offer, recalling her father had quickly remarried.

Yes, Charlotte. I lost count of the times she and my dad suggested I try a different "look." I was keen to please them both and I was very lonely. I had very few friends. Sophia says I have this look, "The Lonely Look," she calls it. I believe that little girl still lives inside me. She's hard to shake.

Tears prick at my eyes. *I think she needs a strong, caring arm around her, not a shake,* I offer.

I watch Tia's internal struggle, tears held hostage, jaw unrelaxed.

She opens her mouth to speak, then stops herself.

That little girl needs our love, I say.

After the session I make notes to steady my unquiet mind.

Finished with my patients for the day, I allow the full weight of Tia's hurting to settle in my body. I acknowledge her physical and psychological scars and wait for the familiar thud of pain, deep and penetrating, to colonize my body. Anger emerges. Being with the familiar devastation, I touch the soft part of my throat, sore and dry. Sadness follows too quickly, I think. My thoughts drift to a piece of clinical work I did as a training psychotherapist with a young woman who spoke often of her three children, all boys, and told me once: *Before they know race, I want them to enjoy color.* Her words have stayed with me fifteen years later. Strong words, true words. Words that evoked a freedom that she had not experienced herself.

Tia carries in and on her body the devastation of structural racism, I write in my notes.

The racism and emotional disconnect Tia's father demonstrated when he ordered his daughter to: *Play nicely; Fit in; Don't answer back; Choose your friends carefully; Don't wear that—too much skin; Have you thought about straightening your hair; Turn that music down; Keep an eye on your weight or you'll end up just like your mother* had whitewashed Tia's biracial body. His response to Black Lives Matter: *All lives matter, Tia.*

Tia's father will perhaps never know what it means to embrace a person of color—and his only daughter—as his true equal whose thoughts, feelings, and beliefs are as valid as his own, I write in my notes, underlining *true equal*.

I had some strong feelings about Tia's father. Feelings that I dragged to peer and clinical supervision where I vexed and felt sorrow. Injustice and anger took hold like an emotional tsunami. I paid attention to the injustice; frustration; exasperation; exhaustion; and objectification. I had felt them all in my own life journey, and now I was witnessing them afresh with

Tia, who had told me that she'd stopped asking for what she wanted and did her best to accept what she had. I decided to locate the tiny door ajar within myself that had survived racist attacks in my personal and professional life. Inside that door was determination and fuel. A desire to find a voice and to step into my power. A need to connect, grow, and change.

A friend and colleague turned my gaze to Zora Neale Hurston's *Their Eyes Were Watching God* and reminded me of the chapter when the main character, Janie, shares with her friend: "It's uh known fact, Phoeby, you got tuh *go* there tuh *know* there."

I agreed with Hurston's protagonist. I had to go where I knew, and that was to call racism out. To find a voice in the haze of white noise.

Concerned with the present, my reveries return to the ongoing work with Tia. I am suddenly alert to the issues. My intentions erect and full of purpose. I concentrate on the psychoanalytical framework, and how the impact of witnessing Tia's racial trauma puts me in touch with my own journey of racial discourse, known as secondary retraumatization. Also, the impact, emotionally and physically, of trauma handed down from generation to generation. I note a rise in my desire, encouraging myself and others to build a better world, step by step. It's the *only* possible way forward.

What's next . . . ?

My mind focuses on the healing needed from Tia's cosmetic surgery and her internalized "father voice" along with her experience of fear and isolation; the death of her mother; the continued attachment with her daughter Sophia, and building awareness of potential reenactment of the mother-daughter relationship.

Was Tia subconsciously distancing herself from Sophia as

Evelyn had when Tia had grown attached to her father? Was art
a threat, or at least the expression of art? I wondered what both
generations of women had felt when they faced something that
felt other, something different to themselves. Something that had
the potential to divide and conquer.

I, like Tia, was raised in a family and community that did
not see me. The emotional disconnect when I attempted a conversation about my identity and being British-born Chinese
with those I shared a roof, a school, a church with, was all
too exhausting as I watched eyes harden against my desire to
be heard, known, and understood. I needed to preserve my
strength, culture, and sanity, I told myself. *She's not like us,* I
overheard uncles, aunties, and cousins say. The story goes that
my estranged grandfather arrived at our home one Christmas
and, as I'd answered the door, my mother close behind me, had
asked: *Who's this funny-looking Chinese girl?* I only have a vague
memory of this exchange and probably for good reason. But
each time I'm reminded of the story by family members I can
still feel the wounds reopen. They bleed.

As the child of an immigrant I've had to rewire my thinking
to understand that we arrive anywhere feeling on the outside,
looking in. *Work hard,* my father would say, *and in the end you'll
be rewarded.*

I wondered what this reward would look like. Surely *home*
is reward enough, I thought.

Tired from the day's clinical practice I remove my shoes
and tuck my legs beneath me. A memory returns, of a much-
needed holiday I had decided to take in 2015 after a challenging
year, both personally and professionally. While I waited,
patiently, aboard a small boat on the Bosphorus Strait, willing the engine to carry me toward the only metropolis on
earth where a country straddles two different continental

landmasses, I acknowledged how exhausted I felt. I was battle fatigued.

The Bosphorus is the thin strip of water that bisects Istanbul, and where Europe and Asia come together—or part, depending on your viewpoint. I hadn't wanted to lose the complexity of this moment. The feeling in my bones when an internal voice, old and customary, reemerged and spoke, *Pick a side.*

The request was impossible, limiting, but not unfamiliar. I was aware of the intricacy of embodying a kind of two-ness, a biracial body. A sense of straddling two cultures, two worlds, two conflicting ideals in one small, confused self. Often, I have struggled with the frequently clumsy language that accompanies a mixed heritage life—the two-ness, the biracial-ness, the duality. Acknowledging it feels like overkill. Not acknowledging it feels like passing and dishonorable. I long for the in-between, the wholeness. The me. Just me.

My mother and father, not unlike Tia's parents, had also competed for my preference and loyalty. Each unaware that their own fears and needs were intruding on my attempts to feel whole. My mother told me to blend in, to do and act as the other kids did at school. My father insisted on the exact opposite, stuffing my lunch box with moon cake and other Asian delights. I was one of two brown children in my class, "the outsiders," and I survived the teasing and cruelty that I neither understood nor accepted. *Oi, chinky! Slanty eyes! Chop suey!* shouted the kids at school. Fingers stretching their mean eyes sideways behind my back. Later, at community college, microaggressions surfaced to ask: *"What are you?"*

The truth is that we are not a "what" but a "who," and how we appear in our skin will never tell anyone who we are. Attempting to define a person by anything other than their humanity can have dangerous consequences.

My exhaustion on the boat as I sailed along the Bosphorus, I believe, was partly down to having conversations—some personal, some professional—in which understanding structural racism still required people of color—myself, my family, my colleagues, and some of my friends—to prioritize white feelings. Tia is evidence of this. My much-needed holiday was evidence of this.

Tia, I write, *wears oppression on her face every day. We must work hard to heal these wounds and dismantle her regret and self-punishment. Acceptance is key, as well as respect for her daughter's victories, struggles, and all that falls in between.*

I set down my notes, turn off the lights in my office, and gather my shoes and rucksack with thoughts of home, two hours away. On the wall opposite, I imagine Sophia's self-portrait. Skin the color of earth, of nature, and uprising skies. My tired eyes lingering over her daring beauty, alive. So alive.

Today she has decided *it's time to work.*

Our seven months together have afforded some trust and alliance and so, sport ready, Tia casts the die and asks me a question: *Where were you born?*

Right here, in the UK, I answer.

She teases and pulls at a pill of pale blue cashmere on her wrist and continues with her inquiry. *I'm curious about your heritage?*

I'm British-born Chinese.

Your mother . . . ?

My mother is white, British, I reply. *My father is Chinese.*

So you're an outsider too, she says.

A sudden crackling aliveness in the room. We are two women connected by a small moment of sharing. Symmetrical in our peripheral living and *outsider*-ness. I am relieved that

Tia has asked about my heritage. Her questions not as a matter of objectification or forced alliance, but of curious connectedness. Subject to subject. We are in this together.

My class and my race have unjustly had me on the outside of things, I say, leaning toward her, *so, yes. I have also experienced myself as an outsider.*

The popular view of a psychotherapist is that of a silent, implacable listener. A blank-screen human who is unaffected by discourse, challenge, similar life experiences and, from time to time, even the most shocking revelations. But in my work with Tia I experience our work as an exquisite affinity. No grand flourishes. Instead, our respectful listening and engagement with each other has the capacity to change and grow us both. And I liken the process to a stretching of the self, or diving into a poem. When touched and moved by the connection and the rhythmic, lyrical words, I am quite simply changed by the end.

What's it been like for you, life as an outsider? Tia asks.

I gather my thoughts, mindful to stay focused on Tia's struggle but simultaneously wanting to remain connected yet boundaried. *Difficult at times,* I say. *And lonely. But over time I've tried to grow comfortable with the discomfort. I've also sought out other outsiders. Turns out there's quite a few of us out there.*

Tia takes the flat of her palm, rubs her chest, and massages her heart in large circular movements. *I feel lonely,* she cries. *My mother was right: the outsider is someone who rarely knows home.*

I move toward Tia. Closer still. A desire to assure her through my words, my skin, and my humanness. *Tia,* I speak. *Too often, the outsider is ignored, sneered at, underestimated, or reduced to invisible. But let me propose that life as an outsider can also exist with a sense of liberation. This is not to dismiss the complexity of our being outsiders, the loneliness, the self-doubt, but being released from society's expectations offers great freedom to define our own values. We have to find a home within ourselves. Home is where we start from.*

Tia wipes her cheek, moves forward in her chair. *That makes sense,* she speaks quietly. *I don't think my mother ever truly felt like she had a home. The hospital where she worked was perhaps the closest she got, which was probably why she worked such long hours delivering all those babies. She was never happier than when she was in that hospital. Coming home to us almost felt like it had been an obligation—and somewhere to sleep, rest her head. To be honest, I'm the same, which is most likely why I'm struggling and frustrated with having fallen out of love with work.*

You and your mother had a strong work ethic.

Tia laughs, shakes her head. *She was forever in those damn overalls and pumps. It's all she ever wore. I used to say to her, "Why not wear one of those pretty dresses, you're not at work now." And she'd say, "There's more to life than pretty, Tia. I got babies, fine and beautiful babies to bring into this world. Now shoo. Go bother someone else."*

It had been a complicated mother-daughter relationship. Tia's mother believing in harsh punishment when Tia was a young girl, an even harder work ethic later passed down, strict weekend routines and, above all else, loyalty. Evelyn was candid regarding her power over her daughter: *No one will hurt you the way your mother can, and no one will love you the way your mother can*; this, offered at every opportunity and spoken with bold, steady eyes. Evelyn longed for Tia, her only child, to be her ally. And Tia's body is still lined and alive with her embroidery—a complicated tapestry of words and mantras. Ongoing, they weave and unravel in every pore of Tia's being, knitting a heavy blanket of loss. Pluck any thread of identity and Tia finds herself longing for her mother's return.

Tia wishes she hadn't feared her mother so much, that she'd told her more frequently how much she needed her;

how she wanted to love and learn from her. Over the years, there have been so many words Tia wished she'd said to her mother—*Teach me; help me use my voice; encourage me to love my body, my skin; insist that I not run scared when Daddy tells me I should dress and eat and talk like cousin Clare; help me tread carefully when speaking because if I express my frustration and anger and exasperation at not being heard or acknowledged as an equal, I will be accused of being an angry Black woman that prescribes to their racist ideas; help me to not fear and align and exhaust myself as I attempt to "fit in"; help me to not feel like I have to change myself and move further and further and further away from you. I miss you. I love you. I am sorry, Mum.*

When she was eight years old, Tia remembers going with her father late one night to the hotel where he worked as manager. The memory and the feelings it evokes unsettle Tia, but she invites me to witness this early snapshot of her life, and insists: *Let me tell you how it went, Maxine.* I sit back, I listen, I wait for her story to unfold. *Let me share what a son of a bitch my daddy was,* she says. You could hear a pin drop.

The thick drawl of a brass band leaking from the ballroom she cannot enter. It was late, close to midnight. The musicians slowed their instruments, the singers bowed, and the room went mute. Applause over the dance floor building, swelling to rhapsodic...

Tired and bored, Tia sneaked a look through the sliver of a half-opened door in the upscale hotel in St. James's. Her father was wearing his usual uniform: a black suit and a blaring white shirt, a puff of red silk peeking from the chest pocket of his neat, fitted jacket. On his pinkie, a gold signet ring still glimmered after years of wear. Tia felt a complicated love for her father as she watched him glide, seamlessly, from small intimate table to small intimate table. One hand resting on the back of a chair as he bent, another resting at his waist. His eyes engaged with the finely dressed men and women.

It was not unusual for Evelyn to insist Tia accompany Robert to work at the five-star hotel. *I need a night off, go be with your daddy,* she'd order, *and keep an eye on him—he lies.* Tia was seven years old when she was assigned the role of sleuth, and she suspected her mother already knew of her father's affairs. Forcing him to take Tia to work at least meant he'd come home at night. Through the walls of her small bedroom, Tia cupped an ear and listened to her mother's accusations and her father's denials. *You're a liar, Robert, and a cheat.* Cheap evidence was revealed—a smudged lipstick stain, a phone number scrawled on a used matchbook, several bar receipts printed hours after closing—but nothing hard enough for Tia's mother to ever leave him.

Tia watched and wondered why her father—*the liar*—desired comfort from other women, *especially when he had my beautiful mother.* Why did the green in his eyes turn firework fluorescent at the sight of the blond women who planted expensive drinks on the small intimate tables? *It was as if he were enchanted.* Blind drunk on the women's lean bodies, catching the blues and grays of their eyes, he placed his marriage hand on the small of their backs, their waists, moved closer toward their necks, sweetly perfumed.

Holding her books and temperamental Walkman, Tia opened the ballroom door a little wider, yawned, and immediately recognized a couple of the tall waitresses she'd gotten to know in the past year, along with the brass band that gifted her sweets, loose change, and intoxicating magic tricks. As the final guests left the ballroom, Tia's father ordered her to wait patiently in the hotel reception. *I won't be long, read your book.*

Later, still tired and bored, Tia went in search of her father and the band with their entertaining wizardry, hoping for disappearing coins, the musicians revealing their circled shine from behind her left ear. She headed toward the dressing room filled with glittering dresses, heels, and combs. Bottles of dark rum. Jars of cold cream swiped with manicured hands. When she opened the door, Camilla the waitress gasped, quickly snapped her legs closed like an automatic door on a happy shopper. She swiftly yanked down her black nylon skirt and tapped Robert's back. The look on his face as he turned was one that resembled *limp shame*.

Tia stared at the growing night outside and wondered when the world would stop hurting her and her mother. When would the moon stop spinning, appear still, luminous and shining like the coins plucked from the soft part behind her left ear. *Never, it never stops,* a small voice spoke in her coin-free ear.

Tia turned away and tried her father's feeling of shame on for size. It seemed to fit.

I know what you did, Daddy, she said in a quiet voice. *I saw you.*

On the drive home, Tia waited for her father to bribe her with late-night ice cream, a cheap plastic toy from the grimy twenty-four-hour service station. She waited for his big sweeping arms, shirtsleeves rolled, to squeeze and hold her all-seeing smallness. Suddenly grown, Tia allowed in the late-night air. Five years more and she might kick it outside, cut loose, and smoke a cigarette. Tia tried to imagine what was playing out in her father's mind: an apology, an explanation, a gentle pleading to understand. Nothing. She checked his face to see if anything moved, his hands, his shoulders. Nothing. She cleared her throat. Nothing. A snivel. Nothing.

Tia envied, hated, and felt confused by the attention Camilla seemed to have teased out of her father. *Why were you doing that thing to Camilla the waitress?* she dared.

Silence.

Daddy?

It was not until Robert pulled up in the driveway that he stared Tia square in the eye. *If you tell your mother what you saw, it will break her heart. You don't want to be the cause of that, do you? I love you, Tia. You know I do. But if you talk about this to her, or anyone else, I will stop loving you. Do you understand?*

There were so many opportunities when Tia might have disclosed her father's *double-crossing, cheating, moonlighting, treacherous, and snaky ways* to her mother, but she chose not to. *Why?* She feared her mother's breakdown, *her madness*. But Tia had also feared her father's rejection should she speak up. *You don't want to be the cause of that, do you?*

Tia tells me the risk of losing her father's love was too great, and this, she believes, is when her love and loyalty took a turn. *I wanted to protect my mum, but I really didn't want my dad to stop loving me.*

Her mother had increased her working day. Tia barely saw her, only on weekends when she tried to stay close to Evelyn, suggesting trips to the cinema, intimate board games for two, and shopping. But Evelyn was tired. Her delivery of babies made her so. The aftercare of the mothers and babies made her so. The after-hours paperwork made her so. *Shall we play Monopoly or watch a movie? I can tease your hair, paint your nails...* Tia offered in a gentle voice, but her mother just needed to rest, to have some alone time. Entering babies into the world was tiring work. *Go play with your daddy,* she said.

Evelyn took her eye off the prize and I wonder about this steady straying—the gradual but certain distancing between them both. Challenged by absence, fatigue, disappointment, and competition, the bonds of love between mother and daughter were beginning to sever. Evelyn's maternal flow was slowly ebbing away.

Tia is quick to reply. *She would say I was just like my dad and not a bit like her. Why you all vague and polite and wanting to read these kinds of books. Read Maya, or Toni, they'll teach you something, girl,* she would say. *It was very confusing because both parents told me I was just like the other. I didn't know where to turn, who to believe and who I should listen to.*

When both parents were working there were young, pretty babysitters who agreed to take care of Tia with domestic gentleness. Tia recalls at least five or six young women reading to her at night. She puzzled over why her mother chose to look after other babies instead of her. She pictured her mother holding their miniature hands and their perfect feet. Their delicate fuzzy heads round like a pearl, smelling of talcum powder. *I didn't understand at the time,* she speaks gently. *I wanted my mum, I needed her, I didn't understand why she chose other babies over me. I promised myself I'd try to do something different with my own baby.*

Later, when Tia's teenage years arrived early, subtle messages were offered clearly. Her father began commenting on her *thick legs,* her *dry skin,* and her *frizzy hair.* He encouraged the idea of giving hair straightening a go, maybe a different kind of dress, something *more feminine.* Sometimes the message *was more subtle, just a little bit racist,* a certain glance when Tia appeared from her bedroom in clothes that welcomed her shape, the volume turned down on music she felt alive with and would dance to.

There is no such thing as a "little bit" racist, I say, *there is only one kind. And I recognize the impact this has had on you, Tia.*

Later, *cruel jokes* and comments were fired at Tia's skin. *Hide like a hippo,* he laughed alone. The babysitters marshaled Tia into different rooms of the house, escaping Robert's racism, acting busy with errands, their jaws clenched. Janie, one of Tia's favorite babysitters, had stroked her head and covered her ears with both palms. *Come on, let's go into the garden,* she would say. *It's nice outside, last one out is a party pooper!*

Back then I felt embarrassed on my dad's behalf. I felt so ashamed when he said these things. I made his racism my problem. I wanted him to love and accept me and the harder I felt this, the further apart me and my mum became.

Tia shuts her eyes, fatigue weighing them closed. *I want to stop punishing myself. I'm tired and I'm allowing the past to define me. I want to respect rather than envy Sophia's sense of self. I have to move on. I have to heal the part of me that was scared to be Black.*

I applaud Tia's courage to heal as well as her radical self-compassion. I rage against the struggle forced against the lives of three generations of women. Their footprints edging along the borders of race and identity and, more importantly, their humanity.

Tia receives an email from one of the partners of the law firm where she works saying there will be a meeting to discuss *inclusion and diversity in the workplace, please attend.* Tia feels her palms start to sweat. Her breath is fast and shallow. She suddenly feels exposed. Tia is the only Black woman in her team apart from Jennifer, a temporary work experience colleague who she's already clocked and checked in with. While Tia is keen to have a conversation with her colleagues, she is also determined not to be a tokenized mouthpiece.

How do you feel about this potential conversation? I ask.

I think it's necessary, but I don't have any expectations. The thing is, we'll be coming at the conversation from different places. And if my colleagues can't recognize that a problem exists in having so few people of color employed at the firm, I will not engage.

I understand, I say.

I worry that my colleagues will think we enter this conversation as equals. But the truth is, we don't. Do you agree?

I listen and feel Tia's desire to have me align with her, a direct and understandable question to test my mettle, my alliance. As therapist I have a professional responsibility to not collude with my patients but to remain useful in helping them think clearly for themselves. But in this instance I meet her and offer, *Yes, I agree, Tia.*

The following day Tia and her colleagues meet in the board-room. Sweet pastries have been fanned out on white, oversized plates. Large silver coffeepots let off steam. Tia is the last person to arrive. There are twelve people seated. Until this moment Tia has never considered herself unlucky, or super-stitious, but as she sits down she feels protective of her voice, her boundaries, and wishes she'd worn her mother's tourma-line necklace—the precious stone believed to encourage balance while shielding Tia from negative or unwelcome energies.

I feel uncomfortable talking about race in a room with mostly white people, says one of her colleagues, who avoids eye contact with Tia. Another colleague, a white man in his fifties, claims how guilty he feels about the lack of BAME solicitors in the law firm where they all work. One woman says she's felt anxious knowing they were meeting to talk about inclusion and diver-sity; *I don't really feel like I have a right to an opinion.*

Tia watches her colleagues nibble on their pastries. Sip their coffee.

I'd like to hear from Tia, another colleague says. Several heads turn her way.

Did you respond? I ask Tia the following evening.

I did.

And?

I asked him why he felt the need to call me out. And then I asked him if it was because I was a Black woman?

Did he respond?

Not directly. He was defensive. He interpreted my question as an affront.

It's not your responsibility to educate your colleagues, I say. *But it is each of our responsibilities to speak truth to power. Conversations can be helpful, necessary even. But only when we acknowledge the symptoms of structural racism. We can all play a part in dismantling racism at work, or at home. Passing on knowledge and skills to our children or those who wouldn't access them otherwise is important. It all counts.*

Tia felt immediately that she was about to become responsible for her colleagues' emotions, but thankfully kicked these feelings to the curb. *For a bunch of lawyers, I am stunned at their emotional disconnect, their nerve and denial.* She looks at me, sighs, *What are you thinking?*

What am I thinking? I repeat, reaching for a sip of water. My throat is sore, again.

I finish my glass of water and pour another.

I'm thinking about white noise. So much white noise in that boardroom.

Tia nods. We lock eyes.

How it masks other sounds, I continue, *how it puts one to sleep.*

She straightens up in her chair, her pupils widen.

I drank a lot of coffee, says Tia.

The day comes when, after all of her hurting, all her reflecting, grieving and gradual healing, the inevitable happens and I do precisely what Tia asked that I never do: I disappoint her. *Please don't be one of those people who disappoint me.*

My flight home had been canceled and there was every likelihood that any subsequent cab ride would have to commit crimes in order for me to make my appointment with Tia at 7 p.m. For the past year Tia had not missed any of her sessions. Neither had she arrived late, which, considering she is a lawyer, a mother, and needs to travel across London to my office, is pretty remarkable. She also informed me she would take her holidays when I took mine. At the time, I had recognized her punctuality and matching vacations as a sure sign of her commitment. I hadn't anticipated that the high expectations she placed on herself, and therefore also on me, wouldn't have thawed in our many sessions together.

I call Tia's phone and leave a voicemail, explaining my flight has been canceled, that unfortunately I will not be able to make our session. *I'm very sorry.*

Five minutes later, this—

Disappointing. See you next week. T.

I admit to feeling mildly irritated after reading Tia's message. The disappointing situation reflected, like a mirror. Haven't we built enough trust in the past year that we might survive one missed session, I think. I suddenly feel angry, defensive. Dismissive. Have I been so ineffective in building a secure base and respect for the work that one missed session equates disappointment, still, in Tia? Doesn't she realize I have no control over the plane's departure? I buy a cup of tea and decide a walk around the airport shops is a good idea. I handle a bottle of my favorite perfume, spray it, inhale its sweetness and place it back on the shelf.

An hour before the delayed flight is due to depart I read Tia's text again. I take a deep breath, my mood now changed. Of course she is disappointed, I think. I've just taken a holiday and now I'm unable to meet her as planned. This unexpected and additional separation will be unsettling for Tia, I think. Perhaps I should have flown back a day earlier and not risked the possibility of a canceled flight. How unprofessional of me, I decide. I've been lax.

These things happen, I gently remind myself, *I had no control over the canceled flight.* Conscious of the ebb and flow of my feelings, I catch my desire to tend the rupture, to repair and preserve our psychoanalytic journey so far. I float the idea of how delicate and transitional our feelings are. How much of what we feel is influenced by past messages, projections, and blueprints from previous relationships. I reflect on my earlier defensiveness and feel relieved to be free of the tyrannous shoulds and musts. An apology is good enough, I think, but understanding Tia's disappointment is imperative.

Perfection. A word that can still bring me out in a cold sweat.

I'd been thinking of the word and the sensation it gives rise to in my body—a kind of zing, like a hot wire, a bolt of anxiety—when, right on time, Tia arrives for her session. The buzzer held slightly longer than usual, or am I just imagining this?

Tia is reserved, quiet. A polite smile, she waits for me to speak. I do not have to jostle to speak this evening. I sense her disappointment.

I'm sorry I wasn't able to make your session on Wednesday, I begin.

Thank you for your apology.

Silence.

Silence.

I understand it wasn't your fault, the flight being canceled, Tia says, *but it put me in touch with how much I rely on our sessions. How much I look forward to seeing you, talking with you. It scared me to think I was dependent on these sessions, and on you.*

I take a moment to absorb Tia's truth.

I understand, I say. *You've taken a risk to rely and feel attached to me and our work. But I'd like to reframe the dependency issue. Perhaps the perils of attachment and intimacy are not that we risk feeling disappointed, but that we risk feeling things we did not expect to feel. Things we have tried hard to control or avoid. To rely on someone other than yourself. I wonder if seeing and experiencing yourself differently is a greater risk?*

Tia nods. *It would have been so easy to feel angry with you, to cancel my session tonight. And it would have been just as easy to say nothing at all and seethe in silence.*

I think you're describing an either/or. We're back to the binary, I say.

Exactly. I want to do something different now, to be with the in-betweens and feel disappointed and be able to talk about it rather than acting out or abandoning my own wants and needs.

I like the sound of your "in-betweens," I smile. *Knowing we can survive potential ruptures is healing. If one is conscious of internal saboteurs and self-destructive efforts to protect ourselves from risks, the relationship can endure, strengthen even.*

Soften even, Tia adds.

Soften even, I say. *I like that, too.*

In the corner of my office beneath a framed copy of *Time* magazine with a portrait of Freud that asks, *Is Freud Dead?* is a small bonsai tree. A gift from a training psychotherapist given after she qualified. I am fascinated by the tiny tree's beauty. Its slow growing and captivating presence.

Tempted to share with Tia my learning of *Ma*—the Japanese concept of space and time—I wait. *Ma* is the fundamental space that life requires in order to grow and evolve, and can apply to anyone who may be interested in pausing, reflecting, or simply being. Space, or the "in-between," encourages a person's progress, and their art. The character for *Ma* (間) combines door (門) and sun (日), and together these two characters depict a door through which the light (日) shines, hence enlightenment. When growing and caring for a bonsai tree, one attempts respect for the space in between each branch. This allows light in, and as it illuminates softly the leaves and surface of the bark, the emerging buds, the tree will grow. I wonder whether to share this small interest of mine with Tia or whether to allow our own *Ma* to settle, encouraging the present to matter. Spiritually inspiring space into the therapy room works similarly to *Ma*. Feelings surface, defenses melt. I am silent.

Quiet.

At any given moment in the session the therapist is reflecting and making choices about what to focus on and what to pursue. I think about where else to scatter seeds of hope, when to water them, and when not to. When to allow a necessary stillness: free of action, free of words, and free of intervention. I think about what the patient is presenting and how best to stretch her feelings, to hold and catch the in-between—*Ma*—with the hope that the space between her responses can be better understood by her and by me. I think about my own journey, commitment, and inquiry in her journey, her story, and reflect on how best to exchange what I hear as a comment on our therapeutic relationship. What is being said, or not said, and what is being communicated nonverbally?

This invitation into the patient's world is both a gift and an honor. Being open to think and feel about the issues a patient brings to her therapy, one begins to embody her struggles and sometimes victories, which eventually encourages healing and greater understanding for the therapist. When we walk gently in the lives of others, we make a commitment to connect and understand. We—therapist and patient—develop a relationship in which stories of desire, connection, growth, and change fill the room like perfume; salutary heady scents saturating the air.

What do you want? I ask eventually, breaking the silence, the *Ma*. An attempt to bring back our inquiry to Tia's desire.

Tia looks at me. Her hand goes automatically to her collar as though to settle an imaginary scarf or tie. I am reminded of the little girl seated at the precisely laid table, fiddling with the large silk bow at her collar, cousins patting her hair. I am mindful of Tia's still unlived life and the ongoing possibilities.

To make a home of my body. To feel and know I belong.

Imbued with happiness for Tia's self-pride, I feel my face, my jaw, soften.

I believe I'm getting closer, she says.

The next hour is spent talking about the two men in her life, Sophia's paintings, work, and a recurring spasm in her lower back; *it's right here,* she massages with her fist.

Both men claim to love her. Let's name them Thomas and Ralph. And both men are her friend and her lover. *They are both good men.* Tia is undecided which relationship, which man, she will choose to live with eventually. Tia loves them both. She asks me if there is an "in-between" way of knowing which relationship would be best for her: *they've both been part of my life for a long time, Ralph since university.* I suggest she think about the home within her body and whom she imagines sharing it with. *Both,* she says. *That's the thing.*

Three large canvases hang in the hallway of Tia and Sophia's home. Paintings that capture three generations of women: grandmother, mother, and daughter. Evelyn, Tia, and Sophia, painted by the gaze and hand of Sophia. Their faces are stories, a lineage and ancestral living and surviving that spans seven decades of life. Tia gazes at all three intricate portraits when she leaves and returns home. Sometimes she talks and sings to them. Sometimes she strokes the canvases with her fingertips and follows the contours of Sophia's paintbrush, skin alive with delicate lines, eyes like mined jewels, winking. She has grown to love the paintings and uses the stillness and beauty captured in her mother and daughter's beauty as *an opportunity to fly.*

I love you, I miss you, she shines.

At work, Tia begins to chip away at warped power constructs and the iceberg of power relations. When she senses microaggressions directed at her or other colleagues, she calls them out. If colleagues look to her to educate them and *to make it all better, less uncomfortable,* Tia sets firm boundaries for herself and her work. She needs her energy for the new cases she has taken on recently, her desire returned to act on behalf of her clients. Occasionally, colleagues ask what can be done to address unity. They want answers. They inquire about "diversity and inclusion" in the workplace and Tia replies by saying intervention is useful in bystander situations. Or perhaps more financial support and sponsorship for trainee lawyers. *I could say nothing, or I could say too much in a really ineffective way. So instead I choose to call it out. Everyone is looking for a resolution.*

Perhaps those who want to rush ahead to the resolution are people who are not really affected by the struggle, I say. *It's not possible to forge ahead to the end point without having challenging and messy conversations first.*

Yes, seeing race rather than seeking unity is necessary for changing the system, says Tia.

And what about you? I ask.

When I look in the mirror, Tia adds, *I know the decision to change my face was a result of believing a quick fix would solve everything. I'm ready to forgive my younger self. I'm ready to acknowledge that struggle and racism is ongoing, that I'm in it for the long haul.*

In Tia's evolving life narrative, the illustrations she gives are of herself as a source of empowerment, not as a person of objectification, or as an object of hate and ridicule. Not only is

she surviving the devasting comments made against her in earlier life, but she is finding a way to mobilize her future without
escaping the legacy of her past. Tia knows what she wants, and
although she's in it for the long haul, she is in it. She is here.
She is setting life boundaries. She is speaking truth to power.
She is inviting desire, creativity and drive to push forward.

*I find it interesting when you talk about your desire to make a home of
your body, I say. To feel and know you belong. Everything you've talked
about tonight resonates with this desire: which relationship you will
choose; the family paintings in your home; your mother; your daughter;
the conversations and organizing at work. But I'm wondering where the
back spasms fit into all of this?*

Tia removes her cardigan, sets free the button at her collar.

They seem to leave as quickly as they arrive, she says. *It's as if
they're acting as a reminder of something—I'm not sure what. Perhaps
they happen so I don't get too comfortable.*

And what would happen, I ask, *if you did get too comfortable?*

I'm not sure.

The body holds the score, I say, *perhaps the pain in your back is a
symptom.*

*Maybe. Or maybe the spasms are testing my spine. Confronting my
posture, reminding me of my lack, attacking my flaws. My dad's body
had the luxury of simply living, but my mum's body had to survive.*

*You believe the Black body has to survive, while the white body is
free to be, to live without fear?*

*Perhaps. If the body holds the score, my mum would have won, hands
down.*

Ingesting Tia's words as seriously and respectfully as she has
spoken them, I say, *Your body is good enough. So many times you
were told that it was not, I'm here to tell you that it is. You are. You are
enough, you are more than enough and you belong. Right here, at least.*

This moment of meeting opens Tia's eyes, wide.

Lack, flaws, survival. They're old stories, right?
Right.

With all of my might I assure Tia through my skin and my body that *The pain in your back is the symptom, not the problem.*

My back is the symptom, she repeats, *not the problem.*

Hope.

As usual, I hang on to hope.

I grab hope by the throat, the belly, and ask that it remain. I want it to anchor us and inspire us. I want it to ignite passion, elevate creativity and affect drive. Hope: a contrast to dread. We need hope. And we most certainly need to refuse the despair, the despondency. You are enough, Tia. You will make a home of your body. You will know and feel that you belong. I will hold the baton of hope and victory until you are ready, and when you are—take it, and run.

Conversations turn to Tia's life, the everyday. Occasionally they are heavy, sophisticated but unburdened by any talk about race. I discover more of Tia's interests, bask in her good humor and her desire for a new home. I learn that she is a keen and strong swimmer with a fascination for synchronized sequences that she watches on a small television set in the kitchen while Ralph cooks her favorite food. Pans he bought with him when he moved in six months ago are pulled out of the cupboard and rattle. She enjoys watching him cook. The way he sprinkles, delicately, spice to make her salmon zing with heat. He swivels a move toward her, kisses her forehead. Her cheek. Her mouth. And her body, at home with itself, responds by pressing her palms against his chest, his heart. *Make sure that salmon burns my mouth,* she smiles. When Tia shares this with me, three years now into our work, I remind her of the earlier struggles compared to what she experiences and feels now. I mirror back her words: *To make a home of my body. To feel and know I belong.*

Feel like you're any closer? I ask, playfully.

A little, she smiles, she laughs.

I think a little is an understatement, I shine back.

All right then, more than a little. You win!

No. We *win,* I say, locking eyes.

Life experience is the architecture of our identity, and it occurs to me that our identities are forever evolving. When one's life experience is made fearful and ostracized by those who are hateful, uneducated, and scared, with their attacks on humans with skin, culture, and race different from their own, the impact is devastating and terrifying. Racism forces the individual into incredibly conflicted territory. It has the power to make one feel inferior, un-belonging, hated, exposed, and ignored—*What are you?* It chips away at one's sense of core self, adding a dimension of distrust, as well as isolation. In Tia's grief and working through and being with her mother's death and the racism she survived, Tia had built, understandably, a lonely and protective fortress around her—*I've always done everything on my own.* To live fully in her identity meant grieving past experiences where she survived, at a cost, structural racism from her family and from pockets of society.

Connecting through and with me in her therapy allowed Tia to live fully in her identity. She was not only able to be more intimate with her daughter, partner, work colleagues, and friends, but also with herself. To become more loving of herself. Previously her desire to be present and honor her daughter's choices had been hindered by Tia's own ghosts in the nursery. Earlier survival against her family's and in particular her father's hatefulness had been internalized and turned against herself, resulting in a distant and sometimes dismissive relationship with Sophia. Engaging in therapy encouraged Tia to name and feel anger, grief, and disappointment for these hate crimes which, over time, she was able to heal from and transform into radical self-love. Now, her commitment to herself and the cause of calling out racism is uncompromising, angry and yet full of hope. No longer are these feelings of rage and disappointment turned inward and against herself. Anger is now fuel poured over injustice. A touch paper lit in honor of herself and those she chooses to love.

We all long to belong. The process of othering, when one is perceived and treated differently because of their skin color, is essentially a dehumanizing act where *an other* is made into *the other*. The objectified and dehumanized Other is forced outside into the cold instead of into a moral world where all its inhabitants are required to live, side by side, human to human. To be seen, respected and celebrated by our family, friends, work colleagues and loved ones. Home is where we start from. But what is home when we are told that we do not belong, that we are not welcome. We must therefore make our home; take it, own it, claim it. Home is ours. Home is where we start and end.

Tia reassessed her position as survivor and daughter, which in turn enabled her to reevaluate her relationship with the people in her life. As with many therapeutic relationships and experiences, Tia's commitment and desire to make a home of her body taught me humility. She arrived believing: *There are two types of people—those who show up, and those who don't. Please don't be one of those people who disappoint me.* A binary approach to her thinking. She now leaves knowing the "in-between" is where growth and change reside. The pleasure Tia took in our difference, too, has pleased me. As Tia's therapist, I am more than capable of getting it wrong, of misattunement, and of not truly understanding the pain survived by a patient. Tia arrived for therapy in need, as so many others do. And as therapist, I was able through training, experience, and knowledge to help— not to relinquish or lead, but to participate with commitment. I hold her story in my heart. I believe the real hero in this story is the learning and the relationship between two women, side by side, who could truly see one another and encouraged healing and growth amid the white noise.

Love him, and let him love you. Do you think anything else under the heaven really matters?

James Baldwin (1956)

Love in the Afternoon

Bikinis the color of tangerines and flamingos sashay past their deck chairs, low and striped. Bill and Agatha remove their relaxed clothing and sun hats and move closer toward imminent bliss as they bend, slowly, their sandals loosened from hot, tired feet. A warm breeze sweeps across the hilly sandbanks and secret inlets, landing on their silver hair, and it's all Agatha can do not to take Bill's face in her palms and kiss him tenderly on the mouth. But something kills her desire to kiss the man she loves. Instead, she stares down at her crumpled one-piece, her delicate liver spots and papery skin. Her son's words suddenly reappearing and declaring that she is *too old, too forgetful, and too foolish to fall in love, especially at your age.*

They watch a sandcastle being made by a child with ruddy cheeks. A collection of pale shells pressed into a crumbling turret; seawater disappearing as it's poured by the boy's busy hands, the chub of his knees hidden by the sand. It is close to teatime and Bill senses a rumble in his tummy and pats the empty feeling with his fingertips. *I'm a little peckish,* he says. But Agatha is distracted, her reply delayed. *Mm, me too,* she eventually offers, preoccupied—her gaze fixed on two horizontal mothers turning like a chicken rotisserie, their svelte bodies, narrow waists and perfect round bottoms changing color, golden. The women swipe across their chests and foreheads to remove their glistening sweat, then lower their sunglasses while settling on their backs. What I'd do with a body like that, Agatha thinks fancifully. I'd wear a skirt above my knees. Dance naked. I'd enjoy every living, breathing second of owning a body like that. She imagines herself as a young woman in the arms of a budding Bill, a fistful of white cotton bedsheets as he makes love to her away from the sun, deep sensual gravity. She closes her eyes and holds on to the image, elaborates on some finer details and encourages her skin to soak up August's glorious heat. She sighs, her breath escaping like a punctured tire while Bill offers the idea of *ice cream, a bag of chips?*

Agatha opens her eyes. *Lovely,* she shines, *I think I might like both.*

Bill takes Agatha's hand, kisses it, places his palm on top to secure a feeling. She watches his face relax as he turns his body toward her. *I think we should get married, don't you?* He smiles.

Agatha wants to say: I do, yes, I do, but something prevents her. Instead, she smiles and, bare-limbed and tanned, reaches over to kiss Bill's cheek. *Married? Goodness, we'll have notched up four marriages between us.* Another smile.

Lucky number four, says Bill.

Go on, be off with you, she plays, with gentle shooing. *I'll have a bag of chips. Lots of salt and vinegar.*

Agatha reaches for her beach bag made of straw and checks her mobile phone that lets her know she has three missed calls from Alistair. She wonders how his weekend visit with the kids is going, and if he's managed to erect the complicated bunk beds purchased online, and whether her grandsons, *poor little dots,* are settling into their new routine. Agatha wishes her son wasn't *such an ass.* It is a wish felt deep within her bones.

Darling, she writes in a text message, her fingers slow yet assertive, *I'm at the beach with Bill but I'll call you tonight. Love you, mum xxx*

An hour or two later, Bill and Agatha head back to the guesthouse that overlooks the beach where they've been staying for the past ten days. For a minute they stop to watch a tiny crab clambering over a pile of careless rubbish: a chocolate bar wrapper, an empty fizzy drink can and squashed cigarette butts. Agatha collects the rubbish and stuffs it in her bag, the act reminding her of all the times she relentlessly cleaned up after her first husband and, later, her only child. She doesn't like the act of littering—it aggravates her. Neither does she approve of the crab trying to make a new home in such mindless mess. When the crab lands in a tiny pool of water next to a circle of small rocks, it sends up curls of sand in its disappearing and Agatha is immediately calmed.

Always the mother, says Bill, taking her free hand.

Returned to the guesthouse, Agatha steps out of her dripping one-piece. She watches her body in the bathroom mirror and expresses some tenderness for herself, thinking she looks like a giant jelly baby, while gently dusting away stowaway sand from her stomach, her thighs. Her face has gained freckles in the last few days and she likes the way they remind her of when she was young and loved to sunbathe, a sprinkling of cinnamon on her nose and cheeks, hair with extra bounce from the seawater.

What are you doing in there? Bill calls.

Brushing the sand off.

She quickly throws an embroidered silk shawl across her shoulders and enjoys its immediate softness, her body enveloped with its delicate tassels that gently kiss her breasts...

When she opens the bathroom door Bill is standing waiting for her, naked. He takes her waist and leads her to their cotton bed. He has drawn the blinds, pulled back the sheets, and sprayed himself with cologne. They embrace in silence, the shawl falls to the ground. Bill kisses her calm breasts, mirrors her delicate strokes and Agatha notes her body is neither shy nor impatient. Arms open, she sighs into his mouth, her body responding with thrill to his touch. Intuitively, they find one another's rhythm and grow speed in their desiring, eyes straining, clenched.

Now comes rest post their lovemaking. Agatha is close to sleeping, eyes flickering. Her hands are relaxed, upturned and heavy on the pillow. Bill drapes her shoulders with the embroidered silk shawl, covers her legs with the cotton bedsheets, and fetches a glass of water before planting it on her bedside table. As he climbs into their bed, he believes, and this he will share later with Agatha, that *I've never felt happier, more content, than when I'm with you. Who knew?*

Agatha awakes first. Her late-afternoon sleep imbued with dreams of her body adrift in a tiny yellow sailboat, Bill working the oar. She'd dreamed of staring back at the guesthouse where music, twirling dresses, and fairy lights garnished the lively terrace—a dream, a wish, a postcard. Three hours of sleep-infused bliss, she turns to Bill and whispers, *I love it when you hold me.* It is only when Agatha reaches for the tumbler of water and checks the clock, *Gosh, is it that time already?* that she is pulled away from her sensual nest and reverie. She stands and takes her phone from her straw bag, makes her way to the outside balcony that overlooks the terrace that moments ago she was dreaming of, and waits patiently to hear her son's voice.

Hi, this is Al. Leave a message after the tone. Beeeep.

Oh, hello darling, it's Mum. Just calling you back. I hope you and the boys are having a nice time. Anyway, I'm sending you love. If we don't speak later, I'll see you when I get home on Friday. Take care now. Click.

Agatha knows that had Alistair not been unfaithful to the lovely Elizabeth she would have almost certainly returned his call earlier. But she is angry with him, still. And unable to tell him how she really feels because *right now, he's such a mess. I just have to love him as best I can and know how, but I'm disappointed. I really am.*

It is not often I receive a phone call from a potential patient seeking therapy during their retirement years, particularly if they've not ventured into analysis previously. But there was something about Agatha, a retired nurse, and her message, that had swelled my heart. Her almost fizzing disclosure that she'd finally found love and wanted to talk to somebody about it. I confess to having felt more than a little curious, suspicious even. After all, therapy fights darkness and balms pain; happy romantic love is rarely a reason for entering a therapeutic alliance. I swiftly opened my diary, noting my zeal, and picked up the phone.

I was met with a gentle voice, good-humored and with enough assertion to secure an initial consultation. *Oh, thank you for calling back,* said Agatha. *I'd like to start therapy. I'm in love, you see.* But something told me this was just the tip of the analytic iceberg. After all, does anyone seek therapy to talk about falling in love? Perhaps I'd grown into a careful pessimist, a killjoy, a love Grinch? In any case, I was fascinated and agreed to meet Agatha the following week.

If love was the true reason Agatha wanted to begin therapy, I was indeed curious, but I also wondered whether it was an unconscious cloak for something else. I told myself that this was perhaps of no real concern—after all, it is a psychotherapist's duty to take what a patient brings as a "what is." It is not our role to underestimate a patient's desire for seeking solace in falsehoods or misinterpretations, and neither is it of any interest. Of interest are the ways in which the patient copes and frames her topic for inquiry (in Agatha's case, her celebration of falling in love) and the potential distortions she might tell herself, and me. These imaginings and creative inventions do not make the patient's struggle any less justifiable. They can in fact open up deeper analytic inquiry for the patient. But first we must understand the purpose of the patient's fantasies and their importance. What is it that cannot be shared or explored without these twists in reality? And what do these flourishes used by the patient to make meaning and sense of their lives set out to achieve? As therapist, my role is to remain curious and openhearted, not to shame the truth out like judge and jury.

Twelve weeks into her therapy, I greet Agatha in my waiting room and, as we walk the relatively short distance to my office, she tells me that while on holiday she's *missed our little chats.* I offer a smile, mindful to contain the session until we close the office door, and begin. The rules of engagement quite different in therapy to those of ordinary social situations.

Are you quite well, dear? she asks.

I settle into my chair.

Yes, thank you, I say. *How are you, Agatha?*

Rested, tanned, and a little fatter but that's what holidays are for, aren't they, she states more than questions, running quick fingertips through glossy gray hair. She swaddles her chest with a beautiful turquoise pashmina, holding on tightly to its soft edges. *Hasn't it turned chilly all of a sudden?* she continues. *I even thought about putting the central heating on last night. We have so much to catch up on; I really missed you. Bill proposed we get married.*

Oh, I say, the speed of her words landing while I attempt to keep up.

I didn't say yes, but part of me wanted to. A pause. *Part of me would love to marry Bill.*

I reorientate myself, checking the clock, a minute barely passed. *Something stopped you from accepting Bill's proposal?* I ask.

It feels too soon. We've known each other for less than a year. Is that a new plant over there?

I turn my attention to where Agatha is pointing. A white orchid resting on my desk that wasn't there before she left for her holiday in Cornwall.

Yes, I say, *she arrived last week.*

She's beautiful. I love orchids. I don't like it when their flowers die, though. Because then they're just sticks and leaves, aren't they? Ugly. I don't have the patience to wait for them to reflower and usually end up throwing them away. I'm an instant gardener. What about you, are you patient? Will you wait for the next flurry of flowers?

I find myself, as is often the case with Agatha, being drawn into friendly chitchat, her enthused thoughts and curiosities ricocheting from wall to wall while my concentration is tested. If I am not careful sessions can fly by with little inquiry or mere mention of what is *really* on her mind. I have reflected on this while gently guiding her back into a quiet field where analysis can resume. I have also considered whether Agatha is lonely. Her enthusiastic outpourings and desire for contact, albeit sometimes fast-paced and distracted, are evident in the way her eyes dance and shine in our sessions together. Quite often my hunch and intuition is to remain very still in response. I like to listen carefully to Agatha if the moment allows, and where possible I attempt to be present to the rumblings underneath that of which she speaks. I have also wondered in our three months together if her zealous distractions are a way of avoiding feelings. Anxiety, perhaps? Or discomfort? But above all, I have wondered if Agatha's relatively late love-finding has put her in touch with feelings of intimacy that, until recently, have been missing. *I don't believe I've ever truly loved a person romantically until now,* she'd told me in our first session, *even though I've been married twice.*

I look again to the orchid, *I'm relatively patient,* I say, *so I'll most likely wait for the next flurry of flowers.*

Flurry. I have mirrored her word. I think of more words that evoke a similar feeling: whirl, burst, bustle, gust, and brouhaha. But I am free-associating and wonder why this is. I suspect it may have something to do with Agatha's entry this morning and observe that her lively conversation style is most likely connected to excitement or anxiety.

You mention the possibility of marriage feels too soon, I continue, edging Agatha back into the field. *You met in September of last year, yes?*

Agatha nods. *And I came to see you in January.*

Yes, you did, I say. *But if I remember correctly, you and Alistair's father had been together for less than a year when you married?*

Indeed, Agatha frowns. *And Kenneth was even less than that.*

Agatha was nineteen years old when she met Kenneth, her first husband. Her parents had been in the market for a new car. *We were a big family, so needed a big car. Dad settled on a Morris Marina. Blue, I think it was.*

Kenneth was twenty-six, tall, charming, and swarthy. *He loved American cars, fast cars: Chevrolets; Buicks; Mustangs.*

Morris and Co. was well known for its imported American automobiles and was family-owned with Kenneth's father at the helm. Kenneth worked front of house in the open-plan showroom.

I remember when he shook my hand, thinking it small and cold, like any other. But he was so handsome he took my breath away. He told my dad he'd settle for a lower price on the condition that he take me out on a date. Dad jumped at the chance. Such things would never be said today.

Thank goodness for that, I'd replied.

Agatha and Kenneth were married two years later, much to the relief and approval of Agatha's parents who'd encouraged the union and were glad of the space freed up at home that they shared with their remaining four children. Agatha was the eldest girl, bookending her three brothers with her younger sister, Mary.

I couldn't wait to leave home and be free of all my responsibilities, including caring for my younger siblings. But as it turned out, I replaced care with care and became a nurse.

Sadly, the marriage soon shriveled. Kenneth's wandering eye landing on various young women also with an interest in fast cars and tennis. His weekends were spent entertaining potential clients on and off court while Agatha cleaned, dusted, and baked in their childless home. When Agatha raised the possibility of starting a family, Kenneth, who suffered with mild depression, said it wasn't the right time. *We need a bigger house, maybe in a couple of years. Anyway, you're young, we've got plenty of time.*

He cared for me in his own way, Agatha told me. *I was very comfortable and we had a beautiful home. I never wanted for anything. But I can't say we were ever in love. What could I possibly have known of love at nineteen?*

Later, Kenneth began to neglect their marital suppers, returning home in the early hours, with Agatha leaving burnt dinners on top of the stove to make a point. *I felt incredibly lonely and sought out friendship at my local church,* where she was momentarily soothed by *kindness and the lord's prayers.*

I couldn't help but feel incredibly sad at the thought of Agatha as a young woman home alone with only a radio and daytime television for company. The highlight of her week was when she would help out at the church bake sale or entertain her in-laws who swore blind they hadn't tasted food as good as hers and *grew fatter by the week.*

When are we going to see some kiddies running around this gorgeous house of yours? her mother-in-law poked.

We're trying, aren't we, darling, said Kenneth, patting his wife's belly, *but Agatha's body doesn't seem to want one just yet.*

Agatha smiled into her plate through gritted teeth. *Oh, I'm ready, and so is my body, Kenneth, if only you were home long enough to make one!* she fumed.

Privately I knew I was stronger than him, Agatha said, *but women weren't encouraged to think such things back then, let alone speak them. I thought his victories over me, at least in the first years of our marriage, were little concessions made so he wouldn't go off in a huff.*

When Agatha expressed an interest in training to be a nurse, Kenneth responded by saying it wasn't possible and that she was needed to take care of him and their home. Sometimes he was cruel, suggesting she didn't have the smarts to be a nurse—*And anyway, why do you want to work when you have everything you need here? I look after you, don't I? Anything you want, you get.*

I want to be a nurse, Agatha argued.

Pfft. Why are you so ungrateful, do you know how many women would love to have what you have? To live the way you live?

Many, I suppose. Why don't you go find one?

Her reply, like a single chess move, had Kenneth retaliating.

Maybe I will.

Close the door behind you.

Agatha realized she'd accepted a husband who was not interested in being loving, even though he desired to be loved. *I feel ashamed that I was in such a loveless marriage,* she said.

There is no shame attached in acknowledging a lack of love in one's early relationships, I offered, hearing Agatha's story.

Maybe, she said, *but there is shame knowing I wasn't loved by my parents. I was terrified of them. They didn't always have the words, the*

language, to say how they felt, so they'd lash out at me and my siblings.
From one day to the next I never knew if I was going to be hit or kissed.

Most psychologically or physically abused children have been taught that love can exist alongside abuse. Indeed, many parenting adults will teach this message to their children. In some extreme cases it may even be said that the abuse is an expression of care and love.

When I was a child I remember minding my own business in the school playground when a boy in the year above pushed me to the ground and pulled at my hair. Crying, I ran to a teacher, who told me he'd done this because he liked me. These early messages are dangerous and unacceptable because they tell a young mind that violence and love (or in this case, likability) are entwined—that they are one and the same.

Love and abuse cannot and should not coexist. This warped and faulty thinking can shape our perceptions of love as children and as adults. It is a trauma bond. I have worked with many patients who arrived at therapy believing their parents or partners were abusive or cruel because it was the only way they knew how to show love. And many of the unacceptable behaviors survived by my patients have continued into their romantic adult relationships. For a child who is emotionally abused or neglected, rationalizing being hurt by those who are meant to care and love them is often a survival mechanism. To fully acknowledge that one's parents are capable of cruelty or abuse is almost unbearable for an adult, let alone a child.

Over the years, I have witnessed an overwhelming number of patients who have been courageous in acknowledging their dysfunctional family beginnings and survived them. Patients who were neglected and physically and emotionally abused, and in the same breath were taught they were loved. When one is raised in a family where abuse takes place and yet care is given, confusion

and gaslighting occurs, and the patient has difficulty acknowledging the extent of the trauma they have survived. They also
believe that whatever happened to them wasn't that bad.

But I guess it wasn't all bad, Agatha told me. *My mum was affec-
tionate sometimes. And my dad, well, he did his best to provide for us
all. It was only when I didn't do as I was told that it turned . . .*

That it turned . . . ? I persisted.

*That it turned nasty. And who could blame her with five children
to look after.*

No number of children condones the act of violence, I said.

Pressed to talk about care and trust in her early life, Agatha
shared that she had felt cared for at times but unloved. As the
eldest child there were many expectations placed on her to
support her mother, who ordered her to cook and clean their
home as well as keeping her father, a railway mechanic, *amused
and fed* when he returned from work in his heavy boots. Playing cards and making supper helped Agatha survive acts of
lovelessness. These moments of intimacy, albeit through food
and games, offered her shards of connection and a *sense of being
useful.* Indeed, Agatha became very good at offering her love,
her usefulness rewarded with scraps of affection from both her
mother and her father. She was less concerned with receiving
love and as a result had later accepted and chosen men who
were emotionally wounded and happy to take her love without reciprocation. Over time, she experienced friendships and
romantic relationships where her need to be loved was unmet
and instead was faced with neglect, unkindness, mistrust, and
sometimes cruelty. Agatha engaged in relationships that focused
on care more than love because they felt safer—the demands
not as deep as in loving relationships, the risk not as great.

Church was the one place where Agatha felt genuinely
happy, connected, and nurtured. Here, she talked freely of her

desire to be a nurse and made friends with Margaret and Tom, a brother and sister who encouraged her by listening and gifting her books and introducing her to people who worked in various health centers and hospitals. On the weekends when Kenneth was busy with tennis, Agatha, Margaret, and Tom helped out at Sunday school and later prepared tea for the church attendees.

Church was like home for me, Agatha shared.

There is no happy ending to this chapter in Agatha's life.

Five years into the marriage, Agatha had been running a hot bath when she received a phone call to say Kenneth had been killed in a car crash.

I still had the bath, it helped soothe the shock. Something told me he wasn't alone in the car. When the police finally handed me his belongings, I found a receipt in Kenneth's wallet for a hotel room on the night he died. It's painful when you feel hatred toward a person you're meant to be grieving. I imagined that if we'd loved one another I'd have felt a different kind of pain. But instead I had to imagine his last moments with another woman. At first I felt angry and then indifferent. The indifference was far worse than my anger.

I had taken a moment to feel in my body Agatha's grief and disappointment. The complication of her husband's death entwined with his infidelity. My first thoughts were that he was young—Kenneth was thirty-one years old when he died—and that Agatha, a widow at just twenty-four years old, was left to experience her indifference alone. *There must be a simple explanation,* said her in-laws. *Kenneth would never do such a thing. Not in a million years, not our Ken. I suspect she was a client test-driving the car,* Agatha's father-in-law lied.

They were always in cahoots, those two, Agatha explained.

The real kicker was that three months earlier, Agatha and Kenneth had stayed at that same hotel for their wedding anniversary. But the night had felt loveless, with Kenneth excusing himself shortly after dinner—*Better get to bed, early start tomorrow*—leaving Agatha alone with her sherry and feelings of indifference.

Grief can be a celebration of love, I offered. *If we have loved we will grieve the loss of that person, the relationship that once was. I'm sorry this was your ending together. It seems your grief only highlighted what was wished for with Kenneth, as well as what could have been. The indifference highlighted your longing for something different.*

The saddest part for me was not missing him. How could I? I wanted to miss sharing a life with him. I wanted to miss him holding me, loving me. Me loving him, but he was never around long enough for me to miss him—even when he was alive.

Agatha leans forward, her concentration returned. She is back in the quiet field.

So, with this in mind, I say, *do you think your conflict in marrying Bill is really connected to only having known him a short time? Or is there something else at play?*

I suspect there might be, she answers.

That is?

Agatha pauses. *I love Bill, I want a life with the man I love,* she speaks softly.

And this feels like a greater risk? I ask.

Yes. And then there's Alistair. He doesn't approve. He thinks me old and foolish. I don't know if I can marry Bill while his marriage is in tatters.

So coming to therapy is as much about your conflict with love as it is about—

Guilt, she demands.

Guilt, I echo, nodding my head, *I see. So how much of a struggle are you having to claim your love, Agatha?*

She bows her head. *I'm really struggling,* she says. *It's so complicated. In a way I've always put Alistair's needs before my own, but this is one time I don't want to and I feel guilty because of that.*

I understand, I say. I pause. *But what if we were to reframe guilt? To think of it as resentment turned inwards.*

Go on, she says.

Perhaps it's easier to turn a negative feeling upon yourself rather than acknowledge your son's disapproval and your disapproval of him, I say. *You understandably don't want to see him suffer any more than he is but at what cost? Your love with Bill? It's possible that you're turning this resentment upon yourself rather than living your truth to avoid conflict. To want is an action. When we commit to our emotional experiences, in your case loving Bill, desire can be satisfied if you're aware of your fear and any self-destructive efforts to protect yourself from its risks.*

I watch Agatha thinking, her eyes fixed on her pashmina that she loosens and sets free from her body.

So I tell myself we haven't known each other long enough, which protects me from conflict with Alistair.

Perhaps, I say.

Agatha stares again at the orchid.

Or maybe I tell myself this so it gives the two people I love the most time to get to know each other?

Perhaps, I repeat.

Or could it be that it's an excuse for what I fear most?

Which is?

Failing. Or maybe it's because I've finally found someone who I want to love and be intimate with? Someone who doesn't just care for me but someone who is loving of me? It feels so different and frightening. Perhaps because it's so unknown, Maxine.

I understand, I smile. *But perhaps it's worth the risk, Agatha. What do you think?*

I think there's a lot of "perhaps," says Agatha.

A lot of love, I smile again.

★

It was awful, Agatha tells me in our next session.

She takes a sip of water. I note she is calmer today, less distracted, less fizz, her sentences more coherent. We are fifteen minutes into the session, most of which has been spent with Agatha remaining very still and silent, the only moments of reprieve by way of releasing her cries and tears. Tiny animal sobs. Her concentration is fixed on the matter at hand.

She explains the supper, the ruined seabass.

Alistair is late.

Agatha checks her watch. *Shall I call him again?* she asks Bill. *Did you leave him a message?*

Yes.

Then I guess we just wait for him, says Bill.

Close to an hour later, Alistair arrives. Agatha notes the tinge of alcohol masked with mint on his breath as she opens the front door and hugs him. His eyes are dark and his forehead imbued with a sadness that has created lines and an expression of angst. *Come in, darling,* she says, stroking his cool cheek. *Is everything all right?*

Traffic, says Alistair, thrusting a bunch of pink roses at Agatha's chest. *Something smells good.* This gift, we will learn later, was a cruel and insensitive offering.

Seabass, Bill and Agatha chime, then laugh, but instead of smiling or joining in, Alistair shrugs out of his jacket. *Speaking for each other already?* he sniggers.

Bill and Agatha throw each other a glance and ignore the comment. *Let me take that for you,* says Bill.

Bill and Alistair settle at the kitchen table, a vase of pale lilies wilting in front of the panting oven. *Shall I change these for you?* asks Alistair, pointing at the lilies. *I know pink roses are your favorite.* He pours himself a large glass of wine and rips a bread roll in half. *Wine could do with a little more chilling,* he scoffs, not caring that his mouth is full—Bill getting a front row seat of the chewed-up carbs. Having prepared the lovely home-cooked meal, Bill ironing the white cotton tablecloth before setting down scented candles and carefully selected wine, Agatha feels a stab of anger and hatefulness at her son's rudeness that quickly morphs into guilt. *What if we were to reframe guilt? To think of it as resentment turned inwards,* she remembers. Too right, she thinks acidly to herself while flipping the shriveled fish onto a serving platter; I resent his rudeness. Agatha feels immediately better, her move from guilt back to anger more real, more honest.

When she lays the banquet of seabass and vegetables on the table, Alistair turns jubilant, tapping his jolly bulge as if to notify it that something yummy is on its way.

This looks delicious, Mum, he revels, tucking in before Bill and Agatha have had chance to pick up a fork, a dribble of butter leaking from his mouth. Agatha leans over and wipes it for him.

I'm not a child, swipes Alistair.

You could have fooled me, says Agatha.

Three bottles of wine later, Alistair collapses on the couch, but not before he's justified his infidelity and given every opinion under the sun as to why Bill and Agatha shouldn't live together: *Elizabeth has taken no interest in me whatsoever since the boys arrived. You two should stay as you are—you're crazy to move in together.*

I don't expect you to be happy for us considering your marriage is in pieces, but I do expect you to hold your tongue, Agatha spits, while loading the last dish into the dishwasher and slapping the door shut. *I'll be upstairs, Bill. There are blankets and pillows in the den.*

Bill covers his love's angry son with a warm blanket and unties his brogues.

I'm sorry, Alistair says, taking Bill's hand. *I'm lonely and drunk.*

Go to sleep, says Bill, tucking a piece of paper in Alistair's trouser pocket.

The next morning Alistair discovers Bill's note when he awakes, head thumping, mouth fried:

If we're to be friends you will apologize to your mother after last night's outburst. There's only one thing worse than a lonely, drunk man and that's a lonely, drunk man unable to say sorry, Bill

How much nicer things are the following afternoon when Alistair has gone; driven himself away with his self-inflicted drama and tiresome digs. Bill and Agatha stretch out in their bed, heads wearing warm pillows, a feather-filled quilt tucked around their bodies and holding them tightly. They find themselves making love, twice, in the soft midday light. The act is gentle. Needed. Agatha holding on firmly to Bill—a life raft—as thoughts of Alistair crash around in her mind like waves in a storm. Love in the afternoon.

Try not to worry, love, says Bill.

I can't help it, says Agatha.

She wonders if she should call Elizabeth and reason with her to give Alistair another chance, but knows the answer already and who can blame her? Instead, she pictures Alistair as a baby: a mass of blonde curls and a gummy smile. His love of dinosaurs and outer space constant companions until his teenage years. She does this quite often, especially when she feels powerless, the pictures in her mind offering sentimentality that is soothing yet melancholic. It must be her fault, she thinks. I should have done more, said more, loved him more when his father died—*cancer*—guilt finding its way to her chest and pressing down hard, harder still. *What if we were to reframe guilt? To think of it as resentment turned inwards.* She closes her eyes and asks herself if the guilt she is wearing is resentment turned inwards, but realizes it is in fact disappointment. That Alistair behaved so appallingly at supper was unacceptable. But what is more disappointing, she thinks, is that he abandoned his family *for a quick bit of skirt*.

Suddenly, memories of her first husband resurface, reminding her of the time when lies and talk of tennis games were guises for infidelity. She supposes her son told similar lies. *Though it must be far more painful for Elizabeth than it was for me,* she thinks, *because she actually loved Alistair.*

Agatha notes she has used love in the past tense and her feelings of powerlessness return. She pictures Alistair as a baby again, a cellular blanket swaddling his tiny entirety. How she wishes she had been loved as a baby, a child, an adult, the way she has loved Alistair. *I think it's my parents who I truly resent,* she will speak in one of her sessions some weeks later, her memories called back and acknowledging that had her parents been loved well by their parents, they might have offered that love to her, too.

Everyone who has observed the growing process of a child from the moment of birth sees clearly that before any language is born, or even before the identity of the mother or caregiver is recognized, babies acknowledge affection and care with looks of enchantment and sounds of pleasure, sweet gurgles of joy. Each day as they grow and evolve they will respond to care, offering affection themselves by smiling and laughing at the bright sight of a welcomed mother or caregiver. I am reminded of the important work of Harry Harlow and his observations of *The Wire Monkey Mothers,* his discoveries changing and informing how we understand early attachment.

The experiment involved Harlow separating infant monkeys from their mothers immediately after birth. The baby monkeys were then placed in cages with access to two surrogate mothers, one of which was made of wire and the other covered in a soft toweling cloth. In the first group, the cloth mother provided no food while the wire mother did. This was done by attaching a milk bottle to both surrogates. Both groups of monkeys spent more time with the cloth mother, even if she had no milk, resulting in the monkeys only going to the wire mother when hungry. Once fed, the baby monkey would return immediately to the cloth mother for most of the day, craving her soft and warm physical presence: an embodiment of motherly care. If an unknown or frightening object was placed in the cage, the infant monkey would take refuge with the cloth mother, its secure base. The cloth mother was far more effective in minimizing the infant's fear. The experiment also concluded that the infant was more exploratory when the cloth mother was present, supporting the evolutionary theory of attachment that it is the security and sensitive response of the mother and caregiver that is important as opposed to the provision of food. The conclusion was that infants feel safer, more secure and connected when soft nurturing, warmth, and contact is offered; in essence, "the body" over food.

But as we know, care is just one aspect of love. If we are to be loving in a true way, we must make love an action. We must recognize that love is not just a feeling because when we actively love we have a responsibility to that person that assumes accountability. For me, love, like desire, is a verb not a noun, as some might have it. Accepting love as an action means committing to respect, trust, recognition, conversation, and affection. We are not passive in the art of loving another human being; one doesn't simply "fall" in love, one fights for it, grows with it, commits to and respects it. Love is as love does.

He did call the day after to apologize and I'm glad about that, but I'm still feeling . . . She searches for the words, gives up, and instead throws her hands in the air, shakes her head and cries.

I can see you're incredibly upset, I name.

And confused. And disappointed. I don't know why he can't just be happy for me.

She swipes away another tear. *Your orchid has lost some of its flowers,* she points.

I turn my attention to the orchid. *She has,* I say. *What shall we do?*

I don't know, but at least she has a few flowers left.

She does, I say, *but rather than waiting to see what happens, I think I'll give her some feed and some water.* I stand up from my seat and find the tiny pink bottle of feed, my watering can, add water and pour it into the orchid's plastic pot.

Agatha smiles.

Love is an action, I say.

Love is also a discipline, as is our healing. Reflecting on love as an action with Agatha, I focus on the agency and energy that makes love possible. Love is not passive, nor docile. It requires commitment. The Wounded Healer, an overused phrase in my opinion, was coined by psychologist Carl G. Jung. Although it is helpful when thinking about patients and how their stories impact my own wounds and healing as a psychotherapist, I'm under no illusion that any therapist, or human for that matter, is ever fully "healed." Our healing is ongoing. What I believe we do is create conditions where therapist and patient embark on a joint discovery, and while the therapist has particular knowledge and experience, she is by no means a healer with all the answers and the power to fix the patient. The concept of the Wounded Healer positions the therapist on a pedestal—a precarious and impossible expectation that will ultimately disappoint the patient and without doubt cause the therapist to fall from a great height.

When Agatha said, *I don't know why he can't just be happy for me*, I'd felt deep empathy for her. We have all, perhaps, had a situation when we have wanted a friend, family member, or loved one to be happy for us after a longed-for life event presents itself. And when that love or enthusiasm has been denied or refused, it hurts. I am thinking of the time when I was offered a college bursary to attend art college, a dream of mine in my late teens that was met with disdain and fear. Still, I went, angry that certain friends and family members hadn't celebrated with me. I understand now that they didn't have language to tell me that they felt scared at my leaving, that they would miss me. And it was only much later that I was able to meet their fears with compassion and empathy. One might say it takes one to know one, and of course we can never know and encounter all that our patients have or are in the process of experiencing. But a shared moment, or a desire, universal or otherwise, to help patients with what we as therapists have learned and are healing from, is a way to connect and soothe—together. It is relational.

I set down the watering can and return to my seat.

Agatha is still watching the orchid, eyes glazed.

I believe she has turned her attention to the orchid because she is hurting. It is, perhaps, a pleasant distraction, even though the orchid's flowers are dying. In nurturing the orchid I'd hoped to offer Agatha some moments to honor her feelings, and that in watching me feed the plant's roots she might be able to acknowledge we are not completely powerless when we are angry. Flowers will return. They will again flourish if we tend and nurture them, though perhaps when restored they will appear changed because of the time spent healing and growing. A fresh bud of hope.

Alistair must be really hurting, she says.

I think you're both hurting, I offer.

The truth is, she says, *without Alistair I would never have been able to love Bill. You see, Alistair taught me how to love and how to be loved.*

An incredible gift, I say.

It was, it is. If love is an action we have both acted on our love. Mother and son. I owe him all the love.

I feel a prick of tears in my eyes. *Does he know this?* I ask.

No, but perhaps I'll tell him. Just as soon as I've got over my anger and disappointment.

Perhaps your anger is protection against your pain, I say. *There is more energy felt when we are angry, which counteracts any feelings of powerlessness. It must be difficult to witness your only child hurting so much and to watch his current behavior. That he isn't happy for you and Bill lacks generosity. Is it putting a strain on your relationship with Bill?*

Agatha takes her time to answer.

I've never wanted to love anyone as much as I want to love Bill, she says, *and remarkably, it seems I can let him love me too. I wish Alistair could be happy for me, for us. For so many years it was just him and me after his dad passed away. We had such a special bond.*

This isn't the first time I've learned of a patient's evolved openness to love after parenting a child—particularly if the patient has survived neglect or lovelessness in their formative years. Without the sustenance of early attachments from one's parents or caregivers, the child and later the adult believes they are unworthy of being loved. It is the parent and child bond that teaches us that we are lovable and wanted, that teaches us how to love ourselves and one another. In early childhood, some of us might remember being told we were loved when we were good and behaved in a way that was pleasing to our parents and caregivers. In turn, we learned to mirror these affirmations of love when they pleased us. If love was conditional and missing when it was most needed, or if we as children felt unable to be our true selves, authentic and free, at the risk of being denied their love, a great peril is created. This danger was too great potentially, because what would happen if we voiced our truth knowing we would disappoint our parents and caregivers? Isolation? Abandonment? Violence?

What I have taken and understood from these stories of early childhood deprivation is that it has sometimes felt safer for patients to love their child before the possibility of romantic love might be imagined and realized. *I don't even know if I can love,* one patient told me when her only child left home for university and she was thinking about the possibility of an intimate relationship. Later, she was thrilled to discover her capacity to love and to be loved was rather splendid. But not until she had worked through and let go of the grief concerning the love she'd not received as a child, having had no means or voice to speak and heal from her heart's longing. Another patient shared, *Something got healed when I was loved by my daughters. The love was, and is, very deep. Early scars were soothed and I am loved, they are loved,* she said, *and I am grateful.*

There has also been anger and despair expressed by patients—resentment often brewing—who believe it is they who have had *to put the hours in and do all the work.* In many cases healing has required years of psychotherapy to balm their feelings of lovelessness. As a therapist, I attempt to bring the patient's attention to their hurt. Together, we try to find words to express what was lost in not feeling loved or wanted. *We cannot change the past,* I have offered, *and there is no going back. But when your grieving has eased you have a choice to once again act on love, to let your heart speak—if this is what you want and desire.*

Agatha is silent, her gaze now adrift. *We had such a special bond*, she repeats before wiping away more tears, *I don't know what's happened between us.*

I imagine it has something to do with Alistair suffering while you are in love, I offer. *Unfortunate timing, some might say, or inevitable considering your desire for Bill. Alistair gave you an incredible gift in sharing love and creating a very special mother-son bond. But it feels important that you and Bill claim your love, even if that means there is conflict with Alistair.*

He'd prefer it if I was on my own forever. He'd like to have it that his father was the last man in my life.

How old was Alistair when his father died?

Thirteen.

That's an awfully long time for you to be alone, I say.

I made a few friends after Tom, Alistair's father, passed away, but the aggravation and guilt I felt was too much to bear. I thought it best to wait until Alistair settled down and had a family before I could. Gosh, saying that out loud makes me sound like a martyr.

She looks to me for what I imagine might be confirmation or annulment.

I'm interested at what cost, though? By that I mean what happened to any desirous energy or longings you had to have a partner?

I put it all into my work. I was a good nurse. Committed, passionate, a favorite, some might say, to the children who came and went. I loved my work. I felt very validated and useful. Tom had been so encouraging that I train to be a nurse after Kenneth died, and in some ways this kept me close to him. I knew he'd be proud of me and my work.

Are you sure you didn't love Tom? I ask, playfully.

Agatha's smile returns now. *Tom was lovely*, she says, *and we had some very special times together. But we married because we cared very much for one another, not because we were in love. We were a good fit. Best friends. We both attended church, had similar interests; I liked his family, especially his sister. He was kind and I was lonely, as was he. I imagine we would still be together had he not died of cancer.*

Unlike Kenneth, Agatha's second husband had warm hands. Tom was a furniture restorer and a man of few words whose stoic character and broad shoulders had grounded Agatha. *He would spend hours in one of the outbuildings where we lived, a tub of spring onions, a wedge of cheese, and the radio on* while he tended broken chairs, adding soft upholstery to objects that had long been forgotten. Tom had been taught by his father, *also a card-carrying introvert,* to French polish, upholster and plane wood with such care and sensitivity that Agatha would feel *immediately calmed* as she watched him at work. *He put a chair in every single outbuidling and there were lots, so I could sit and be with him.*

In listening to Agatha's description of marital life with Tom I couldn't help feeling soothed myself. The envisioned care and restoration of "things" being brought back to life acting as tonic in a world of vast and disposable consumerism. But it also brought to my mind our conversation regarding orchids, and how Agatha would simply toss them away once their flowers had died off. I wondered if Agatha had been trying to restore something in her own life since childhood, perhaps her lovelessness, and in watching Tom at work had felt calmed, reassured even, in the rebuilding and healing of objects dismissed and forgotten.

I'm trying to picture you sitting with Tom in one of the outbuildings, I say. *I'd be interested to hear more about why his work felt so calming for you.*

I sensed his love to bring things back to life, she says, *much like he did me, after Kenneth's death. He had so much love for these old pieces of furniture. Even if something was on its last legs, he touched and held it with such tenderness and care. Once, he must have spent a whole month* restoring a child's rocking horse for a family we knew. Everyday I'd pop in to watch the horse's transformation. It was a beautiful experience.

He wasn't disinterested in the horse's recovery, I say.

Exactly, he didn't just toss it away. He believed in it.

Silence.

I think I might know where we're going with this, says Agatha.

I nod.

She clears her throat. I probably throw orchids away because that's what I've known and experienced. The absence of love replaced with violence and indifference when I was a child made me feel unlovable and therefore disposable. But Tom was different.

Can you say a little more? I ask.

Tom showed me care and respect, she continues, he was thought-ful. And very kind. I still wasn't ready to love when I married Tom—I didn't know how to love. But having Alistair changed everything. Back then, I was more concerned with caring because if you cared and were useful you might get a tiny scrap of recognition.

You're referring to your parents, or Kenneth perhaps? I ask.

Both, she snaps.

A pause.

We'd been married for fifteen years when Tom was diagnosed with cancer. It was such a shock for Alistair and me. We watched the cancer ravage his body, she cries. Alistair would wheel him out into the garden when we visited him in hospital. There were masses of rosebushes. Pink roses became my favorite flowers—Tom loved their scent. He'd ask that I pick a few so he could smell them and take them back to his hospital bed. There were roses at his funeral.

I understand now why Alistair's gift of pink roses upset you so, I say.

Exactly. It felt cruel.

Silence.

Handing me roses won't bring his dad back, says Agatha. And nei-ther will his cruelty. I need to talk to him.

What do you want to say?

I want to say that just because I love Bill doesn't mean that I love him any less or that I've forgotten his father. I want to say he has to stop being cruel and dismissive. And that I love him, even though his pain makes him hateful. I want to say pick yourself up—tell your family that you're sorry until you're sore in the throat!

Straight backs. Shoulders drawn and alert. We are suddenly sitting upright. Previous chitchat pays no mind to today's session and has instead been replaced with Agatha's life force. Her learning and loving is empowered, words alive and reclaiming in her own language a desire to be seen, felt, and understood. Feet firmly anchored to the ground, she is rooted. I feel her assertion and understanding—the use of which she is now reclaiming for her desire.

Wise words, I nod. *It's time,* I say. *We have to end for today.*

Agatha is surprised but not shocked when she opens the front door and finds herself faced with a home littered with food-stained plates, limp washing draped over wire hangers, and the smell of dank despair. She covers her nose with her gloved hand and climbs the stairs, collecting bottles, abandoned clothes, and empty family-sized crisp packets on her way. When she reaches the top of the stairs she takes a deep breath and steadies herself with the help of the wooden banister. She is tired. Lying on the bed in pajamas, her child, curled like a bean, a baby prawn. The bed takes their weight and she strokes his damp head. Alistair in turn moves closer. *I'm sorry, Mum,* he says. *I'm a mess.*

She spots an empty wine bottle on the bedside table and sighs. *I should have encouraged you to clean up your toys when you were a child,* says Agatha.

What? says Alistair, puzzled.

Children learn from practical acts how to cope with emotional mess and I didn't prepare you well enough. I did everything for you, which my therapist might say is a type of neglect, and after your dad died I did even more for you because I couldn't bear to see how much pain you were in. I also put my own needs on hold and made you my life, my world—but now I want Bill in my life, Al. I love him. You have to understand I don't want to be alone anymore. Your spite has to stop, as does the self-pity. I love you, Alistair, but I don't like you very much right now, especially after what happened last week at supper—the roses were particularly cruel.

That's not surprising. I don't like me much either, he replies, *and I'm sorry about the roses. It was a cheap shot.*

Yes it was.

I didn't mean the things I said about you and Bill but the timing couldn't be worse. Bill's a good guy.

When he sits up she notes his weight loss, and in an act of maternal love pulls the bedsheet up to warm him and removes her gloves, their fighting now ceased.

Why did you have the affair, Al?

I was lonely, he is quick to speak. *Elizabeth is always so busy with the boys. I constantly feel like a spare part. She has everything covered, all the time. I'd hoped we'd be happy, the four of us, but I feel like I'm on the outside, looking in.*

Have you tried to be more involved? Or told Elizabeth what an incredible mum she is? She probably has everything covered because she has to. Where were you when she was putting the boys to bed at night? She told me you'd stay out at night without so much as a phone call. And now we learn it's because you were having an affair. Actions have consequences, Al.

I miss them so much, he says.

So tell them. Tell your family how sorry you are. This separation won't heal itself. You'll have to make a gigantic effort if you want

Elizabeth to forgive you. Stop sitting around, moping and drinking.
Do something about the way you feel. Love is an action. And right now
I don't see much love. Look at this place: it's a pigsty!

Alistair leans into his mother, the sweet rocking of limbs.
She longs for something potent and wordless to happen: *change*.
Later, over coffee he tells her that he longs *to turn back time*, and
in the same breath wants to desperately *move forward*.

Between her body and his, Agatha and Alistair cradle their
love where there is enough room for apology and forgiveness
yet no space for air. In their embracing there is learning, listening, and understanding. Love in the afternoon.

Winter has arrived, a dusting of snow on the ground.

Outside, delicate snowdrops nod, sway, and shiver. Warming
my fingers around my coffee cup, I water with my free hand the
once blooming orchid now changed: a mere shoot with new
and tiny unformed leaves. I recall how Agatha had thought this
stage *ugly*. *I don't like it when their flowers die, because then they're*
just sticks and leaves, aren't they? From my office window I watch
a family of determined thrushes pecking at the fat balls of nuts
and seeds hanging from a birdfeeder. Eventually, my attention
returns to two Paula Rego prints both framed but not yet hung.
I had the idea to secure them next to my creaking bookcase but
when the family of lively birds arrived, I was pulled away from
my task of tapping nails into walls.

Moments of distraction are fine of course and inevitable for
any psychotherapist. These mind wanderings can offer flashes
of much-needed respite amid moments of emotional discourse in clinical practice and even provide amusement in less
compromising situations. But they are also a way of soothing
discomfort, overlooking thoughts, disavowing feelings, or kill-
ing desire. These insistent and resourceful distractions not only

serve as a reminder of life's challenging circumstances but also as a way out from our feelings when life serves up struggles.

I hold up the first print entitled "Love." It is one of a series of paintings named *Stories of Women* by Rego that shows a woman in a dark, patterned dress lying on a scarlet bedsheet. Her head is resting on a pillow, hands pressing down on her heart, her gaze somewhere else. The painting is beguiling, exhilarating, and harrowing and I am moved each time I stare at the unflinching delineation of love. Earlier, I wondered if the woman held her heart out of love or heartbreak—Rego's play on emotions are worryingly alike. Indeed, if the title "Love" was not known to me I would certainly not be able to detect whether the woman was holding her heart out of love or out of loss.

Agatha came to her therapy in love—*I'd like to start therapy. I'm in love, you see.* At the time I suspected that this declaration was simply the tip of the iceberg. I was suspicious, one might say. Skeptical. Unable, like with Rego's painting, to detect if it was love Agatha was feeling, or something quite different. And if so, what? I recall both my curiosity and my cynicism thinking romantic love is rarely a reason for entering a therapeutic alliance. However, Agatha reminded me that we are all experts in knowing nothing; this, an early learning that was taught by my training therapist. And while my learning and clinical experience are helpful, Agatha gifted me the experience and opportunity to see that therapy not only fights darkness and balms pain but is an excellent and necessary place to explore, witness, and understand matters of the heart.

That Agatha and I were able to examine her frightened and desperately unhappy childhood, the deaths of her two husbands, the infidelity of her first husband, the birth of her son and all that occurred in between was not only necessary for understanding some of the choices she made later in her life, but has also honored her life journey.

Most people want to know and understand more about the art and act of loving, or at least are inquisitive. *What is love, exactly? No one teaches us how to love; Is love an illusion? Do you think he, she, they, love me? Do you love me? Love is a drug; Love sucks; When will I find love? Love is just capitalism's attempt to have us buy into the fantasy; Love is being a grown-up; I long to love; I need love; Love is a battlefield; Love is power; Love, love, love*—patients have told me over the years. And I have been fascinated to learn, feel, and participate in these explorations. To love is a deeply personal and unique experience. It is for us to decide if our blueprints of longing and living without love will remain and continue, or if we will encourage the wounds of our hunger for love to heal.

Agatha showed me an openheartedness and capacity for love in her later years, and it was mighty. Her daring supreme. She reminded me that pain is not our destiny but our reason; and no matter what has happened to us in our past, if we are open to love and being loved we can live freely. This is not to say we forget our past, but with therapy, we can allow hardships to live inside us differently, knowing the past is just that: past experiences that no longer have power over us as they once did. To choose change is to embrace a love that is empowering. Recognition and acceptance for those who love us allows healing to begin and grow.

Agatha also showed me one of the richest and most ancient of truths: love heals. As Agatha's therapist, I attempted to shrug off my love Grinch and my cynicism for a cloak of hope and respect. Cynicism is rooted in fear and despair and hopelessness. Therapy, I was reminded, is not just about how we ease our embodied pain and psychic suffering, or healing from an unquiet mind, but also an opportunity to make ourselves awake and ready to receive the love that is waiting for us. That is, the love we haven't yet met, experienced, or perhaps even know—the love we want and need. And in Agatha's words: *At sixty-seven years old, I'm just getting started.*

The most sublime act is to set another before you.

William Blake, *The Marriage of Heaven and Hell* (1790)

Thorn of Hope

For weeks their final conversation seeps across the borders of her days. She has memorized the afternoon: warm, late, and scented; and the words he unwillingly spoke: confused and adrift. She repeats these words over and over and out loud for no one to hear but herself. And she pictures him: defeated, a wild-eyed gaze evading any hope or rescue she had for his unquiet mind.

He'd appeared too thin that day. His shoes were too big, scuffed, laces undone. How she'd wanted to hold him, hard, *Sweet baby*. To pull him into her body—his home once for nine natural months—and to speak quiet, tender loving words that might balm his entire hurting. These words, Beverly hoped, would haul him away from the dark forlorn waters that wished to drag him under and make him sick. But he had turned away from her and instead poured himself another drink. His third. Kept in a leather hip flask, in his breast pocket, in his loose navy overcoat.

Are you hungry, darling? she'd asked, watching the raw edge around his nails.

Not really, Ma.

Still, she offered him lunch, his favorite: *spaghetti bolognese*. Stacked and stored in a chest freezer in the unlikely event his appetite returned. *Or I can make you a sandwich. I have ham.* But her *faffing* had caused him to pull away. She watched his body knot and curve at the mention of love and care.

Across the weedless lawn, an ancient maple tree swayed. It

was home to birdsong that at one time he'd been able to hear, to see, and take joy in. He'd sat and slept and read beneath the maple as a boy. But on this warm and scented afternoon he saw only shadows. The branches of the tree were no longer a cooling shade from the sun; they had turned into tentacles, the trunk a rich demon. Leaves had become eyes. Soon, necessary messages would arrive through the roots of the tree, whispered from beneath the earth's surface. Beverly held his hand in hers, knowing a balanced grip on his mind was now lost.

Every so often, a psychotherapy referral will shake me to the core. It will test whether I'm equipped for the work, have adequate clinical experience and skill, enough smarts and sufficient heart space. Beverly was one such referral, and I noted on reading her assessment that I approached the possibility of us working together with deep, penetrating caution. She had requested to meet with a female therapist who was based in central London. With emphasis, the assessor noted that *the therapist must be a mother.* We spoke in the morning, and by noon the following day Beverly was sitting opposite me with the look of a woman who had given up. A woman who had nothing to live for.

She takes a breath. A moment for herself. Grief worn on her face like a fresh bruise. *A week later he committed suicide,* she says, with the trace of a sad and beautiful Scottish accent.

I note Beverly's height in the chair, the straightness of her back, hair peppered with silver. She is a distinguished-looking woman. Her clothing is chic yet comfortable: a soft blazer and loose jeans. When she looks at me, brown eyes so full of pain, I believe I can see grief orbiting her like Saturn's rings. We are silent and I encourage the weight of Beverly's words, her loss, to percolate in my body.

I understand you're a mother, she continues.

Yes, I am, I say.

And I am no longer.

Is a mother no longer a mother when her only child commits suicide? Beverly's role had now disappeared, but I wondered if perhaps she disavowed herself as a mother so soon after Monty's death because she was in so much pain. There is almost nothing more traumatic, more agonizing and brutal than the death of one's child. It leaves a gaping hole with so many questions, and of the multitude of losses people suffer, the loss of a child takes the longest to heal and to rebuild lives thereafter. Monty's death was premature and violent. A mother who grieves the loss of her only child grieves a person who embodied her being, a person central to her life's journeying and sense of identity. In this complex bereavement, I wondered if Beverly unconsciously feared the grief process. I wanted to explore *"And I am no longer"* further, but first a gentle settling into the work must begin.

I gather my thoughts. If I speak, I fear I may insult her, because in this moment of grief and suffering nothing but the return of her only child can bring about comfort. I am sure of this. An image of my own son flashes up in my mind and I honor Beverly's painful reality. My unchanged role as a mother feels momentarily cruel, insensitive, and exposing. I'd like to find words that will magically make everything better for Beverly, but of course no such sentence exists, so I say the only thing I can say:

I am deeply sorry for your loss, Beverly.

She nods.

I can only imagine how much pain you must be in.

Beverly holds her breath and it's as if time is suspended, much like Monty's age, just twenty-six—*Sweet baby.* Her eyes widen. They are charged with despair. Beverly takes both arms, palms outstretched, and reaches them around her entire body. She bows her head. And she rocks. Back and forth.

Perhaps the movement and the holding of her hurting body are the catalysts to release a cry so primal and so raw that I note a wave of nausea finds my throat. I sit with her cries. Noise that oscillates from ancient screams to deep, bellowing sobs. I move my chair closer. After many minutes I remind Beverly, *I am here, I am with you, you are not alone.* Beverly stays rocking.

I don't want to be alive anymore, she insists.

She wipes away fluids, nose and mouth, with the back of her wrist. Her eyes shine amber. They are raw with hurt.

Your only child has committed suicide, I say. *And there is no immediate escape from your reality, or your suffering. But death is not the answer, or the cure. Can you talk to me about your pain?*

She pauses.

Last week I wanted to walk out in front of a car, she says. *Anything that was moving fast. I wanted to feel the same pain that Monty felt. I thought that if a car hit me, I'd have some idea of his suffering. It isn't fair that he suffered more than me. He must have been so frightened, so desperate, and so alone. I should have insisted he come home and stay with me. He'd stopped taking his medication, and he was drinking again, I could smell it. But his unwellness scared me. All I could see was his madness. I felt so helpless.*

In this grief, Beverly attempts to become him. She digs out his clothes—left in the guest bedroom painted peach, that was once his childhood bedroom painted blue. She pulls on his hoodie to make breakfast—*eggs*—left and later thrown away because she can't welcome anything good in her belly. She pops his remaining pills that he'd abandoned on the dining room table and waits for the numbing sensation to drown out the *whys, what ifs,* and *if onlys.* And she blasts, on repeat, his favorite bands on the stereo, making herself scream the lyrics, not caring if anyone hears her.

She forces her feet into his shoes: big and scuffed, and gently ties the brown laces while trying to picture him in his last moments. *What were his last thoughts? Had he showered in the morning? Eaten breakfast? Had he stroked his beloved cat Tilly before feeding her? Had he tried to call anyone? Anyone? Why not me, his mother? Why not? Why—*

In quieter moments, when the distraction of music is overshadowed and the pharmaceutical wonders no longer work, crying acts as a salve to Beverly's sorrowful thoughts. She takes out one of his old toys, a tiny yellow rabbit, kept in a shoebox on top of the wardrobe and whispers his name, *Monty, darling*. In these moments she is with him again, mother and son, *Ma and Monty-Moo*. And she strokes the ears of the tiny yellow rabbit against her cheek as he once did, wishing she could hold her baby close, closer, sweet lullaby songs.

What type of medication was Monty taking? I ask.

Antipsychotics. Whenever something difficult happened, he'd stop taking it—just when he needed it most. He split with his girlfriend a while back and it completely destroyed him. So he did what he always did. He turned to drink. We tried everything. Therapy, meds, rehab. Nothing worked. I lost sight of my baby.

I note the quiver of anger in Beverly's voice and wonder if our future work will be about finding ways to internalize and preserve the Monty before he became ill and suicidal. Or perhaps this is too simplistic. Instead, I imagine an earlier Monty sitting beside the hurting and desperate version of himself, with Beverly close by.

Your desire to walk out in front of a car; it has something to do with feeling as Monty did, to do as Monty did?

Something like that.

We will find other ways, I speak quietly.

That's why I'm here.

★

He arrived on bonfire night and slipped out as easy as a kitten, with clenched fists and a shock of raven hair, *Monty.* The midwife and doctor had winced at his nine pounds two ounces and quickly added a stitch or two, which Beverly neither felt nor remembered having until one day she'd touched herself and found the tiny scar. *What a bruiser,* quickly corrected to *beauty,* Beverly thinks she heard one nurse say. She remembers fear meeting her relief after counting fingers and toes, and she stroked the delicate flake on his head, slightly cone-shaped and imperfect. One nurse noted Beverly's touch, how it lingered a little longer around the contours of his *lemon head. We had to use forceps to slow him down,* she explained gently, *he was coming out rather fast. Keen to be with his mummy,* she smiled. And this had calmed her, affirmed her. Beverly smiled in return at the kind nurse.

At home she swaddled him with cellular blankets and learned the ways of breastfeeding. A paperclip attached to her bra strap as reminder of which breast was offered last to *Monty-Moo,* should she forget. She discovered frozen cabbage leaves soothed and calmed the burn in her heavy breasts when Monty struggled to latch on. The 2 a.m. feed was when she felt most calm and content because, although fatigued, it was just her and Monty and the stars. Later, her mother traveled down from Scotland to show her how weaning was done. A blender pummeling the life out of squash and apple and pears that was spooned into ice cube trays, and later popped out and microwaved when Monty turned eight months old. At a year he was nearly walking.

Her husband didn't bond with Monty as much as Beverly had hoped. He'd been loving and helpful to begin with, cooking, helping with house chores and offering to take Monty off her hands for a while and carrying him on his hip to the local parks. But Theo hadn't wanted to touch her body the same way he had before her birth as a mother, cringing as she retrieved the breast pump, breast pads, and magical creams. Many times she'd caught him masturbating in the shower to which she was not invited, a cubicle of solo wet fantasies. And when she did find time to be intimate, sex felt pedestrian and quiet. Her empty body was quickly, prematurely, faced with the sharp turn of his back.

Beverly began to notice that it was rare for the three of them to spend time together, Theo needing a large pull of whiskey most days, and most nights. He began to use words like *Momma's boy*, and she thought his handling of Monty just a little too frantic and curt when lowering him into the buggy. Later, she was charged with being *fussy* and *overprotective*, while Monty was accused of acting *clingy, like a spoiled brat. He doesn't know how lucky he is,* said Theo. When asked how she was finding motherhood by friends at dinner parties, *Sons and Lovers* was a frequent reference guised as a joke. The nod toward D. H. Lawrence's novel a sly way of accusing Monty, who when reaching manhood wouldn't be able to love because his mother was the strongest power in his life.

What do you understand of Theo's envy? I ask in one of our sessions.

He had a difficult childhood. His father was a functioning alcoholic and his mother was depressed. She was lovely, but completely preoccupied with her husband's drinking. Theo always felt like an afterthought. I guess he was jealous of mine and Monty's relationship, of the care and love I showed him.

I had some ideas of how Theo's trans-generational trauma may have impacted Beverly and Theo's relationship. *When we envy our children,* I say, *we deceive ourselves. We perhaps think too little of the child and too well of ourselves.*

I have listened to mothers, fathers, and guardians complain

how ungrateful their children are, how they never had the opportunities their children have, the material comforts or loving parents—*Spoiled rotten,* patients have said. *They don't know how lucky they are; At their age I was working a weekend job, helping my mum and looking after my siblings; I find myself being withholding and I don't know why; He's so entitled; I feel so angry and resentful toward her.* For the most part, envy is unconscious. How do we unhook ourselves from envy and reach an acceptance of ourselves and our way of life so we can enjoy and feel proud of our children's successes and happiness? Envying one's child is a psychological debacle, and if we are not careful we stand to lose not only our mental serenity, but also our child in the process.

Over time I've found exploring a patient's deprivation, often a prerequisite for jealousy, is helpful in healing envy toward their child. We envy what we do not have and cannot imagine having and experiencing for ourselves. And when one witnesses their child achieving and recognizing a life that was not available, or made possible for themselves, it is incredibly painful. I have in my mind Tilly, a talented artist and writer whose parents were emotionally unavailable, and on dark days punishing and negligent. They too had been artists—the mother a poet and the father a frustrated painter whose work was received with lukewarm critique. Tilly's son, who unlike herself had *glided into art school, everything he attempts he achieves. He simply takes everything in his stride. There's very little conflict and confusion about what he wants and needs to achieve his dreams.*

He has you as his mother, I offered. *You've spoken of your commitment to supporting his artistic talent and journey to art school.*

Tilly nodded. *I wanted to do something different to what I'd experienced. I want to support him but sometimes I feel so jealous at how easy his life is.*

I had leaned toward her. *Now would be a good time for me to say how respectful I am of the commitment you've shown your son. You've offered what William Blake cited as "The most sublime act," which is to "set another before you."*

Tilly locked eyes with mine, a marvelous smile.

But, I continued, *it will be healing to talk about the cost of this. The potential conflict inside of you. Perhaps how tiring and reminding of your past it feels to be so committed. As a child and teenager you longed to be cared for, for others to want and take an interest in you. Owning and acknowledging the deprivation you experienced as a child holds meaning and gives context to the envious feelings you have toward your son.*

A year or so after our work ended, I received a letter from Tilly saying she was due to exhibit her paintings in a gallery in central London—*Would you like to come to the opening, or is that a breach of boundaries?*—and had embarked on another course in fine art. *I'm by far the oldest person in class but I don't care. I'm doing what I love most: writing and making art.*

A year or so after our work ended, I felt proud and relieved. I had visited the gallery, but not on opening night. Her paintings were large, expansive, more daring. Their palette of color much changed from Tilly's previous work. I wrote to Tilly and congratulated her. She replied, saying: *I love your word: daring—*

Outside, a nagging car alarm interrupts my reverie. Beverly reaches for a tissue. *I'd do anything to feel envy toward Monty,* she says, casting her gaze to the floor. *If only he were still here.*

She had suggested date nights to Theo, couples therapy, and a holiday. *Mum can take care of Monty,* who was a year old and happy to spend time with Granny and Gramps. A trip was planned to Venice. Theo's love of gothic architecture might delight his senses, and she imagined walking and sailing toward Venetian splendor, sculptures inspired by classic mythology and engineering marvels. Her own love of antiquated gardens would also be enjoyed. The hope that when Monty reached nursery age she'd enroll in the horticulture course she'd longed to take. In the early days she and Theo had dreamed up the perfect scenario, where he'd continue as partner at the architects practice he'd worked long and hard to build, with Beverly as landscaper. *Horticulture extraordinaire!* he'd said. *You can leave PR and do what you've always wanted—to be outdoors, every day, with nature.*

The trip to Venice hadn't gone as Beverly had hoped. Theo had spent hours on his phone and laptop finalizing a pitch for a restoration project in Westminster. His moods had turned erratic and his drinking, she noticed, began before midday. *We're on holiday,* he said, noting her expression when he cleaned out the hotel room's minibar. By 3 p.m. he'd fallen asleep, trips to the Basilica Di San Marco, Doge's Palace, and Peggy Guggenheim Collection taken alone. She noticed that she flinched a little too often when they were having dinner together, preempting his rudeness to waiters if his order took more than a few minutes to arrive, or if his wineglass was left dry. On the few occasions when she'd telephoned her mother to check on Monty, Theo had scoffed and later punished her with his absence. One night Beverly had been woken up by a forceful tug, the smell of scotch on his breath, his entering of her momentarily confusing and severe. When she told him to stop, he slapped her.

When Monty was three years old, Theo served Beverly with divorce papers and left the family home.

I was relieved and slightly depressed when he left us, Beverly says. *We had the house but no means to run it. Maintenance was arranged by the courts as well as weekend visits for Monty, but it was messy and deeply upsetting. Any opportunity Theo had to make life difficult, he would. Often I'd take Monty to his house and he wouldn't open the door. He was either drunk or had forgotten Monty was staying with him for the weekend. I began to feel very uncomfortable leaving Monty with him.*

I can understand why, I say.

I would dread it if he answered the door, and if he didn't. Either way, Monty became very distressed. So, for six months I stopped taking Monty on the weekends. Theo didn't get in touch to ask why. Then he stopped paying maintenance. It took over a year for the courts to act on it, and by this time I was in so much debt that I took a job at a local garden center.

For the next five years Beverly worked full-time while studying horticulture in the evenings and on the weekends. *It helped with my depression, doing what I loved, but I realize I wasn't as present for Monty as I should have been. There was no letup, and what with Mum in Scotland, help was sporadic and expensive. I was very lonely. I used to dread the summer holidays. If I didn't work, I didn't get paid, and there are only so many favors you can ask of your friends.*

Beverly noticed the beginning of Monty's stammer sometime around his eleventh birthday. *We were at a burger restaurant and when Monty came to place his order, as I'd encouraged, his cheeks grew red. He couldn't get his words out. I ordered on his behalf, not wanting to cause him or the waiter further embarrassment. In hindsight, I wish I hadn't,* she says.

Was that the first time you'd noticed Monty's stammer? I ask.

I'm ashamed to say it wasn't. School had mentioned he'd become increasingly withdrawn. It was an effort to get him to talk. I often found myself speaking on his behalf. I think part of me thought it would pass. That he was just shy.

What happened next? I inquire.

I took him to a speech therapist and that really seemed to help, but to cut a long story short we came to realize that Monty was depressed and angry. Angry like you wouldn't believe. Angry about his dad, the

divorce, not having the friends he wanted, the fact I was always work-
ing, that he had no one to take him to football. The few times a year
he'd see Theo would end in tears, leaving Monty feeling desperate. On
his thirteenth birthday he said he no longer wanted to see his alcoholic,
deadbeat dad. Then shortly after I met Mike.

Tell me about Mike, I say.

Her remembrance is expressed by the softening of her gaze.
Mike's lovely, she begins. *Kind. Funny,* she smiles. *We were together*
for six years. He was incredibly supportive to Monty and me. We're
still very good friends.

A pause.

We met when I thought no one would ever find me attractive again,
at a weekend propagation course. He was already working as a land-
scaper and we just hit it off. A year later Mike moved in. Monty was
nearly sixteen at this point and had fallen into a—she pauses—*shifty*
friendship group. Lots of risk-taking, loose rules, fast sex.

Mike had pointed out how reserved and frightened she was
around Monty. At first, Beverly was reluctant and understandably protective of their relationship, explaining how it had just
been her and Monty for the past twelve years. That it would
take some time for Monty to adjust. That she kept her purse
and jewelry hidden was not lost on her, however.

Six months later, Monty's best friend, Robert, died in a car
crash, and this had tipped him over the edge. It was the catalyst
for most things that were to follow. His drinking and drug-
taking were out of control, and anyone who attempted to get
close was shot down. Beverly threw herself into work. It was
the one place that kept her from feeling that she wasn't *com-*
pletely useless.

Shortly after his eighteenth birthday Monty demanded that
Beverly *make a choice: me or Mike.* She chose Mike, if there is
such a thing as choice when commanded to make one.

I was so lonely and in need of a love other than Monty's, says Beverly. *I wanted Mike, I needed him. I'd spent so much time on my own or just being a mum. But I knew being in a happy relationship again would come at a cost. Monty watched Mike make me happy and this upset him. He felt excluded. Even though Monty was making a life for himself, he didn't think I needed one too. He'd turned very self-ish and entitled.*

Beverly tried, endless times, to explain to Monty how alone she felt. How she wanted a companion who had similar interests—someone she could be intimate with—but Monty insisted: *He's not right for you. We don't need him. I mean it, Ma, it's him or me. Make up your mind.*

How is such a decision that is so crucial and so complicated made in such haste, I wonder? Was Monty really so misattuned and unseeing of his mother's wants and needs? Had he turned selfish and entitled, or was he trying to communicate something else? What had Monty feared most when he forced his mother to choose between him and Mike? The effect it had had on Beverly was that she'd felt cornered, bullied, and as she fought to claim her desire of a romantic and loving relationship, it was decided that Mike would stay.

The consequences, Beverly speaks, *were horrendous. He smashed up the kitchen, hurled mugs and plates to the ground. I felt scared of him. You choose him over me?* he'd screamed. *You're such a bad mother. You're a selfish cow!*

Two weeks later, after many attempts at conversation and healing, Monty told Beverly, *I'm moving out,* though their separation was relatively short-lived. *If I'm honest,* Beverly says, *I enjoyed it when it was just me and Mike. Our home felt so calm and peaceful. It was fun—just the two of us. But I feel so guilty saying that now.* Once Monty left, Beverly realized how frightened and anxious she'd become around him. Her shoulders and jaw tensing in his presence. She was exhausted at tiptoeing around, careful not to upset or *set him off. I was relieved that he'd found somewhere else to live,* she says.

From the age of sixteen, Monty had been working at a local carpentry firm, and after a two-year apprenticeship and the painful rupture with Beverly, decided to move in with his then girlfriend, Janey. The relationship was short-lived. Janey, Beverly soon discovered, was pregnant *and a frequent pot smoker,* though this had no bearing on her decision to terminate the pregnancy. *I would have kept the baby,* Monty later told Beverly. *I would have liked a son or daughter to look after. Someone apart from myself.* Janey's decision to go ahead without discussing the pregnancy with Monty had unsteadied him. *Why would she do that?* asked Monty. *I want to move back home, Ma. Is that okay?*

The office was quickly turned back into a bedroom and once again painted blue. A new bed, plants, and cotton sheets were purchased. Every Thursday night was dedicated to pizza and a movie. But their eighteen months apart seemed like years to Beverly. Monty had changed considerably. His humor and gentleness seemed to have melted, and instead sprouted anger, contempt, and cruelty. She found his jokes ugly, dark, and off-key. Veering toward sinister. His violent tone and para-noia scared her, and his choice of friends and interests were at best shaky. He started to cover his body with tattoos. Mean and aggressive ink that sprawled snakes and skulls and broken hearts across his chest, back, and arms. When Beverly asked him why he was harming his body with these images, he replied, *It's my body, stay the fuck out of it.*

Mike often left the dinner table or the movie—carefully chosen to avoid potential conflict—early. Beverly walked a tightrope of appeasing both men in her home. That Monty left his half-smoked joints, clothes, and dishes around and stinking

caused her no real concern, Beverly convinced herself. She tried
to put aside how happy she'd felt when it was just her and
Mike, and instead curled into a denial that left her rejecting of
calm, fun, and peacefulness. Her own wants and needs took a
back seat. Mike began to withdraw. But what was important,
Beverly told herself, was that Monty was back home where
she could watch over him, take care of him, cook for him, do
as she'd done for him as a boy.

It is uncomfortable to think about fear in relation to our
children. Fear of losing them, fear on their behalf, and fear of
them. Beverly felt all manner of fear regarding Monty. She
feared his anger, his erratic behavior, and his tattoos. She feared
what his bench-pressed body might do to her in retaliation. She
also dreaded waking up to a message that he was in a police cell
or a ditch. The way his eyes darted toward the block of
kitchen knives at the mere mention of tidying and cleaning his
room had her shrinking with terror. *I'll clean it when I want,
I'm not a fucking child,* snapped Monty. Beverly dared to retaliate. *So stop acting like one.* She feared her rage toward him, her
powerlessness. She was wiped out. And she hated how it was
impacting her relationship with Mike. One night Beverly
dreamed that Monty set fire to the house while she and Mike
were in bed asleep. When she woke up she checked his room
for lighters and matches and ordered several fire extinguishers,
which she hid on each floor.

I wish I'd got help for him sooner, says Beverly. *I didn't know
smoking pot could lead to psychosis. My little boy was suddenly lost
to me.*

There were two processes at work, a double bereavement:
the heartbreaking death of Monty lost to suicide, and the earlier loss of the child that had been funny, kind, and gentle. I
could see how despairing Beverly was, how torturous it must

have been for her to watch her child plummet from mild drug-taking to psychotic episodes.

In a moment of complete desperation Beverly called Theo. When she heard his voice she broke down. Theo was gentle and patient and sober, his ten-year chip (offered every twelve months by Alcoholics Anonymous to mark his sobriety) collected earlier in the year. She wished Monty would attend AA too.

Beverly explained how Monty's refusal to take his medication was out of control, that his psychotic episodes were more frequent than ever, more violent. She told Theo how her and Mike had been struggling to connect and support each other. *Mike's had enough, so we're taking a break. He's moving out,* she said, and Theo listened.

I don't know our Monty anymore, he's a complete stranger to me, she cried.

The following week Monty was admitted to rehab, his first of three attempts to get clean and sober. After his second treatment he decided to move out of the family home again to live with friends.

I was living alone wondering what I'd done wrong, thinking I was such a bad mother, says Beverly. She glances at the clock on my desk. *Men are always leaving me, why is that?*

This idea of the bad mother, I say, *I'm not sure how helpful it is.*

Beverly nods, shrugs.

Are you familiar with the term "the good-enough mother"? I ask.

Writer, psychoanalyst, and pediatrician Donald Winnicott coined the phrases "good-enough mother," "ordinary devoted mother," and "there is no such thing as a baby, only a mother and baby," to name a few. Winnicott's work on parenting was culturally progressive and relatable. At a time of seismic social change, post–Second World War, he spoke on the radio directly to mothers and was a natural and compassionate communicator expressing sensitive and complex issues with reassurance and deep understanding of human development. The "good-enough mother," he believed, is one who adapts to the child's needs. An active adaptation that eventually lessens. The mother is by no means "perfect," but "good-enough" in that the child feels a slight amount of frustration.

Aged sixty-seven, Winnicott wrote a poem about his own mother called "The Tree":

> *Mother below is weeping*
> *weeping*
> *weeping*
> *Thus I knew her*
> *Once, stretched out on her lap*
> *As now on dead tree*
> *I learned to make her smile*
> *To stem her tears*
> *To undo her guilt*
> *To cure her inward death*
> *To enliven her was my living*

I've heard the phrase before, Beverly says, kneading the calf of her leg with her thumb, *the "good-enough mother,"* she repeats.

I think it's a very helpful phrase, I say, *one we might think about together.*

Okay, she speaks quietly. *If you say so.*

Poor timing, I think to myself, and make a note to revisit Winnicott's theory when Beverly is more open to exploration. Instead, we discuss ICE numbers. In Case of Emergency numbers. These numbers, we agree, will be called if fear and hopelessness feel undeniably present. *I am familiar,* she says, *with the Samaritans.* Other numbers will reach the phones of family, friends, Mike, her GP, and myself. A circle of care.

We're nearly at time, Beverly, I say. *How are you feeling?*

She shrugs. *Angry, hopeless. Not good enough,* she says.

The next six months are fraught with anger, guilt, and despair.

Hope diminished, and like a thorn in her side, Beverly seeks out opportunities to project her feelings of hopelessness and anger wherever she can. She appears at Mike's house drenched in sweat and rain, no overcoat. She wants him to see her soaked to the skin, to take her into his new home, undress her, and dry her body with a soft towel. She wants him to spoon feed her like a baby while she cries, *Why the hell did you leave me when I needed you most?* Mike fetches a sweater, a spoon, and warmed soup. *I'm sorry,* he says.

She leaves messages on Theo's phone before dawn and screams what a terrible father and husband he was, a drunk. *Do you remember what you did to me in Venice, you monster?!* Theo returns her call when he awakes. *I'm sorry,* he says.

She binges and purges on spaghetti bolognese, Monty's favorite, while attempting to track down Janey, *that—,* and considers writing to her: *See what you did to my only child, my Monty-Moo. You took away his baby.* She writes a list of the friends who didn't care; the imagined dealers who made him sick; the therapists who didn't do their job; the girls who told Monty they loved him and left. She rakes through her mind to recall anyone who had hurt Monty, anything that might have contributed to his suicide. *I hate the world, and everyone in it,* she howls.

She sees Monty everywhere: street corners, at the kitchen door, beneath the maple tree in the garden, at the dry cleaners, the bank, floating above her bed, supermarket queues, the train tracks in her dreams. Everywhere. She dreams of him clutching the giant panda she'd paid too much money for after Monty threw himself to the ground in pure frustration because he wasn't able to knock coconuts off their plinths. *How much?* Beverly pleaded with the friendly tattooed guy at the fairground.

There are days when she feels mild respite from her suffering, but then guilt quickly takes over: *How dare I feel okay? How dare I forget he is gone?* And the punishment starts up again like a wild horse bucking on hind legs. She drinks, eats, burns herself on the stove, bumps into walls and doorframes that refuse to get out of her way. She smashes things, hurls things, bashes and shatters and punches things. She starts arguments in the garden center, coffee shops, and the supermarket, forcing her protesting trolley into the middle of the shopping aisle, just daring someone to challenge her. Hurt and rage consume her. If only she would cry. Instead, she demands contact—a desire so great to push against something, someone. It is violent and exhausting. Beverly wishes she could control how she feels. She wants to press a button, flick a switch that will make her feel different, better. *I'm so tired,* she says.

That's the thing about grief: it's immune to control. It does what it wants in its own time. It is stubborn, strong-willed. Grief remains in our minds and hearts much longer than anyone who is grief-stricken wants or sometimes can even bear.

At night Beverly clings to Monty's tiny yellow rabbit, rubs its soft ears against her cheek until, mentally and physically exhausted, she eventually falls asleep. When she wakes up from failed dreams, the grief starts over again, a rolling, relentless hell lived on earth.

Most of Beverly's sessions are wrought with anger, guilt, and powerlessness, until we eventually, and with relief, reach tears. I encourage her tears.

Beverly is exhausted.

I am exhausted.

We are in this together.

I am reluctant to take a break at this delicate time. *Take a holiday,* suggests my supervisor. *You will be no help to Beverly or your other patients if you're exhausted to the point of collapse.* I go away and lie horizontal beneath the sunshine. Tiny cool drinks are delivered, books are read, the sea cradles my body, soft delicate holds. I rest. I breathe. I rest.

Grief joys, joy grieves, on slender accident. I speak Shakespeare's words out loud for no one to hear but the sea.

My thoughts drift, momentarily, to Monty. His suicide. How alone and deeply unhappy he must have felt to tragically outwit his life on earth at the only price possible: his death. He had lost in order to win. Every day he woke up to a nightmare. Voices, pain, suffering, and addiction ravaging his mind and body. Suicide was the one thing Monty believed he had control over.

Freud believed we are born with a death instinct, and that "The goal of all life is death." This theory caused great controversy among psychoanalysts at the time and remains a lively topic of discussion today. That all human behaviors are motivated by drives and instincts, as Freud cited, is not the method I use in my work as a psychotherapist. Therapy today is less focused on innate drives toward death and destruction— Freud's death instinct is lost in modern psychotherapy—and instead focuses on the catastrophic failure of attachment when feelings of suicide take hold.

Before leaving for my holiday I had encouraged Beverly to lean into her circle of care and offered her my email, should she need to be in contact. This overture is sometimes enough for a patient to feel they are being held in mind at particularly fragile periods in their therapy. *Thank you, it means a lot that you'd do that,* says Beverly.

Beverly also decides to take a holiday and works in her garden.

She forces her hands into buckets of soil. She likes how grounded this makes her feel. The earth offers her an opportunity to be present rather than constantly distracted by her memories or dread for the future, the sun casting warmth and reaching her shattered heart. She pushes her palms in the soil further still, wrists disappearing, and stretches her fingers. She tries to lose herself in her garden. Sawing, digging, planting, and pruning. A tapestry of violets stretching past the immaculate lawn. One day she hallucinates riding a magic carpet of her velvety violets to a land where death no longer exists, only a nirvana of life and the living. Monty on a swing.

She leans over and smells the garden's many flowers, snips their fleshy stems, and lowers them into vases to dot around her home. Delicate petals offering beauty to fight off dark thoughts.

She also plants perennials. This gives her hope and modest certainty that life and color and growth will return next spring. She builds a new compost bin from wooden pallets and feels reenergized when she hurls in masses of broken tree branches, sodden leaves, old soil, grass clippings, and undesired raw foods. The tossing of this waste, although she's done it for years, takes on a new energy. She is grateful for the brown mass that will eventually come good in the end. Her body, that has been mostly still since Monty's death, starts to ache and she soothes it with warm, sweet-smelling baths. She welcomes the hard climb of the stairs to her bathroom, her muscles overworked, and is pleased to feel something other than guilt and grief. Throbbing arms, back and thighs. *My body is waking up,* she thinks.

Beverly enjoys the nonpharmaceutical therapy of her

garden. Pills slow her down, they make her *groggy and fat*—a veil of vague and remote feelings shielding her from anguish and despair. She wonders if she should reduce her medication now that she's engaging with a talking therapy. *Grief needs to be felt,* she repeats out loud, while running hot baths.

On warmer evenings she returns to the garden and gathers fistfuls of magenta snapdragons—Monty's favorite as a little boy—and pictures him beneath the ancient maple tree pinching their tiny flowers with his thumb and forefinger. *Snap, snap,* she'd hear him sing while she tidied and pruned. She pulls one of the tiny magenta flowers off its stem. *Snap, snap,* she says, she cries.

Grief needs to be felt.

Growing through grief is one of many powerful ways we might, as humans, heal our suffering. For years, the balm of nature has been written about by those living with mental illness and grief. One precious gift gardening offers is the way it contemplates and consecrates time. It grounds the gardener in a present both conscious of and undistracted by the ongoing cycles of seasons stretching across past, present, and future thoughts and feelings. The poet Ross Gay wrote: "The gardener digs in another time, without past or future, beginning or end. As you walk in the garden you pass into this time, the moment of entering can never be remembered. Around you the landscape lies transfigured. Here is the Amen beyond the prayer."

Virginia Woolf also found sanctuary in her garden, writing: "I was quite unable to deal with the pain of discovering that people hurt each other, that a man I had seen had killed himself. The sense of horror held me powerless. But in the case of the flower I found a reason; and was thus able to deal with the sensation. I was not powerless."

I am reminded of the time when I visited film director Derek Jarman's garden in Dungeness on the shingled shores of Kent. A trainee psychotherapist and keen gardener myself, I'd sat watching Prospect Cottage, small rings of flint protecting, like circles of care, the wild and scented flowers. Jarman mourned loss after loss as the AIDS plague destroyed his friends one by one. Every time, he grounded himself in the boisterous life of earth, of soil, bud, and bloom.

At the end of each gardening day Beverly eyes the many diaries kept in an aged cardboard box, daring herself to read them. Her plates of spaghetti bolognese are slowly changing to delicate soups, fish pie, colorful salads, and crunchy vegetables picked from her garden. She enjoys their earthy freshness in her mouth and is relieved her taste buds are no longer indifferent to nourishing food. Flowers on the verge of death are left a little longer to dry and shrivel in carefully placed vases. She tells herself they have a few more days of life left in their petals, their stems and their leaves. On the days when she pulls the flowers out of their vessels, she notes herself feeling mildly accepting of their ending. And at the cusp of the night she cries and pushes the diaries a little further out of view. Years of confessions, wonderings, celebrations, and secrets she imagines, written down in Monty's loose hand. Grief must be felt.

On the evening before we are due to meet after our holidays, Beverly decides to pour herself a large glass of wine and reaches for Monty's diaries:

Age 11: I pretended to be an airplane. I was so fast. I flew really high and waved at everyone who looked like ants on the grass. It made me happy. Craig Bishop was a helicopter. He couldn't keep up.

Age 13: Dad forgot my birthday again. It's not like he has another kid to think about. Dickhead.

Age 15: If I could be anyone I'd be James Dean. So cool. Who wants to get old anyway?

Aged 18: Ma chose Mike. No one hurts you the way a mother can. I'm moving out tomorrow.

Aged 19: Me, a dad? I hate Janey for not telling me. How could she just kill our baby? We would have been good parents. I still love her, though . . .

Age 22: Work is crap. Life is shit. What's the point?

Age 25: The meds seem to be working. They help stop the voices and drown everything out. Big K owes me money. I owe C money. It's all fucked.

And finally:

Age 26: A lot of you cared, just not enough. Ma loves me. Ma loves in a way that I never could.

Outside, spring has arrived without her even noticing. Beverly stares down at her body, hardly recognizing its expanding shape. The holiday offering her time to build muscle, to eat well. Today she'll eat eggs with tiny bread soldiers. She will dip each one into the bright runny yolk and take her time to taste, to chew, and allow her belly to feel full and satisfied.

Knowing Monty felt loved feels like air in her lungs. The morning balm of clement sunshine approaches. She showers and applies hand cream to her scuffed hands, pins a comb to her hair. The morning shards of light are so brilliant they ache behind her eyes.

Noon. Our first session together after the holidays.

I feel refreshed, rested, and ready to begin our work again. Beverly arrives on time. I notice the smartness of her clothes.

Her face is tanned and her hair is pinned and secured with a tortoiseshell comb. A delicate pink has been applied to her cheeks and mouth.

Moments of healing during bereavement are much like watching and tending seeds growing on a broken, shaky windowsill—light casting slow hope. As therapist, I am committed to holding hope that the patient is unable to see or feel for herself. Beverly's hope until now has been thorny. It has turned upon itself, casting judgment, fury, powerlessness, intense guilt, shame, and isolation. And it has attempted, understandably, to cover and conceal what lay beneath that which was profound loss.

How are you, Beverly? I begin.

How am I? Beverly asks. She pauses. *I've had some dark days, but I don't dread waking up in the mornings. I'm eating again, too.*

Another pause.

How was your holiday? she asks. *You look well. That color suits you.* She points at my blouse: silk and coral.

It was very restful. I enjoyed it very much, thank you, I say, I smile.

I realize this is the first time in our ten months together that Beverly has asked me a question unrelated to Monty. Usually, when another person can be seen, noticed, engaged with on topics other than the person they are grieving, gentle healing is most likely occurring. It is a moment when the bereaved can see beyond their loss. This is a hopeful sign, I think.

How is your garden? I ask.

It's beautiful, she says, and tears immediately fill her brown eyes. *I don't know what I would have done without it. It's kept me sane, seeing everything growing. Life.* She looks away, dabs her tears with a tissue.

Your garden sounds very healing, I add.

Yes. But I worry I'll never want to leave it. Just thinking about going out, talking to people and going back to work fills me with dread.

Say a little more, I encourage.

I worry people will judge me, Beverly says. *That they'll blame me for Monty's suicide. What kind of mother was I to allow my only child to get so sick?*

We had returned to what Beverly believed was her bad mothering.

I wonder if punishing yourself is somehow more manageable than being in the grief, I say.

I've struggled to move beyond the blame.

Perhaps your anger serves to protect you, I say.

How so?

If you didn't feel anger, what would replace it? I ask.

Beverly looks at me with damp eyes. *Absolute torture, so much pain. My body just can't take it anymore,* she says, the sharp edge of her suffering in every word.

I understand. As Monty's mother you may have felt completely responsible for him. That you should have had all the answers, all the cures. But it's important to acknowledge he was his own person, an adult with struggles and pain and choices. Events, life, and his surroundings led to his tragic death, I say.

I finally read some of his diaries, Beverly says, reaching for her bag. She pulls out two. Yellow Post-it notes peeking from marked pages. *May I?* she asks.

Of course.

Beverly reads Monty's words. Entries dating back to his teens up until the day he killed himself. This entry offers her some mild relief. Her unconditional love for Monty known and expressed in his words, his diary. Beverly takes her time and looks to me to respond, which I do: *Monty knew how much you loved him,* I speak quietly. *He knew this as a boy and as a man.*

*I'm glad you've been able to read his diary and know this—to accept
and understand this. He felt your love, Beverly. You have been holding
yourself together for a very long time, and tolerating such insufferable
pain. But you are finding different ways to metabolize your grief now. I
hope this helps you feel less distressed, less blaming of yourself as Monty's
mother. Good enough,* I say.

Silence.

I love you, Maxine.

Love, I say, *such a precious thing.*

When Beverly was a child, probably no older than five or six,
she would push around in her little buggy a plastic baby, her
favorite toy, named Peter. Peter went everywhere with
Beverly. She loved undressing and redressing Peter in clothes
her mother had made or bought from various charity shops.
Her favorite outfit was a lemon sleepsuit with a matching knitted bonnet that was soft to the touch. She loved rocking him,
feeding him, placing him beside her at the dinner table. *Where's
Peter?* her mother would ask, as though he were a family member. *Has Pete finished with his plate?*

When newer plush toys—rabbits, elephants, and the like—
were given on birthdays and Christmas they never quite made
the grade, and they certainly didn't make it into Peter's buggy.
Then one summer while at the beach, Peter got lost. Beverly
turned hysterical and began screaming, as did her mother.
Beverly's father looked everywhere and tried to calm both his
wife and his daughter. Still, Peter was nowhere to be found
and when they arrived home, no rabbit or elephant was able to
soothe Beverly's heartbreak. Later that week, a small bunch of
wild flowers was placed in Peter's buggy. Beverly's father didn't
know if it was his wife or daughter who had placed them there.

It wasn't until Beverly was thirteen that she discovered she had been born a twin. Her baby brother had died at birth. A complication involving a lack of oxygen to his brain. Suddenly, feelings that she'd not quite been able to fathom as a little girl, such as deep loneliness, a disconnect with other children, and constantly searching for something or someone she couldn't make sense of, made sense. And there was, of course, her mother's loss too. That she'd introduced Peter to the family, including him in daily meals, activities, and day trips was perhaps a way of coping with her loss. Had watching Beverly and Peter playing together soothed that which was not spoken of?

It's almost as if that early loss set a blueprint for all future losses, Beverly says. And this is the moment when she answers her own question asked months earlier, that being: *Men are always leaving me, why is that?* I offer up the possibility and question of whether she can move from the position of the one left to the one who has survived.

I never truly understood the meaning of survivor guilt until now.

Noon, and close to a year into our work, Beverly removes her beret and marshals her skirt so she can sit comfortably. She is silent for several minutes. *I need to talk about what I want today, and the guilt that comes with that,* she says.

Please, I encourage gently.

Beverly clears her throat.

I want to talk to Mum about losing our sons. She closes her eyes, raises both palms. *Let me start again,* she says. *I want to talk to Mum about her baby, my twin, dying. And I want to talk about Monty's suicide.*

I ease back in my chair, respect and admiration sensed for Beverly's felt clarity. There is courage in her voice when she names her loss.

And I want to have an honest conversation with Theo and Mike. Both are long overdue.

Very good, I say.

I realize me and Mum have never talked about Peter, she begins.

Peter? I say. *Your favorite toy?*

Yes, but I think we both know Peter was my baby brother, don't we? Beverly takes a sip of water. *It will be good to talk openly about what we've both lost. Mum had me, but I have no one. I'm a mother without a child to love.*

It's good to hear you reclaim your identity as a mother, I say. *I don't know if you remember, but when we started our work together you said that you thought you were no longer a mother after Monty's death.*

I do remember, very clearly. I am still a mother. Good enough, she smiles, *even though Monty is dead, even though I have no grandchildren. I've been thinking about starting a community growing project with the local council when I get my strength back. Perhaps with young people. Somewhere they can learn about growing things—fruit, vegetables, flowers. Gardening has always helped me.*

Sounds like a wonderful idea, I say. *Very healing, very growing,* and much like the life of a therapist, I think.

I wonder if I should mention guilt, one of the two matters Beverly had wished to talk about when she arrived. But it seems desire has become the topic for today's session. I will wait for another time, another opportunity.

Beverly leaves messages for her mother, Mike, and Theo. She asks that they call her back when they have a moment, making sure her voice is calm and steady. That way she knows they won't call her out of concern or pity. She wants to move beyond their charity to a place where she can be honest. Messy. Real. And able to speak her truth. She wonders what might be needed in terms of adaptability, resilience, and healing. She remembers reading something, once, somewhere, that as

humans we are mostly adaptable to our environments, our situations and our lives. That those who adapt are the ones who
ultimately survive and thrive.

The following week the matter of guilt is raised and revisited.

How do you think I'm doing? Beverly asks.

It's not unusual for those who are grieving to ask their therapist if they are doing better or worse than other patients who
have survived significant loss. Mostly, patients believe they are
doing worse because of the well of sadness and depth of pain
they feel.

Good enough, I answer. *How do you think you're doing?*

I feel so guilty when my days are back to ordinary, says Beverly. *If
my mind wanders to anything other than Monty, it's like I'm betray-
ing him in some way. Feeling sad shows him how much I miss him. I
can't ever forget him—not even for a moment.*

I suggest Beverly attempt more compassion for herself and
that she try to remember Monty in a more natural way, rather
than punishing herself if her thoughts wander elsewhere.
When a person is actively searched for they become less available. And if Beverly were to stop searching so hard, I thought,
the pieces would combine into a complete image of clear and
rich memories of Monty.

I remember the time I wanted to walk out in front of a car, she says.

I remember saying we'd find other ways to grieve, I reply.

And we are.

As she speaks, I am aware of how resilient she must be to
endure so much pain.

Posters and flyers are dropped at local schools:

*Are you a keen gardener? Interested in giving back to your community,
looking to meet new friends, and stay physically and mentally active?
We are recruiting volunteers to help transform green spaces . . .*

And to Beverly's surprise, dozens of young people sign up to volunteer at her community growing project. She also talks with her mother at great length about baby Peter. The loss of their sons is acknowledged and both mothers are locked in their sadness.

They speak of the unbearable suffering, different yet the same. *Monty had a life, it was short-lived but he at least had some time with us, unlike my baby brother, your son,* says Beverly. *I'm so sorry, Mum.*

Her mother cries while they reach and hold hands together. Neither woman speaks as their bodies attempt to regulate the significant loss of their sons. Eventually, Beverly lets go and wipes her damp palms along the length of her denim calves, her body doubled over, anguished. *How do we ever get over this, Mum?* she asks.

I don't think we do. How could we? her mother says. *They were our babies.*

Beverly reaches for her mother's body and presses her own body against her, holds her tightly. A gentle swaying. Tiny lioness noises. Nothing will disturb this moment of deep pain and deep recognition of each other. Their bodies rocking as if they are cradling their lost sons, their babies. A funeral held for their lioness hearts.

They are brothers, two years apart. They look the same. Let's call them Mark and Matthew.

Beverly finds herself gravitating toward the two boys, both with wild hair, granite eyes, and half smiles. She suspects that if they were to risk a full smile each, they may feel *too vulnerable or daft*. They are proud boys with hard exteriors and potentially soft hearts. Their Nike Jordans are worn and scuffed, laces held together with slivers of tape. Both boys live on the estate behind the Community Growing Project. Beverly likes it when they call her *Miss*. It makes her feel younger, playful, and relevant. Occasionally, after an afternoon of work she offers Mark and Matthew ham sandwiches wrapped in greaseproof paper parcels and leftover macaroni cheese. The boys wolf down the carbs and wipe their mouths with the backs of their nail-bitten hands. Beverly enjoys their appetite and how quickly it is calmed with work and food. She likes how delicately they tend exhausted bees and wandering ladybirds, hands cupped before gently releasing the tiny coworkers into long grasses and chokes of hedges. But mostly, she likes the way they laugh.

Beverly also plants a cut flower bed. Here she grows dahlias, ranunculas, sweetpeas, roses, and foxgloves. Sometimes she cuts the roses' stems too soon, a tight pink bud, tender and not fully grown, truncated before the exquisite frill of full bloom. When she places the roses in cold water they seem to live longer this way. Silently, she wishes there were a rose named Monty.

She suspects Mark and Matthew have chosen the project instead of community service because they think it might be easier, and perhaps less shameful. *Cleaning and sweeping up other people's crap just ain't for us,* the boys confess. But Beverly doesn't mind. She likes that they arrive on time twice a week after school and on the weekends, too. The three of them sit on wooden sleepers ready to be drilled and hammered to make raised beds for the vegetables, ancient trees whistling overhead. They talk about girls, school, and music. Occasionally, they talk about the items they wish they hadn't had to steal. But mostly they talk about girls. Mark knows his older brother is in love with a girl called Violetta. *She's way too posh for you, bro,* he says. Matthew agrees.

Hey, Miss. You got kids?

I used to have a kid.

Used to?

My son committed suicide last year.

That's too bad, Mark says, *I'm sorry.*

I'm sorry too, says Beverly.

Beverly gets them to work in what will soon be the vegetable patch. She hands them both gloves and overalls and spades. *I want you to dig over that whole area there,* she points. *This is where we'll be planting potatoes, tomatoes, and green beans. So let's get to work.*

Bossy, ain't ya, Miss? Mark says.

The suicide of one's child is possibly one of the most heart-breaking, demanding, and painful therapeutic journeys a therapist and patient can dare to commit to. The therapist must assemble all manner of learned experiences, felt and academic, for the clinical work with anyone who has not only witnessed but survived the violent departure of a loved one. And the patient will be tested, relentlessly, if she has enough courage, strength, vulnerability, and resilience for the task. Both therapist and patient commit to participate in a most agonizing loss. The therapist holding the heart, mind, and backbone of the patient as she slowly, tentatively and sometimes reluctantly heals from the trauma of her beloved child. Suicide has teeth, it growls fury and snarls at love. It is hopelessness. Cruel. It goes for the jugular. And is persistent for some, I'm told, and relieving for others.

Some patients with suicidal thoughts talk of the potential act as the one thing they have some control over—of losing in order to win. They feel lost, wrenched from hope and loved ones. And desperate for the other side of life, the only thing that made living possible, one patient described. Suicide casts a black shadow over those who survive, leaving them to experience and grieve the loss of their child. Feelings of survivor guilt can be so powerful, that growth and healing are believed almost impossible. One never knows whether balm will emerge from the debris of the most severe self-destruction of suicide. Its darkness fights love on all accounts, attempting to destroy hope, faith, and connection of any kind. I have listened to people accuse those who commit suicide as lacking courage, as being selfish, self-centered, victims, and narcissistic. But as a therapist and Samaritan for many years, when listening to someone with suicidal intentions I am faced only with a deep, penetrating, and sometimes invisible agony that speaks to the aloneness and existential disconnect. A deep sensitivity to the world, touch feels like ice and fire to their skin; noise, human contact, and nature are experienced as intrusive, sometimes terrifying and completely overwhelming. From the moment one wakes up to the time one rests, the voices speak to end it all, that the pain will never end, never. Not until you die.

Avoiding cruel, dismissive, and thoughtless stereotypes toward those who are feeling suicidal is necessary to not perpetuate an already desperate self-state. When one claims a suicidal person is a coward or selfish, they are sending a message to an already hopeless and depressed person that they are weak and worthless. They are saying that those with suicidal feelings do not count and by doing this they reinforce the voices, already in their head, that wish them to end their life.

It is not selfish to feel suicidal, it is human. Painfully human. And if anyone tells you otherwise, don't listen. Walk away. Such words do not belong alongside humanity.

Next week is the one-year anniversary of Monty's death. It is too late to plant snapdragons so instead Beverly purchases a cherry blossom tree and digs a hole. She waters the bare roots and sinks the tree, covers it over, and with the heel of her boot grounds it deep into the soil. She stakes it. Waters it some more.

Marks and dates a copper tag and makes sure the cherry blossom tree is level and proud. Then she buries his tiny yellow rabbit.

There, Monty-Moo, she says. *I think you might like the view from here . . . I miss you with all my heart.*

This is what we want—

I want to hold you tightly, to kiss you on the mouth—

Terri

I want my family to see me—

Kitty

I want my body back, healed—

Ruth

I want a baby—

Marianna

I want to do something different now—

Tia

I want a life with the man I love—

Agatha

I want today—

Beverly

I want to desire *my* way—

Maxine

For women, the need and desire to nurture each other is not pathological but redemptive, and it is within that knowledge that our real power is rediscovered.
It is this real connection, which is so feared by a patriarchal world.

Audre Lorde, *The Master's Tools Will Never Dismantle the Master's House* (1979)

Conclusion

My turn . . .

I find myself in another restaurant. No fish tank this time.

Forty years later I am still sensitive; not *too sensitive to live*, but peacefully and fiercely sensitive all the same.

My dining partner and I are both in shock when we order our food. Pak choi. Lotus root. Broccoli with oyster sauce. I watch my brother ward off his tears and steady his breath. He tells me he wants to yell, fight, take flight. Exit. I reply saying that to want something is *no bad thing*.

Moments ago, we, the first and second children of our parents, had discovered our father died six months ago. Upon hearing the news of our father's death I am unable to quiet myself until I grip my brother's hand, my lips and heart both quivering.

I'm so sorry for the loss of your Baba, the restaurant owner said when she came to take our order. The second her words were set free, I watched her face change. There was a look of panic in her eyes, and lines appeared across her forehead. If she could have lassoed those condolences back inside her throat, I believe she would have. But what is spoken cannot be unspoken. What is known cannot be unknown. With the delivery of death comes a cruel and penetrating certainty.

The restaurant owner turned her gaze southward, and her breathing became difficult. *You didn't know?*

We did not, I replied, struggling to settle my thoughts, my uprooting.

Our food arrives, and an image of my father appears in my mind like a vibrant snapshot, an untouchable dream. I slide his presence to one side along with my plate. And I replace it with a reimagining of my origin story. The enormous domestic fish tank returns. I want a different ending this time. My rules. I want to desire *my* way, not the way I was ordered. This time, desire is on my watch, my turf, and my terms. I refuse my father's hand and sashay to the fish tank alone.

I invite the fish to somersault and spin and glide. No hiding at the back. We are no longer swimming against the tide but *with* and *for* the water. When I challenge my father and his slippery-sidekick waiter, I disrupt their attempts to humiliate and shame me. Both men lean in, snickering—but fear no longer overwhelms me. It is instead replaced with desire: passionate, devoted, fascinated, sensual. I reclaim my body. From object to subject, from girl to woman, from hiding to seeking. I am wearing a different outfit from the one he ordered me to wear that day. And eating delicious food that glistens with calories. I do not care that it is *fattening*, that I am *greedy*. Greed only derives from deprivation anyway. I order for my mother, my brothers, and myself, too. We feast like kings and queens.

Finally, yes, I am sensitive. Thank you, Baba, for placing the word under my nose, so I could smell its sweet rapture. It is this sensitivity that inspires and fuels my wanting. It grows and swells until I sob with triumph and relief.

I realize in this moment that I am writing myself and my patients homeward to claim the *want* within ourselves. A newer voice is in motion now, pushing its way through my writing and my work as a psychotherapist. It is clear, unapologetic, accountable, and advocating. All this time, I have been swimming toward liberation and a deeper understanding of desire in *What Women Want*, and this is ongoing, expanding. We are traveling together, with and for each other. We know what we want and will have it—and it will be rich, and creative, and empowered.

I began writing *What Women Want* with lineage in mind. As the daughter of a white working-class mother and a patriarchal Chinese father, I have been both witness to and disrupter of a particular cocktail of oppression. If desire is my engine, then curiosity is the pedal and accelerator. Any tyrannous "should" and "must" are the brakes. Often when we think or talk about desire, we believe the moment of wanting is an isolated experience, but it is not: there are always undercurrents, origin stories, experiences, tales, and bonds that have been handed down from our forebears that have influenced us—for better or worse. These stories are inside us, however hard and fast we keep running from them. By understanding and respecting my own lineage as both a therapist and a patient, I have been able to take the risks needed to face my wanting as I attempted to embody my truth.

As we grow, our challenges in life grow too. In my early twenties I began my therapeutic journey as a patient on the couch, not knowing the shape my desire would take, or if it would take shape at all. In my thirties I began my psychotherapy training, hoping to connect with other desiring people in need of connection and who also believed themselves too sensitive, too hurt, too damaged, too lost, or too strange. Now, as a practicing psychotherapist for fifteen years, I believe the art of therapy is a uniquely breathtaking and beautiful undertaking. As therapist I cannot help but be changed and profoundly moved by my patients. Journeying with another's growth and change is a tremendous privilege. Perhaps a patient believes she is merely of clinical interest, or simply work, and has little personal and emotional impact on the therapist, but this is not true. My patients affect me deeply.

The women in this book all have something in common: a curiosity to set sail on an exploration and conversation about what they each want and desire. There are no neat conclusions to the stories and lives of Terri, Kitty, Ruth, Marianna, Tia, Agatha, and Beverly, no plain triumphs over struggles that will never again eclipse their lives. Psychotherapy, I have attempted to show, is about encouraging ways to think more clearly, to open up understanding and inquiry that may have enduring value for people long after the therapy is ended. For Terri, it was the reclamation of her sexuality. For Kitty, it was a desire for her family to truly see her. A healing body free of rage and fear was what Ruth desired most. And for Marianna, it was the experience of unconditional love that comes with being a mother, a love like no other, and the courage to stand on her own in her desire, without a man, to attain it. For Tia, it was a life that offered pause and a home within her body. Agatha wanted to share her final years with the only man she'd ever loved. Finally, for Beverly, a life worth living after the suicide of her only child was what she desired most.

It perhaps goes without saying that the struggle to speak and understand our desire is ongoing. Language will remain patriarchal as long as it is permitted to oversimplify feelings. If we are to respect our desire, our erotic energy empowered, we must remain in conversation together. It is my hope that *What Women Want: Conversations on Desire, Power, Love, and Growth* has shown how collaboration between psychotherapist and patient is very much about a collection of moments where two people are changed by their connection. Every therapeutic relationship is an extraordinary privilege, in which two people attempt to tolerate confusion, struggle, grief, and sometimes psychological triumph in a bold and intimate way.

What Women Want was inspired by the incredible women and girls I have listened and talked to in my working lifetime, as well as those I am yet to meet. You are all gentle and fierce, brave and committed, and the heroines of my every day. Thank you. I am still learning.

Let us support one another when we are fearful of crossing our threshold of longing. We will need each other to sustain desire's momentum, and also to lean into one another when we are tired and doubt our capacity for growth and change. And we will need all the love, determination, resilience, and sensitivity to honor the empowered and beautiful want inside ourselves. Long live our commitment to each other—to our Desire, Power, Love, and Growth. And long live our continued journey as desiring women, as we open our hearts and dare to speak:

This is what we want . . .

Acknowledgments

My gratitude begins with the seven women in this book who, with big, open hearts and commitment, offered their stories for publication. If there was any doubt that two women in a small room exploring the universality of our wanting was worthwhile, fear not: you are all testament to that inquiry. What an honor to be in conversation with each of you; may your figuring out long continue. Thank you: Terri, Kitty, Ruth, Marianna, Tia, Agatha, and Beverly; I am still learning.

This book began its life as a conversation with my spirited agent, Eugenie Furniss, a fierce and gracious advocate for *What Women Want*, who believed, wholeheartedly, that conversations on desire would sit proudly on the shelves of those who are curious about desire, power, love and growth. I'm grateful to Venetia Butterfield who felt something in those early pages and took a risk on my voice and believed our women (and me) would feel a sense of belonging and home within Hutchinson Heinemann. Anna Argenio, my editor, awes me and has dazzled and delighted with her potent edits and wise guidance, making *What Women Want* a beautiful collaboration. Thank you, Anna, for encouraging my wild daring and growth as a writer. Praise for the design team, who made me cry when I glimpsed our smart, intimate, and beautiful book jacket, the copy editors and fact-checkers. And everyone at Penguin Random House who made this book real.

Thank you also to Shoshi Asheri who invited my nature reserve, welcomed, my in-betweens and dared me to cross the threshold. Our moments together are expansive, beyond. And, Dr. Lynne Layton for her clinical guidance and rich conversations on how we might grow and nurture passion for civic life so it can take its rightful place beside work and love in the consulting room.

Love also for my family, friends and loved ones. You are my purest joys. Dexter, Kirsty, Toni, Charlotte, Martyn, Mark, Chi-Chi, Anthea, Caz, Greg, Christine, Mister T—I love you all.

And so it ends as it begins, with thanks to our seven women: awake, empowered, and growing. To want and desire *their* way has been a beautiful and sometimes terrifying undertaking. Thank you for inviting me to listen, learn, and grow with you. Your courage and vulnerability, commitment and desire, victories and curiosity are nothing short of extraordinary. I am changed.

Quotation Permissions

About the Author

Maxine Mei-Fung Chung is a psychoanalytic psychotherapist, clinical supervisor, and writer with over fifteen years of clinical experience. She lectures on gender and sexuality, trauma and attachment theory at the Bowlby Centre and was presented with the Jafar Kareem Award for her work supporting people from ethnic minorities experiencing isolation and mental-health problems. *What Women Want* is her first work of nonfiction.